LE TISSIER

LE TISSIER

by
Jeremy Butler

Thomas Publications

First published in Great Britain in July, 2005, by
Thomas Publications, PO Box 17, Newport,
Shropshire, England, TF10 7WT

ISBN 0 9512051 7 X

Printed and bound by Cromwell Press, Trowbridge

Contents

Introduction

It's not the heat-seeking missile Matt Le Tissier guided past Tim Flowers that stands out most in my memory, nor the flick and chip free-kick that beat Wimbledon. It's a moment never picked up by the television cameras and one no doubt forgotten by most Southampton fans.

The time I really marvelled at Le Tissier's stunning talents came in a bland old defeat by Sheffield Wednesday. I was sandwiched into my favoured Milton Road end as David Hirst, who was in the opposition ranks in those days, smashed in one of his rocket drives from fully 30 yards to condemn The Dell to an afternoon of misery.

Then, in the blink of an eye, it happened, way down near the Archers Road end. Two Wednesday defenders were hunting Le Tissier down as he ran away from goal. Suddenly, magically, he was gone! The chasing pack were still racing towards to the East Stand but Le Tissier was now heading the other way. To this day, I don't know how. The embarrassed Wednesday players probably didn't know either and sadly, it was never highlighted and never replayed on television. But the fact is that Matt was capable of such genius - and no-one was.

That, in my eyes, was his greatness. Not the show-stopping strikes, the last-day saviour routines or the loyalty he showed to Saints fans. It was the fact that every other Saturday, I would turn up knowing that this man could astound and astonish me with a piece of skill I would never have imagined possible. It made supporting Southampton different to pledging my allegiances to the likes of Charlton or Fulham.

As I travelled round the country in subsequent years as a football journalist, the Saints were always a welcome addition to the conversation because of the inevitable discussion about Le Tissier's merits. Can supporters of Portsmouth and Middlesbrough honestly say the same?

Le Tissier has been the endearing focal point of my love affair with the Saints - one that began with the April Fool's Day 5-0 thrashing of Blackburn in the promotion season of 1977-78. Two years earlier, I had stood by the Woodman pub on the route taken by the bus carrying the FA Cup-winning heroes but was too young to take in the full sense of the occasion.

So it was players such as Phil Boyer and Ted McDougall who fired my passion to be a supporter; one that has seen me travel throughout England - and more recently to Bucharest - to endure pain, heartache and that nervous twitch that arrives in April. And I was lucky enough to grow up watching Le Tissier's career develop on the pitch and read all about it through Graham Hiley's extensive reports in the Daily Echo, which have been a huge help in compiling this book.

My aim when I set out to write his story was to tell it without the sycophantic superlatives thrown about like confetti by national journalists as goal after goal flew in. They have not been necessary here. His tale has enough drama, frustration and joy to stand on its own feet. I have simply tried to convey the memories of a majestic career, so those who were thrilled by his talents can relive the moments.

Acknowledgements

The author and publishers would like to thank the Daily Echo in Southampton for their generous supply of photographs, allowing access to their cuttings library and for their enthusiastic promotion of the finished product. In particular, we are grateful to Jez Gale - but also to Adam Leitch, Margaret Kerton, Ian Murray, Jo Richardson, Dave King and Peter Bullwinkle.

Also, we recognise the Saints fanatics at Hagiology Publishing, whose books, 'In That Number' and 'Match of the Millennium,' have proved invaluable for reference purposes.

The design skills of Tricia Freeman in producing the cover for this publication are greatly appreciated as well.

Preface

Le Tissier watched David Batty's cross sail into the box and noticed out of the corner of his eye that Angelo Peruzzi was hurtling towards him. The Italian keeper's ill-judged decision to come out of his goal had marooned him in no man's land and left an empty net beckoning. Le Tissier simply had to guide the ball over the line before twisting away to celebrate his new status as an England hero.

But for once, the man whose unerring accuracy would secure him 209 first-team goals for Southampton was a yard out in his calculations. His effort dropped wide of the right-hand post and in an instant, his international career was over. One of England's greatest talents was about to become Glenn Hoddle's sacrificial lamb.

Le Tissier's brilliant trick to lose his marker earlier on was an indication that his skills alone could get his country back in the game. But just as so many managers had done throughout the player's career, Hoddle panicked - and it was the exceptional who suffered while the mundane triumphed. Les Ferdinand was sent on in his place as England unsuccessfully chased an equaliser.

While any of ten outfield players could have been dragged off without complaint on that February night in 1997, Le Tissier was left carrying the can. England ended up defeated by Gianfranco Zola's goal in the crucial World Cup qualifier and the Channel Islander was marked down for the scapegoat's role.

There was no way back this time and his international career must rank as one of the worst wastes of talent this country has seen. But while the rest of the world missed out on witnessing an array of skills so sensational that he was fated as a footballing god, one tiny atmospheric ground on the south coast was the stage for a shining light.

One club were saved time and again from the wilderness by the remarkable abilities of a humble man born with an extraordinary gift. Matt Le Tissier is rightly revered as a legend – and here's why.

1986-88

Boy Wonder

Y EARS before the rough justice he received at Glenn Hoddle's hands, Matthew Le Tissier's career had exploded into life on one of those magical Dell cup evenings. The willowy teenager's amazing scoring feats in the junior ranks were no secret but his unusual name was still just a whisper on the lips of Southampton fans. That's until a cold November night in 1986 when he knocked Manchester United out of the League Cup and cost Ron Atkinson his job.

Saints had battled to a 0-0 draw at Old Trafford but were two up in the replay and tormenting the Reds when Le Tissier bounded out to replace Danny Wallace. It was not long before he gave the first glimpses of a talent that would dazzle a generation of adoring supporters.

There was no sense of fear as he galloped on to a bouncing ball on the edge of the area. Mere mortals might have panicked when faced with the knowledge that beating Chris Turner would not only secure a famous cup win but also rack up a first goal in senior football. It would certainly have been too much for most spotty teenagers - but not this one.

He was so sure of his ability that there was no hint of anxiety as he approached the chance, angled his foot and lifted the ball over a bemused goalkeeper with the perfect weight to ensure it dropped neatly under the bar. Football had just witnessed the birth of a legend.

That was not the end of the Le Tissier show that night. United's dispirited defence failed to pick up his run from a corner and he thumped home a header from Jimmy Case's perfect delivery. The two goals made headlines. His name was splashed across the back pages and sports editors were quick to identify the brace as a major reason for Atkinson's sacking 36 hours later.

United's boss might have remained in a job had Chris Nicholl not been strong enough to stick to his plan of hauling Wallace off to protect his swollen ankle. Le Tissier said: "The manager was holding Danny's number ready to bring him off when he scored our second goal. It would have been easy then to let him stay on but, fortunately for me, he went through with it and I scored twice.

"The first was disputed. It was a clearance by Peter Shilton, and Colin Clarke went up for a header. The ball came off the defender and I ran through and chipped the keeper. United claimed it was offside but because the ball had come off one of their men, I was played onside. And my second was a rare header from about six yards from a Jimmy Case corner on the right. It was a memorable night, one I certainly won't forget."

That stunning contribution was the launch-pad for a career that would see Le Tissier smash a remarkable 209 goals in 540 games and win eight England caps. It was an appetiser for a sensational scrapbook of feats that kept Southampton in the top flight year after year, against all odds; a hint of the 16 seasons of tricks, dazzling, mazy runs and crafty nutmegs to come.

His four appearances and one goal for the second string in 1985-86 had proved that his goal-scoring feats in the youth team could be carried on at a higher level. He had scored an astonishing 59 times in his first season with the youths, including six in one game against Brighton. But for the next couple of years, the player spent more time entertaining during the warm-up than in games and he started 1986-87 as he had ended the previous one - in the reserves.

By allowing him those few run-outs in the reserves, Nicholl had checked that he could cope with the jump from Boys Own antics against kids to skipping away from tackles by frustrated old pros. Now, the Saints boss gave him his head by sending him on from the bench at Norwich in the third game of 1986-87. Southampton led 2-0 at one point but an 82nd minute winner by Steve Bruce saw the Canaries home 4-3.

Nicholl was fuming about the collapse and decided it was time to start with the eager youngster in the following game. He could not have picked a better fixture. As a kid in Guernsey, Le Tissier had drooled over the skills of Glenn Hoddle, idolising the England star's skills on the ball, his ability to drop 50-yard passes on a team-mate's toe and his knack of pulling off the spectacular.

The apprentice was presented with the chance to compare himself with the master when included for his full debut at The Dell on September 2. His family quickly booked flights and ferries to ensure they were present - and were not disappointed. "It was a nerve-wracking moment," he said. "I knew my whole family were in the stand. It was a big game and the thing that made it special was Glenn Hoddle being in the Spurs team that night. It was all my dreams rolled into one."

While Glenn Cockerill supplied the passes for Clarke and Danny Wallace to score in a 2-0 win, Nicholl picked the precocious Le Tissier as a star in the making. One sublime moment saw him pluck Matt Blake's pass out of the air with a deft touch before rolling the ball behind the Spurs defence into Wallace's path. The striker had only the keeper to beat but, in his haste, dragged the ball horribly wide.

"He had the confidence to get the ball and have a go at Mitchell Thomas, who had just been picked for England," Nicholl said. "In fact, he almost became arrogant." He kept his place as Saints were pulled apart by Nottingham Forest in a 3-1 defeat four days later and his chances of further opportunities were boosted when local hero Steve Moran was surprisingly sold to Leicester for £300,000.

A League trip to Old Trafford was deemed no place for the young Le Tissier to parade his skills and he was probably happy to be on the bench as Tim Flowers shipped five goals on his debut. With Nicholl attempting to sort out Saints' defensive woes, Le Tissier was also left out as Liverpool were beaten 2-1 and Wimbledon were held to a 2-2 draw.

He was back on the bench as Saints went ninth with a 4-1 win over Newcastle and, on October 14, was handed a professional contract to give him a double celebration on his 18th birthday. His confidence was sky-high, although Nicholl kept him pretty much reined in until telling him to strip off in the second half of the early-November trip to Sheffield Wednesday - four days after his dramatic impact against Manchester United.

The game was already out of reach but Le Tissier was intent on seizing his chance. When the opportunity came, it was matched by an assured finish, one that would become a trademark. Martin Hodge became the second keeper in a week to watch the ball sail over his head from a delicate finish - this one dug out from the edge of the Wednesday penalty area.

Now everyone was beginning to believe the claims of Saints youth-team coach

Off the bench and on the score-sheet. Le Tissier exquisitely leaves Martin Hodge stranded in the game at Sheffield Wednesday in the autumn of 1986.

Dave Merrington. "After we had Matty for 18 months, I said we have a player on our books who is a genius and people laughed at me," he said. "They appreciate him now."

Le Tissier was playing largely in the wing role that he occupied for much of his early Southampton career, the club having almost missed out on signing him despite his goal-scoring exploits in the Channel Islands. The club's development officer, Bob Higgins, had been tipped off by Barry Ferguson, secretary of Guernsey's schools, about 'a gangly 14-year-old' but said: "He didn't stand out, although there was something there. We invited him back to train with us during the school holidays but were still not sure about him.

"He had a short spell with Oxford after that, nothing transpired and he came over to Southampton for a third time, and clinched it. We took him down to our Gurney Dixon training centre at Lymington and that's when he really started to show his promise. But he had a fitness problem; not enough stamina. He wasn't eating properly - too many chips and chocolate bars - and that didn't help. Once we got him on a better diet, with more fresh meat, it paid dividends."

Even after Le Tissier had convinced Higgins there was enough ability in his boots to make it as a professional, he still had to pass a test of loyalty to remain in the club's plans. "It was after Matthew had joined us on schoolboy forms that the crunch came," Higgins added. "He had been picked for his first stint of under-18 duties on the substitutes bench and, when we gave him the news, he became very upset.

"It transpired that the match clashed with Guernsey's annual fixture with Jersey, and Matthew had been selected for the Guernsey youth side. He desperately wanted to play in it but was given an ultimatum: turn out for Saints or forget a career at The Dell. Credit to the lad, he chose us and not long afterwards, became an apprentice."

Le Tissier's devotion to his island was understandable. The area was ingrained in him as he grew up as one of four brothers, all of them sports-mad. His mum Ruth said: "Everywhere in the house was a football pitch. The doors were goals, the bottom of the windows were posts and they continuously played. On Saturday mornings, we used to take them down to the fields to play football. We would watch them in their various age groups, then bring them back. Matt's dad, Marcus, would strip them off at the front door as I would run a bath. All the dirty clothes would be put in a shed. The boys would run upstairs, have a bath, then go and watch Marcus play."

The close-knit community were excited by Le Tissier's talents from an early age - and not just at football. One of his teachers, John Henry, saw the youngster astound his peers with his all-round sporting ability. "He was also a superb cricketer," he said. "He played in the junior league and I think he still holds the record score of about 140.

"But my earliest memory was before he started at the school. I was taking a group of boys out for a game and, as I did, I saw a junior match and a nine-year-old Matthew was taking a corner. His teacher said to me: 'Watch this, Route A.' He took the corner and it went straight in.

"Ability-wise, he was out of this world. I didn't teach him very much. I just had to keep him in check more than anything. I remember we were playing a school we should have been beating fairly easily and Matthew was in one of his lackadaisical moods. I looked at my watch and said to him: 'Matthew, one minute to go.' He picked up the ball, beat six players and scored."

It was once Le Tissier came under Merrington's wing that Saints realised just how big a talent they had on their hands. "He is the most exciting prospect I have ever worked with," the coach added. "The lad is full of confidence and I always gave him his head in the youth side. It would have been a crime to stifle talent like his. He scored goals that took your breath away."

The player, by now having fans licking their lips at the prospect of just what he might do to top-flight defences, enjoyed the chance to get among lesser markers by netting two goals in the Full Members Cup defeat of visiting Hull on November 25. He was sharp enough to capitalise on Mark Wright's knock-down to fire home and, just two minutes later, casually tucked in a second when George Lawrence's cross was partly cleared.

The goals didn't win him a prolonged first-team run. When he did make it back into the starting line-up on January 24 against QPR, it was for only one game, Nicholl explaining: "If we rush him, we might spoil him. It's tempting to put him in, sit back and wait for the goals to flow. But it's not that simple. His strength has not yet caught up with his size and he lacks the resources to go for a whole game. He has hardly had any reserve experience having made a massive leap straight from youth football. So if you throw him in too quickly, he will get shell-shocked and go backwards at great speed. The learning process has to be gradual."

He was sent back to the reserves to improve stamina levels that must have suffered from his continued brief use as a substitute. Three games in the Football Combination brought one goal - against Luton on Valentine's Day - but Saints were struggling in his absence and a run of one win in ten matches prompted Nicholl to hand him the chance he had been longing for.

He used him as a sub in the second leg of the Littlewoods Cup semi-final, only for Liverpool to score three times in the last 24 minutes to book a place at Wembley. The Reds had held out for a 0-0 draw at The Dell in the first game despite Paul Walsh's 48th minute sending-off and so blocked Southampton's route to a final for the second year in a row. They knocked them out of the FA Cup at the same stage in the previous campaign.

But with Saints under a cloud, there was good news for Le Tissier when he was recalled to the starting side for the League clash at Anfield on February 28. The move failed to inspire Nicholl's men as he teamed up with Lawrence and Wallace in a defeat secured by John Aldridge's goal.

Le Tissier soon lifted everyone with another blast of his potential. On a Dell pitch

Hat-trick time for Le Tiss. On a bitingly cold day at The Dell, Leicester were put to the sword by a rising star who was only just 18. Here, he beats a lunging challenge for one of his goals in a 4-0 victory that remains an obvious personal highlight.

affected by snow, Leicester were victims of a master-class from the teenager, who danced his way through their defence to collect an eye-catching hat-trick in a 4-0 win. His predatory skills were to the fore as he closed in to meet Wright's knock-down from a first-half Gerry Forrest free-kick and beat Ian Andrews. After Gordon Hobson crashed home when Wallace's shot came back off the bar, Le Tissier followed up from Andrews' save to coolly sweep in a side-footed effort for his second.

Until now, Saints fans had only been treated to deadly close-range finishing but that all changed with eight minutes left. Picking the ball up near the half-way line, he glided past one blue shirt after another as he surged at the heart of a shell-shocked defence. As three men converged, the gangly teenager barged through on goal, kept control of a bobbling ball and unleashed his shot. He appeared to have wasted his magical work by firing too close to Andrews and allowing him to block but he reacted quickest by ramming home the rebound with his left foot.

It was a fantastic way to complete a hat-trick on a day when the player could barely feel his frozen toes - and his feat was timed to perfection. His father had not found it easy to afford the airfare to watch games regularly but, luckily, picked the Leicester match for one of his rare visits.

"I still can't believe I did it because my feet were like blocks of ice," Le Tissier Jnr said. "After 50 minutes, I wondered where on earth my toes had gone. When I first saw the pitch, I doubted there would be a game. But I'm glad we played now. My dad had come over from Guernsey to watch me - the first time he has been able to get over since I made my debut against Tottenham last September.

"It costs so much to fly over that my parents can't get to as many games as they would like. And having Dad there made it extra-special. It was lovely leaving The Dell with the match ball, signed by all the lads, and going off for a quiet meal with him. I'd like to think I've done myself some good but there's no such thing as a guaranteed place. It's the manager's job to pick the team and I can only go on doing my best.

"Scoring my first hat-trick in the First Division is very special. It certainly gave me as much pleasure as the first goals I scored for Saints against Manchester United. My game went back a bit when I had a long run on the bench. Just recently, I've played in the youth and reserve teams and now I feel I'm starting to go from strength to strength. I really gained from playing at Liverpool. Knowing I could go out against them and not be out of place was a real confidence booster."

Of his heroics against Leicester, he added: "The solo goal was the best of the trio. I just put my head down and kept running. I remember my first shot hitting the keeper on the foot and I put the rebound away from a tight angle."

It should have been a launch-pad for Le Tissier to book himself a regular place. Nicholl certainly hoped so and, after the player drew a blank in a 3-0 defeat by an Everton side marching to the title, he was in creative mood as Saints smashed five past Aston Villa. His through ball teed up Cockerill for the second but he himself went goal-less. And, after two more matches without netting, he was out in the cold again.

Two games and one goal in the reserves - against Brighton on April 11 - and he was back. The break worked, with Le Tissier stepping off the bench to follow up Lawrence's drive and crash home a late equaliser in the 1-1 draw with Sheffield Wednesday. It was the kind of goal that had his strike partner Clarke purring. "He has a load of skill, he is very tricky and a great crosser of the ball," he said. "For goals a game, he has almost matched me, which is remarkable for a winger. If he looks after himself and learns the ins and outs of the game, he'll become a great player."

Despite showing superstar potential on the pitch, Le Tissier was not living the life of a legend off it. He was renting a mouse-infested flat in Portswood with his girlfriend Cathy and when they moved to a two-bedroom house in Bursledon, they stayed in every night so they could afford the mortgage. Le Tissier could have done with more appearance money but Nicholl refused to budge on his plan to ease him in gently.

The manager was nevertheless quick to salute his finishing prowess before handing him the no 12 shirt for the 2-2 draw with Charlton. He said: "He has tremendous things to offer us in a game but people have to remember that he is only 18 and is still developing."

Le Tissier probably came on a bit more for his stunning right-foot 20-yard drive in the 1-1 draw at Watford, which proved to be his last significant act of the campaign. His exploits, including his flourishing form when he started five matches in March and took the club's Player of the Month award, had not gone unnoticed by Bobby Robson's scouting network.

They called him up for England's under-19 summer tour to South America, only for him to have to pull out with an ankle injury picked up on Saints' end-of-season trip to Singapore. But he refused to let the disappointment ruin his memories of a fantastic debut season that marked him down as one of the most exciting youngsters to break into the English game.

With typical modesty, he said: "I've just been fortunate. The chances have fallen my way. I know they'll be proud of me back home and that makes me all the more determined to do my best. I've taken a big step but still have a long way to go, a lot to learn and a lot of work to put in. It's been an unbelievable year. My expectations last August were to earn a regular place in the reserves!

"My hope for next season is to become a regular at home and away and there are aspects of my game I have to improve on, particularly the defensive side. I am still learning where and when to make runs and how to become a better team player."

Le Tissier's undoubted potential created a buzz around The Dell over the summer and there was great excitement that the winger might turn into a regular match-winner for Saints. But his 1987-88 season struggled to get off the ground as his slender frame encountered problems against the rough and tumble of the man's game, and his acid tongue occasionally landed him in trouble.

He twisted a knee before a ball had been kicked and, on his comeback in the second string at Millwall, was sent off for dissent after only 18 minutes. As he regained fitness in the reserves, he scored twice in the 6-0 defeat of Swindon in early September to earn a run out from the bench for the senior side in the 1-0 defeat of QPR.

A sweet strike in the youngster's first full game of 1987-88 brings a Littlewoods Cup goal against Bournemouth. But it was one of only two that season - and Saints still went out.

That was followed by two more sub appearances as Saints won only one of their opening nine League fixtures, and Le Tissier said: "Chris was trying to protect me a little bit. When I did come in, he used me as a sub after a couple of matches. This went on for 18 months. I know he said he was trying to protect me but I just wished he had told me at the time to save me getting annoyed!"

On October 6, he was handed the no 7 shirt and responded by cracking home an early equaliser in a Littlewoods Cup second-round tie against Bournemouth, only for Saints to embarrassingly lose to their south coast rivals on aggregate. He kept his place in the League and the side's form immediately turned around, with Danny Wallace's searing pace scaring Watford's defence into back-pedalling too far - and allowing him to drill home the winner from 20 yards.

In the next match, Le Tissier played his part in Southampton's first win at Coventry in 32 years, delivering a pin-point centre for Graham Baker to smash home the second as they recovered from two down. He was enjoying the freedom of being able to cut in from wide on the right to torment teams, although he confessed to still lacking the stamina needed to be a constant threat.

"In a lot of my youth-team games, I started off on the right wing but tended to drift across into the centre-forward position and scored a lot of my goals from there," he said. "Getting away from my marker was one of my strong points. The left-back never knew whether to run with me or stay and, in the end, he often left me. I did struggle at first with a midfield role in the first team, mainly with the fitness part and the fact that tackling was never my strong point.

"But I have improved on both these aspects. I find it a lot easier now. I am getting stronger in that role. It is up to me to be positive as long as I can get back as well. All I need now is a few games. The more you play, the more rhythm and confidence you get. I haven't had that luxury yet this season."

Le Tissier continued to struggle to last 90 minutes and was taken off in the 3-0 defeat of Chelsea. A knee injury in the draw with Charlton then meant he had to wait six weeks to break back into the first-team picture as a sub in the 2-2 home draw with Liverpool on December 12. His two goals in the reserves' 5-1 defeat of QPR a week earlier, when Alan Shearer also netted twice, prompted Nicholl to recall him.

He didn't start again, though, until January 9, when he was the match-winner for Saints in a tight FA Cup clash at Reading. It was his first appearance in the competition and he tested keeper Steve Francis before scoring the only goal two minutes prior to the break, latching on to a flick by the bustling Clarke and showing great composure to control under pressure and angle in a drive.

With his tail up, he and Nicholl hoped his previous season's exploits against Manchester United would be repeated, this time in the League. He failed to play a part in either of Clarke's two goals but Saints sprang a surprise by winning 2-0 against a side now managed by Alex Ferguson. And he kept his place for the 0-0 draw with

January, 1988 - and a match winner in his first FA Cup tie. The team on the receiving end of his heroics are Reading at Elm Park.

Norwich. Nicholl was desperate to bring back Cockerill, though, and with Clarke in a golden spell after scoring nine goals in 11 matches, the young pretender was sacrificed again.

Flowers, who had started the season in Saints' goal before the arrival of John Burridge, watched Le Tissier bounce back and forwards from the reserves to the first team, and says: "He wanted to play but I could see why Chris Nicholl did what he did. People a couple of seasons ago were asking why Wayne Rooney was coming off the substitutes' bench, and David Moyes would say he had to ease him through gradually.

"He wasn't saying that because he didn't want to play Wayne Rooney. He was doing it because that was what was best for the lad. Maybe Chris was right to do that with Matty. When Tiss came off the bench, invariably he would score or set one up. When he started games, that didn't always happen and people would be asking why. He was only a young boy, don't forget. He had only left school a year before. He had one unbelievable season scoring goals in the South West Counties League but to put him in the highest league in English football is a totally different proposition. Yes, he had terrific ability - but it's a big step up."

Netting against Portsmouth in the third of a run of three games in the reserves was enough to give Le Tissier's stop-start season another kick. Nicholl selected him for four successive games and he shone enough to be selected by ex-England boss Ron Greenwood as a regional winner of the Young Eagle of the Month award for January. "This season has been a bit of a non-starter for me," the player said. "I have had too many injuries and suspensions and have never really got going.

"I had a run of four games in October and we were unbeaten in all of them. I was quite pleased with my form and starting to feel part of the team but picked up a knee injury at Charlton and that put me back at square one. The injury took about three weeks to clear up, so it wasn't until January that I got back in again. But after four games, I was back on the treatment table after turning an ankle in the Simod Cup at Bradford. I've got to start from now on to establish myself, so I can start next season as a regular."

The injury which had knocked a dent into his 1987-88 campaign came courtesy of a thumping tackle from former Portsmouth hard-man Mick Kennedy in Saints' Simod Cup exit in late January. And, with Nicholl upset at his team's lack of fight in the 1-0 defeat against Charlton at The Dell, Le Tissier was sent packing to the second string once again. It was disappointing - but also a chance to regain some confidence and match fitness as he played in the final eight Football Combination games.

He scored five goals along the way and created many more as the reserves rattled in 19 during his stint. Then, in an unimpressive first-team draw with Luton, he finished the season as he had spent most of it - stepping off the bench to replace Danny Wallace.

Despite his dissatisfaction, there was no escaping the fact that he had the talent to interest the manager of any national side. He was duly selected by Bobby Robson's youth team guru, Graham Taylor, for England's under-20 close-season tour to Brazil, justifying his place by fighting off a stomach bug to score the equaliser with a left-foot volley in the 1-1 draw with Lordrina.

Le Tissier then battled against a back injury in England's second game - a 3-2 win against Maranga, where he scored in only the second minute after the keeper dropped a long throw at his feet. He succumbed to the pain at half-time but could still be proud of his performances in an international shirt. Not that that would spare him a somewhat down-to-earth end-of-term assessment from the stoical Nicholl.

"Matthew has had a poor season by the standards he promised last year," the manager said. "We can't be satisfied with that and expect a lot more from him next season. So will he. Injuries didn't help - he started the season with a knee ligament problem, which kept recurring, and had other physical setbacks which messed him up. The publicity he got when he first came in didn't help either. He has found this year that the game is a lot harder and hopefully he has learned from it.

"He still has a lot to do. He might be a player you tear your hair out at but our results have been better when he has played. I don't mind him being unpredictable because that is an advantage when faced by a defender. But it's important he isn't unreliable. His team-mates must know where he will be and what he is going to do. By the same token, they must provide him with the right service to keep him involved, then he can try his tricks. Dennis Rofe and I have sat and talked with him at length. He has a great deal of potential but we must make sure it does not go unfulfilled."

1988-89

Craving a Chance

THERE was little on for Le Tissier when he picked up the ball on the touchline. West Ham's midfield had funneled back into position and a solid row of four defenders were ready to step in if he found a way through the first layer of protection. The sensible option was to play a simple square pass but that thought never seemed to enter Le Tissier's head.

Darting in from the right with pace and a sure touch, he angled a run between three Hammers players. As the first defender stepped out, Le Tissier shipped the ball from one foot to the other and then sidestepped to his right as an attempted lunge from a recovering opponent missed its target. Now he had a sight of goal….one more player to beat and he was through. A dip of the shoulder created some space and he fired across Tom McAllister to cap a fantastic run with a sweet finish.

Matt Le Tissier was changing from a boy to a man. It was clear that this was not the ungainly player of two seasons earlier, when he bludgeoned the ball past defenders to score against Leicester. In this opening game of the new campaign, he was gliding past markers with a turn of pace and neat footwork.

He had preceded 1988-89 with a welcome trip home to play in a friendly against Vale Rec, notching a hat-trick in a 13-0 win. It was the first sighting of Chris Nicholl's adventurous 4-2-4 system - the one he hoped would showcase the attacking talents at his disposal. Back on the mainland, Le Tissier surprisingly started on the bench as Paul Rideout scored on his debut in a 4-0 defeat of West Ham on the opening day.

But his goal at The Dell saw him restored to the line-up in place of Danny Wallace and he was perfectly placed to nudge home the rebound from Kevin Moore's header to claim an early winner at QPR. Le Tissier then played his part as Saints beat Luton 2-1 to go top, their cavalier style taking the division by storm.

And he made a dream start at Arsenal as he showed his nose for goal to slot past John Lukic from Colin Clarke's cross. Rod Wallace grabbed a second and a surprise win was on the cards until controversy struck. Glenn Cockerill was laid out by Paul

Davis and suffered a double fracture of his jaw - an off-the-ball offence for which the Arsenal man subsequently received a nine-match ban.

Brian Marwood netted a penalty with eight minutes left following Moore's handball but Saints still looked capable of holding out for the win. That was until Alan Smith left them devastated with an equaliser as the referee found an astonishing nine minutes of injury-time. "I feel cheated and so do my players," Nicholl fumed. "It felt to me that we were going to play until Arsenal scored again."

A deflated Saints were beaten 3-1 by Liverpool without the injured Le Tissier and drew 0-0 at home with Derby in a game in which he went on as a substitute. He was introduced too late as the wheels started to come off in a 4-1 defeat at Everton, the forward having scored in his first reserve outing of the season - a win over QPR.

Le Tissier continued in his role as sub during a 2-1 loss at home to Sheffield Wednesday and a victory by the same score at Spurs. But when Nicholl's patience with Clarke finally snapped, it left a gap that Le Tissier seemed certain to fill. Clarke had angered the manager by demanding to leave and was unceremoniously dumped in the reserves and loaned to his former club Bournemouth before being offloaded to QPR for £800,000.

His absence meant Le Tissier had a central role in the 1-1 draw at surprise leaders Norwich and in the 2-0 victory over Lennie Lawrence's Charlton on November 5. In between, the striker took advantage of a Littlewoods Cup outing at Scarborough to score with a technically perfect volley from Graham Baker's clever header. It put Saints 2-0 up but they were still looking fragile and were punished for easing off by being pegged back to 2-2.

An award - and something to drink to!

The Fourth Division pacesetters were intent on taking a prize scalp when they went to The Dell the following week, their resolute defence proving hard to break through until Le Tissier made his mark early in the second half. He was picked out by Derek Statham's precision cross and planted home his header to seal a place in the fourth round of a competition in which Saints had earlier beaten Lincoln.

With games coming thick and fast, Le Tissier set up one of Danny Wallace's three goals as Stoke were beaten 3-0 in the Simod Cup. But Nicholl was finding it tricky to harness the inconsistent brilliance that was Le Tissier. Even fans were questioning whether the man with magic in his boots deserved a place in the starting line-up.

While his team-mates were showing the endeavour and graft required to prevail in matches, the youngster was drifting in and out of the action with a nonchalance that was beginning to suggest he did not have the necessary determination to become a key man in the side.

He was by now just out of his teens and his manager was hoping for more mature performances from undoubtedly his most talented asset. With some supporters making accusations that Le Tissier didn't care enough, the player himself was more than aware of his shortcomings and was desperate to prove he could be a superstar. It was catch 22. Nicholl was convinced he didn't warrant a lengthy run in the side while the player swore he would only be able to recapture the form he showed in the youth team if he was granted a long spell in the starting line-up.

"The manager feels I'm a player who needs a kick up the backside," he said. "That may be true and it may be because of me coming from Guernsey, where the pace of life is so much slower than here, although I think I have adjusted now. But it would really help my confidence to have a long run in the side. I can feel it happening already and it enables me to try the kind of things I was doing in the youth side.

"It does not help me to be in and out of the side. If the manager sticks with me, I know I can reward him. I don't want to sound big-headed but I really believe people have not seen the best of me yet. I can still play a lot better. All I need is a good run. The most I have ever played is eight games in a row, which is not a lot to get to know the players around me."

Le Tissier lived up to his words instantly as his League famine ended against Aston Villa in mid-November. He almost appeared to close his eyes as he nodded home Jimmy Case's cross at the far post and his second left Villa bewildered by his ability to create a chance for himself. Cockerill headed a long corner back into the box and, with one touch, Le Tissier controlled a ball that had bounced up to waist level. As it dropped, he swivelled and hammered a rasping drive into the top corner.

After that 3-1 win, he was the saviour at Old Trafford, where he refused to let the pressure tell as he raced on to Danny Wallace's through ball, held off Lee Sharpe's challenge and beat Jim Leighton with a low shot that helped secure a point.

He then picked out Baker for the midfielder's second goal in a thrilling 2-2 draw with Millwall and remained provider as Moore outjumped Guy Butters to head the crucial goal in the 2-1 Littlewoods Cup win at Spurs. But he was unable to make an impact as Saints slipped out of the top six with a defeat at Wimbledon and a 1-1 draw with Nottingham Forest. He was, though, feeling more confident in his surroundings.

"Now I feel part of things," he said. "That is reflected in the way I'm playing. I feel quite pleased with my form. I had a poor season last year because of my injuries and suspensions, so it was important for me to get off to a good start this time. Now I've just got to keep it going."

He was thriving on Nicholl's attacking system - and not just because he was seeing more of the ball. The boss had devised a set-up which allowed his star man to take players on without the need to hurry back and thunder into tackles. "We are spreading balls out well to the flanks, which keeps me involved," he said. "With three men in midfield, it takes a bit of the defensive pressure off us wingers, so we can concentrate on attacking. But we do need the ball. That's the problem with wingers. If the ball isn't played wide, you don't look involved."

Le Tissier was also quick to pay tribute to his team-mates for understanding his game and working hard to give him licence to try the tricks designed to crack tight defences. He added: "Some things come off and look really good. But when things go badly, they look terrible. I know it can be irritating for the team at times if I go on a run, lose the ball and then they have to win it back in defence. But they have learned to live with that."

It appeared Le Tissier had finally made the breakthrough when named Barclays Young Player of November by England manager Bobby Robson. Three goals in four League games had seen Saints go unbeaten for the month and, allied to his cup strikes, the clinical finishing had caught the eye of the international hierarchy once again.

"Matthew has lovely ability on the ball," Robson said. "He is deceptive, gets past defenders and gets good crosses in. Like all good wingers, he relies on service and when the team are in full flow, the lad can be exceptional. He can also score goals and got some vital ones last month - five in all - which is a good return for a wide player. What I like most about him is that he does it when the going gets tough. He's more consistent than he used to be and I know they are delighted with him at The Dell."

Despite their attractive football and a goal for Neil Maddison on his debut in the 2-1 reverse at Wimbledon's Plough Lane, Saints needed Le Tissier's goals. He failed to make an impact as they were knocked out of the Simod Cup at home to Crystal Palace but his efforts should have been good enough at Newcastle, where he inspired a spirited fightback from Lee Brock's eighth minute opener.

Rod Wallace did the hard work by taking the ball round Dave Beasant and squaring for Le Tissier to quickly shift the ball from his right boot to left and guide it past two players on the line. His second was reminiscent of the opening-day dazzler against West Ham. He latched on to Statham's pass in midfield and headed for goal, only to be

23

met by two players intent on crushing his chances of getting through. Le Tissier rode the tackles, though, and slipped the ball past a diving challenge to arrow home a cool finish.

Rod Wallace added a third but Saints were mugged, almost literally, when Tim Flowers was hit by Rob McDonald while jumping for a 65th minute cross. The keeper was left flat out and concussed for the final quarter of the game. Substitute Michael O'Neill scored from the subsequent drop-ball and the same player equalised deep into stoppage-time while Flowers floundered.

Instead of enjoying the plaudits of two super strikes in the first 28 minutes, Le Tissier was left laughing at Flowers' antics at the final whistle. His concussion was so severe that he did not remember Newcastle's final two goals - and was celebrating a Saints win. "I really believed we had won," the keeper recalled. "It was only when the lads told me the score that I worked out what had happened. I can't recall their last two goals or picking the ball out of the net. I was just functioning on autopilot."

Nicholl's game plan, which had allowed young starlets Le Tissier and the Wallace brothers carte blanche to go for goal, was fantastic on the eye. But the Newcastle result proved that it also left Saints exposed at the back. On Boxing Day, they finished the stronger and stole a late point from Coventry as they came back from 2-0 down. Rod Wallace headed them back into it and Le Tissier served up a pinpoint corner for Moore to power in and nod the equaliser.

The fighting spirit went too far when Russell Osman was sent off for sparking an injury-time brawl but had disappeared at The Dell five days later as QPR cruised to a 4-1 win despite Le Tissier spearing a shot through a busy area to briefly raise hopes.

Even though results were disappointing, Le Tissier's creativity was becoming increasingly crucial and, when Derby's name came out of the hat in the FA Cup third round, he had the perfect stage to produce some magic.

He jinked his way through their defence in the opening half, only to mess up his finish when left with only Peter Shilton to beat. His off-day continued as he missed the target with the whites of the former Saints keeper's eyes again in his sights, this time from Statham's cross, then he saw his centre disappointingly headed wide by Danny Wallace as Saints drew 1-1.

Three days later in the replay, Shilton denied him twice in the second half before Saints heartbreakingly lost 2-1 in extra-time. And his miserable New Year continued as Luton handed out a 6-1 League thrashing before Middlesbrough tucked into the side's soft underbelly with a 3-1 victory at The Dell. At least the youngster could draw some consolation from providing the cross for Moore to score against Boro - the second time the combination had come up trumps in four games.

Sacrificed for the 2-0 loss at Liverpool with Cockerill back to add midfield bite, Le Tissier scored in the reserves' defeat of Fulham but his recall failed to stop the rot as Saints slumped 3-1 in the League at Derby. It was their fifth top-flight defeat in a row, left them 15th and drew an honest assessment from Nicholl. "We were probably the best team in the country in November. Right now, we are playing very poorly," he said.

The boss had to make changes - and Le Tissier was one of the casualties, replaced by Alan Shearer as Paul Rideout was also dropped in a change of system that was rewarded by a 1-1 draw against Everton. The move, not for the last time, sparked rumours of problems between player and manager. Le Tissier was hurt by his omission from the squad just a week after winning a recall and knocked on Nicholl's door for an explanation.

The decision was not unpopular with all fans, some continuing to ask whether the Wonder Boy was worth all the effort. Nicholl, though, assured the masses: "There is no rift. He was disappointed and we had an amicable chat. There really is no problem for him or me as a result. I felt against Everton, you get quite a bit more physical strain and the problem with Matthew is that I never know what he is going to give me.

"He's very difficult to understand but I have to try and I'll keep doing so because he has a lot of ability. I have to work him out somehow. Plenty of fans have written in asking: Why bother with him? But I won't dismiss him like that. He is very clever and has a lot of talent. That in itself is not enough, though."

A goal in the second-string derby with Portsmouth helped Saints to a 4-1 win and he netted again in reserve matches against QPR and Palace. But his frustration got the better of him in the Palace game and he was sent off for swearing at the referee. It was his third red card and earned him a three-match ban he could barely afford as he tried to worm his way back into Nicholl's affections.

Saints had just ended 17 League games without a win by beating Newcastle 1-0 through Neil Ruddock's penalty, the side boosted by the arrival of Barry Horne in a club record £700,000 deal and left-back Micky Adams. With his team feeling more confident, Nicholl brought Le Tissier back as sub in the 3-3 draw with Middlesbrough and in a defeat at Forest.

A victory over West Ham was achieved without Le Tissier, although an injury to Danny Wallace gave him a run in the side for the final five games of the season. It was the opportunity he craved and, by teeing Rideout up with a teasing cross in the 2-1 win at Villa, he helped Saints record two victories and three draws to salvage some pride as well as a final 13th place.

Despite being part of the side who signed off by drawing 1-1 with Millwall at the old Den on May 13, his only appearance on the score-sheet during the run-in was in the reserves' win over Charlton. He had ended the season with 11 goals from 36 senior matches and still had plenty to do to become an automatic choice.

1989-90

Penalty King

MATT Le Tissier approached the new season fearing he was being left behind; burned off by the frightening pace with which Rod Wallace motored into the first-team picture. While Wallace had been instantly included by Chris Nicholl in 1988-89, Le Tissier - for all the plaudits and for all his goals in climbing through the ranks - was still bouncing between the reserves, the subs' bench and a spot on the wing.

This was going to be his make-or-break season. This was the serious stuff. He would either push on to become a star or slither into the massed ranks of players who never lived up to their potential.

He fired a statement of intent with hat-tricks in warm-up games with Farnborough and Swansea - enough to persuade Nicholl to use him instead of Wallace when Saints kicked off the campaign at home to Millwall. Le Tissier justified the decision by delivering a pinpoint corner for Neil Ruddock to head home against his former club but defensive lapses enabled Teddy Sheringham to net the Lions' 89th minute winner.

Days after Saints had announced a loss of £1.125m, he saw Danny Wallace notch twice in a 2-1 win at Maine Road in a demonstration of electric forward play. But Le Tissier was hauled off in the annual defeat at Everton and dropped as Nicholl handed Rod Wallace his starting spot. Then he set about proving his manager wrong....

He soon showed that he was in far too good form to be left rotting in the reserves. Four goals in four games might not have earned the second string a win - in fact they went the first 14 matches before breaking their duck - but it was a clear sign to Nicholl that he should return to the first team.

He was handed the task of replacing Danny Wallace when Manchester United eventually increased their bid for the Londoner from £800,000 to £1.2m - enough to keep the money-men happy as Southampton balanced the books. The deal was a clear sign that Nicholl and the club's board were banking on Le Tissier to come good.

"In some ways, I was sorry to see Danny go because I liked him," he said. "Everyone did. He was a typical Cockney, full of banter. But when he left, it took a bit of pressure off me. His departure gave me extra room and a chance to show what I could do. It meant I did not have to look over my shoulder as much. It was probably one of the turning points of my career because it gave me confidence that I could do the job."

Wallace's last game was a 4-4 draw at Norwich. Le Tissier's return didn't inspire similar fireworks. A 1-1 draw with Crystal Palace saw him frustratingly taken off and replaced by Alan Shearer. He kept his place, though, for the defeat of Derby and was handed back the treasured no 7 shirt for an entertaining draw with Wimbledon, the latter game proving to be a landmark in his career.

Ruddock had twice missed from the spot in the previous season and, when Paul Rideout also failed, Nicholl devised an unusual way to find a successor. Le Tissier had missed his first competitive penalty - taken in the youth team - but was composure personified when rattling home the most spot-kicks in a competition organised on the training ground. Thus he stepped up to take his first senior penalty and prove to Hans Segers how deadly he could be.

He had already beaten the Dutch keeper in the 53rd minute by moving in from the right wing, skipping past two defenders and shooting across him to equalise Eric Young's early opener. Dennis Wise scored another for Wimbledon but, when Segers

Celebrating at the expense of Hans Segers on the day he started to tap into another rich supply of goals.

was harshly adjudged to have brought Shearer down, Le Tissier waddled up, slammed home and started a trend that would see his name become just as synonymous with penalties as wonder goals.

The Wimbledon clash was sandwiched in between the dismissal of York's challenge in the Littlewoods Cup. Le Tissier set up Rod Wallace for the only goal of the first leg at Bootham Cresent and sent Shearer away to score his second in a 2-0 win at The Dell - the Geordie's first goals in the first team since his League debut 18 months earlier.

Le Tissier then had another face-to-face showdown with a keeper. In his next game, QPR were put to the sword by classic counter-attacking at Loftus Road and he converted his penalty to score the second as Saints used the pace of Rod Wallace and power of Shearer in a 4-1 win.

And a week later, leaders Liverpool suffered a similar thrashing, this time at The Dell. It was their first defeat of the season and saw Nicholl's men reach the high point of their time together. Jason Dodd delivered a measured cross on his home debut for Rideout to thump home a near-post header to edge Saints in front. Rod Wallace added no 2 with help from Le Tissier, who then neatly lifted the ball over David Burrows and used the space to pick out Wallace again for the side's third. On this occasion, the Londoner was at the far post to fire through Bruce Grobbelaar's legs.

"I saw David Burrows out of the corner of my eye, so I controlled the ball and flicked it over him," the creator said. "I was never blessed with blistering pace but, if a defender is coming at you so quick that you can knock it round him and get past him, you make yourself look quicker than you actually are."

Liverpool's search for a way back gave Le Tissier the room he wanted and he extended his own scoring run with a close-range header from Wallace's cross. Rideout was denied a hat-trick only by the woodwork as Saints sent their fans into raptures by going third on the strength of bagging eight goals in two games.

A 1-0 Littlewoods Cup defeat of Charlton at The Dell followed before Brian McClair's early strike at Old Trafford was matched within seconds by Le Tissier's intuition. He was alert to Bryan Robson's headed back pass and beat Lee Sharpe to the ball before despatching a low effort past the advancing Jim Leighton, only for McClair to score the winner.

Two less eventful games saw Saints total only one point out of six against Spurs and Coventry and, even when Le Tissier got back on the goal trail at Stamford Bridge, Nicholl's men couldn't win. He was nevertheless starting to make his name as a cool customer from penalties and few doubted his chances of firing Saints ahead from the spot when Chelsea's Graham Roberts clattered into Rideout.

He was proving just as deadly in open play. Three markers were left embarrassed as he carved through Chelsea's defence before angling a finish wide of Dave Beasant. His conjuring should have ensured Saints' first win in four matches but Ken Monkou and Clive Wilson struck in the final quarter to snatch a draw Chelsea barely deserved.

While Saints were struggling to snare wins against football's big guns, Liverpool excepted, the smaller fry were serving up ample portions. Luton were next to be devoured as Le Tissier headed home Jimmy Case's free-kick in a 6-3 Dell demolition that had Nicholl admitting his side would inevitably have some disappointments amid the delight of goal-laden victories.

By now, Tim Flowers was sympathising with opposing keepers over the trauma of facing Le Tissier penalties. He had often suffered as the guinea pig in training and was not surprised when another successful conversion earned a 2-2 draw at Millwall in early December after Glenn Cockerill had been taken out by the keeper.

"He used to practice his technique in training," Flowers recalls. "He used to say: Would you go in for five penalties? I did but never got near them. He also used to do weird things like practice his shooting from 40 yards. I'd think: He's miles away, is he having a laugh? Then I'd find myself at full stretch keeping them out. He'd practice his free-kicks as well because they were a chance for him to score. His eyes would always light up at the thought of taking them."

Even without Le Tissier scoring or providing an assist, Saints picked up points. Before and after Christmas, Rod Wallace hit the target as wins over Manchester City and Arsenal kept them in the top six. Then the Channel Islander went three matches without a goal and even his return to the score-sheet failed to end the hold that visiting Sheffield Wednesday appeared to have on them.

The famine, such as it was, ended from the penalty spot after Rod Wallace was hauled down by the bamboozled Roland Nilsson, and Le Tissier then showed a nimble pair of heels to dart in and put Saints 2-1 in front, only for Peter Shirtliff to quickly thump home an equaliser.

Saints' considerable frustration melted away two days later at Charlton, where Le Tissier started to show off his talents from free-kicks. He curled a shot round the wall to cancel out Rob Lee's early opener and an outrageous back-heel late on allowed Rod Wallace to seal a 4-2 win that stuck in the memory. Even the main man was impressed with his own artistry in executing a pass he was hoping to avoid.

"I was starting to make a run out wide to allow Rod a bit of space but he rolled me the ball and carried on his run," he said. "I was facing off the pitch and away from goal, and the only way I could get to Rodney was to pull out a little back-heel. I used my right foot to send the ball right into his path and he went on to slip it nicely under the goalkeeper."

It was the kind of trick only the game's magical players dream of pulling off. Most earthly beings would have been happy with the penetrating pass that cut open the home defence for Wallace to score his first in the opening half.

Knock-out football was also providing excitement and Le Tissier was instrumental as Swindon were beaten at the second attempt in the Littlewoods Cup after the sides had drawn 0-0 at the County Ground.

Thirty-six minutes into the replay, the packed Dell crowd had almost given up hope, with future Saints midfielder Alan McLoughlin helping the lively Robins into a 2-0 lead. Then came a stunning second-half fightback which brought four goals, Le Tissier playing his part well by curling a teasing free-kick over the wall and past Fraser Digby.

That party piece came on a day when he generally failed to shine but his displays throughout December were recognised as he was named Barclays Young Eagle of the Month. The award won him praise but not a coveted place in Bobby Robson's England set-up. Astonishingly, he was never considered for the under-21 squad.

"I'd very much like to think I could get in the side or at least the squad," he said. "I'm a bit disappointed it has not happened already. If you don't get an under-21 cap, it tends to hold you back from moving up to the B team and the full side. If I don't break through this season, I might have a long wait. I feel this might be my best spell for the club. I am really enjoying my football. We're playing some great stuff and it's a real pleasure being out there.

"Consistency has always been a problem but I feel that goes hand in hand with experience and I've really benefited from having an extended run. In the past, I was under pressure because whenever I had a bad game, the manager would drop me. Now, I don't feel pressure every time I run out. That is the biggest difference. I feel much more part of the team. The system is geared towards wingers and is working well.

"We now have three in midfield and that gives me more licence to do my own thing. Rod feels the same. The two of us also tend to score more with three in midfield because when we had two centre-forwards, we would play more as wingers and didn't have to go inside as much. Having said that, 4-2-4 worked well. We caught teams on the hop for a while until a clampdown on me and Rodney when they put a defender and midfielder on us. I thought the manager might stick with that formation a little longer but teams were beginning to come to terms with it."

Spurs were powerless when presented with the tricky task of coping with Le Tissier and Wallace as Saints' FA Cup campaign started with the kind of win that hinted at a march to Wembley. They travelled to London to face a sided minus Paul Gascoigne, who was out with a broken arm, and Terry Venables' men learned there was a player in the opposition ranks with equal brilliance.

Le Tissier started unconvincingly by blasting a chance against the shins of Bobby Mimms from Case's pass but the midfielder was the supply line again after 29 minutes and this time the right-winger neatly side-footed into the corner of the net as Gudni Bergsson desperately attempted to catch him.

Before the half-time interval, Le Tissier broke superbly from midfield and played a penetrating pass for Barry Horne to slide home from a tight angle. David Howells' piledriver rewarded Spurs' new-found endeavour and Flowers had to produce two spectacular saves to claw away Paul Stewart headers before Rod Wallace finally killed the tie off by following up Le Tissier's header to slam home the third.

Le Tissier's inspired contribution was bringing chances galore for his team-mates and Russell Osman was next to take advantage to earn Saints a 2-2 draw with Everton. The no-nonsense defender had already crashed home from a free-kick to give the side a lead, which evaporated when Norman Whiteside struck with two goals. But with 16 minutes left, Le Tissier turned up in a selfless wide position and crossed low for Osman to volley home first time.

It kept Saints fourth but a splash of cup activity led to a run of two defeats and a draw against Villa, Palace and Luton respectively. It saw them drop to tenth. Le Tissier was quiet in the games and appeared to have been saving his magic for the Littlewoods Cup and a dramatic fifth-round home clash with Oldham.

He left the lumbering Ian Marshall floundering to crack home a 20-yard drive via a deflection off Earl Barrett and, after Andy Ritchie equalised with nine minutes left, kept cool to slot home a penalty when Stuart Barlow checked Horne. It should have been enough to guarantee a quarter-final spot, only for Ritchie to pop up four minutes into stoppage-time and force a replay.

In the FA Cup, Saints made sure they didn't suffer another sucker punch as Le Tissier's corner was headed home by Ruddock to earn a scrappy 1-0 fourth-round win over Oxford, who had recently vacated the top-flight spot Oldham would soon seize. Then it was up to Boundary Park, a ground so cold in winter that it is labelled 'Ice Station Zebra' by manager Joe Royle.

This time it was Saints who froze as Ritchie and Mike Milligan scored in the second half to send Royle's men on their way to a Littlewoods Cup final appearance. It was a double cup heartbreak for Saints, who had been knocked out of the FA Cup by Liverpool in a tie missed by Le Tissier as he nursed a sore ankle.

He was nevertheless drawing the scouts to The Dell in droves, with Spurs regular watchers of his talent. He still had 18 months of his contract to run but the interest prompted Nicholl to safeguard Southampton's star attraction. The offer of a four-year contract was initially turned down, though, as the player attempted to land himself a decent pay rise.

"The manager has made me only one offer so far and we are not far away," he said. "There are just a few little things to sort out. If he makes me the right offer, I am quite willing to sign. The length of the contract does not bother me. The chances are that I will sign but we all want to do the best we can in life, so I will not be rushing into anything."

Nicholl was crying out for his most creative player to turn it on again and keep alive the club's hopes of European football. The Heysel ban was close to ending and Saints, having missed out on a 1986 UEFA Cup spot because of the tragedy, were aiming to feature in England's foray back into competition. Le Tissier answered his manager's prayers in that direction by sparking back to life in the clash with Norwich.

It was hat-trick time again and, of course, there wasn't a scruffy one in the batch as Saints cruised to a 4-1 home win. The scores were level when, ten minutes after half-time, Le Tissier took the ball on his thigh, spun in a flash and powered a shot into the top of the net. His second showed more of his close control as he made monkeys out of two Norwich players - one of them former team-mate Andy Townsend.

Picking up a pass from Osman just inside the Canaries half, he gave Townsend and Mark Bowen a sighting of the ball in appearing to overrun it. The pair set themselves to nick possession but, like a street entertainer, he embarrassed them both by unveiling his latest trick and whipping the ball away as they comically collided. While Bryan

Gunn was probably chuckling to himself over the mid-pitch comedy, Le Tissier picked his spot early and unleashed a fierce low drive that raced past the keeper's fingers and pinged into the net off his left-hand post.

After Kevin Moore also scored, the Channel Islander took advantage of Norwich's disheartened defence to grab his third with four minutes left. He found Francis Benali in space on the left by clipping a pass into the left-back's feet, evaded his marker and raced on to the return to bewilder Gunn with a delicate chip.

That finish may have been the most pleasing on the eye but the footwork for his second goal had thrilled him even more. The master considers it one of his ten best and he said: "I dribbled round Andy Townsend once and found myself in between Mark Bowen and Andy again a few yards later. I just managed to drag the ball between the two of them and they ended up tackling each other as I went away."

Nicholl added to the debate over which of the sumptuous strikes were best by picking out the opener as his favourite. He said: "Matthew's finishing was absolutely brilliant. The last two looked spectacular, although in many ways the first was the best. He had to work much harder for it, turning almost 300 degrees to get a shot in. I enjoyed that most of all, especially as it got us moving."

The goals took his tally for the season to 19 and the fever for him to be called up by England was spreading in the national press. France's assistant manager Gerard Houllier had already been in contact on the orders of national team coach Michel Platini to let Le Tissier know he would be welcomed across the Channel. The French were desperate to pounce as Bobby Robson had yet to include him as part of his England set-up in the countdown to the World Cup finals in Italy later that year.

Le Tissier said: "The World Cup is always at the back of your mind but I'm not going to build up my hopes because Bobby Robson more or less has his squad together. The next one will be the big one for me but anything can happen. Injuries to key players could let you in and it is all about getting your break at the right time."

While the Norwich match was a glorious one for Le Tissier, it was followed by one of those infuriating performances as Saints lost 3-2 against Chelsea after Rod Wallace had fired them into a two-goal lead. Wallace was in the form that made him impossible to cope with, his pace and deadly finishing - combined with Le Tissier's ability to pick him out when well-positioned - leaving opponents shaking their heads.

The pairing worked perfectly when Derby visited The Dell on March 10. Wallace brought down a Le Tissier header to beat the imposing presence of Peter Shilton and open the scoring before the keeper was left exposed as Le Tissier ghosted into the box when Benali crossed from the left. The Saints star had all the time he needed to slot home the crucial second in a 2-1 win.

The victory kept Nicholl's men seventh in the table in a tight race for Europe, although the boss must have known Saints' chances of a top-six finish would hinge on the next three games.

Manchester United came to town for a match sandwiched between daunting trips to Wimbledon and Liverpool - a side now constantly been linked with a £2m move for Le Tissier as they hunted a replacement for John Barnes.

The tough run came at a time when Le Tissier ignored the call from France and pledged his allegiance to England, with Robson assuring him he was in his thoughts. "I've spoken to Chris Nicholl and am pleased that Matt has indicated his future lies with England rather than France," the manager said. "This being so, he comes into serious consideration for a place in the England B team."

Le Tissier responded in his usual way to the encouragement - with yet another stunning display that single-handedly earned Saints a draw against battle-hardened Wimbledon. Plough Lane was particularly intimidating for star players as they knew they would be singled out for the 'special' treatment. It was the kind of game where the faint-hearted would drift out of the action as studs and knee-high tackles went flying in.

Benali took the bait as he retaliated against the injustices around him and was dismissed for launching himself at hard-man John Fashanu just after the hour. Le Tissier might have been excused for wanting to save his talents for the clashes with United and Liverpool. Instead, he humiliated the dirty Dons with his second hat-trick in four matches.

Admittedly, his powerful shot for the first needed a deflection from the leg of Eric Young to loop over Hans Segers. Wimbledon's unscrupulous tactics turned things round to 3-1 in their favour before Le Tissier stepped forward again magnificently for a ten-man team many still deemed to have a soft centre.

Flawless control gave him ample room for a deadly close-range finish that put Saints back in the game. Then four minutes later, Segers was left with the impossible task of guessing which way he would go from the penalty spot after Keith Curle made the mistake of tangling with the electric Rod Wallace.

The predicable late battering was withstood and Saints had a point that would have been given up without Le Tissier's clinical intervention. Even then, the bad feeling continued. The Dons carried on their nastiness after the final whistle by refusing to hand over the match ball, claiming the first of his trio was an own goal.

The display finally tipped the balance for Le Tissier's England career and he was called up for the spring-time B friendly against the Republic of Ireland in Cork. It laid to rest the fears that Le Tissier's international prospects were being scuppered by his loyalty to what were perceived nationally as a small-town club.

"It was getting very frustrating not receiving any kind of international recognition," he said. "I was beginning to wonder if I was being overlooked because I was not playing for one of the bigger clubs. Obviously, it has been a good season so far for me and there had been a few under-21 matches, which I felt I stood a chance of playing in. I have not even been in an under-21 squad, let alone the team."

In an England shirt at last - but this fixture in Dublin was hardly a happy occasion.

While the England front looked bright, Le Tissier's dreams of playing in Europe effectively came to an end when Saints were soundly beaten at The Dell by Manchester United. It was the worst kind of send-off as he headed off to join up with a new set of team-mates.

It was his first outing in an England shirt since the under-20s' tour of Brazil and he failed miserably to take his chance on a pitch hardly suited to his skills. Dave Sexton's side slumped to a shock 4-1 defeat on a mud patch, Ireland's willingness to fight for every ball making it a match for the Saints star to forget.

His inability to find time on the ball and his refusal to fly into tackles saw him dragged off at the interval with a flea in his ear. "Le Tissier and the other new lads will get other chances," Sexton said. "It is their first step on the ladder and will be good experience. Matt did not really get into the match. It would be easy to say he was not brought into it but, at this level, you have to stand on your own feet. Good players get hold of the ball. If you're going to be polite and wait for it, you're long gone. The game will by-pass you."

What should have been a big night for Le Tissier had turned into a waste of time and he revealed his frustration. "It was more like a cup-tie on a non-League ground than an international. The pitch was bumpy and it was 100 miles an hour stuff. It was a disappointing start. I just hope I get another chance to show what I can do. I found it hard to get into the match but was just starting to do so when I was taken off."

His club form was also dipping. Case's firecracker against his old club failed to prevent a brave defeat at Liverpool, where Le Tissier was unable to make an impact. And he struggled as Saints then lost at home to QPR before winning 1-0 at Sheffield Wednesday four days later.

Ironically, just as he hit a scoreless streak, he was being lauded with his first major honour - as the PFA's Young Player of the Year. He finished just ahead of Rod Wallace in the voting, with team-mate Horne not surprised to see the two junior members of Saints' squad neck and neck.

"It was a fantastic time," Horne said. "Those two and a half years under Chris Nicholl were really happy days. You often find managers are the opposite to how they were as players. It's almost as if he had seen the game from one point of view and felt he knew how to counter that. Chris loved creative attacking football and that's how we played. We went 4-3-3 - the three were Wallace, Le Tissier and Shearer.

"We had a good system with an experienced three in midfield - Glenn Cockerill and me either side of Jimmy Case. There was a good balance. It was brave and typical Chris Nicholl and, because of the three senior lads in midfield being so disciplined, it gave Matt and Rod licence to thrill. That's what they did.

"The nice thing about Matt was that he was a generous lad. He would give his time up for local good causes but was also generous in the dressing room. He really appreciated your efforts. I have played with many great players, and the type of player Matt was meant he needed people around him that would do the graft for him. He was the bricklayer and I was the hod carrier but he was always quick to notice your efforts. That says a lot about him."

Le Tissier was back in creative mood in the 3-2 win over Charlton, his cross allowing Ruddock to crash home a header. And he supplied the ammunition for Rod Wallace to fire his second in the 2-0 defeat of Forest at The Dell. Named Saints Player of the Year before the home demolition of Coventry, Le Tissier took 36 minutes to give the fans another reason to cheer by slotting home a penalty after he was bundled over by Trevor Peake.

The inspired Le Tissier continued to sweep the board in the individual honours by adding the Barclays Young Eagle of the Year trophy to his PFA Young Player of the Year award. But probably more important to him as he was handed his silverware were the words of praise from England boss Robson.

"It might be a bit late for this World Cup but Matthew has to be there for the next one," the manager said. "He is lazy but he can win a match at any time and whatever the arena. He has vision, talent and the ability to turn a game. He knows when to run with the ball, when to hold it and when to release it. Chris Nicholl still has a lot of work to do on him but he is fantastic player who will thrill the crowds.

"He has scored only a few goals fewer than John Barnes, who has the back-up of the whole Liverpool team. No disrespect to Southampton but scoring 24 goals for them and at such a young age is a tremendous achievement."

Le Tissier receives the warm congratulations of another Saints legend, Terry Paine, after he swept the board with awards at the club - and beyond - in the spring of 1990.

It was the kind of statement Le Tissier had been longing to hear. "The awards are a great way to round off my best-ever season," he said. "It was great to hear Bobby Robson's comments. This World Cup has come just too early for me but it is nice to know I am in line for the next one and I have set my sights firmly on it. It has been a tremendous season. To win this award, the PFA Young Player and the Echo Saints Player of the Year trophy is quite something. The PFA one probably means the most as it is awarded by a my fellow professionals but I am thrilled by them all."

Tellingly, Nicholl revealed a manager's frustration when he joked about the awards. "A lot of blood, sweat and tears have gone into these awards - and they have all been mine!" he said.

His confidence boosted by the plaudits, Le Tissier was on form at Highbury in Saints' next game. He threaded through a return pass to allow Horne the chance to crash Saints into a 47th minute lead but Arsenal crushed the faint hopes of a top-six finish once and for all when Lee Dixon punished Ruddock's hand-ball by converting from the spot and David Rocastle scored a late winner.

It became a case of double London despair with Saints going down 2-1 against

Spurs in their final game despite a late header from substitute Andy Cook - teed up, of course, by Le Tissier.

With his contract negotiations rumbling on, Le Tissier might have been excused for wandering round White Hart Lane dreaming of what it would be like pulling on a shirt of the club he supported as a boy. Spurs boss Terry Venables had already been in touch to discover whether Le Tissier fancied the move - something that turned the player's head.

"We got to the point where we agreed on wages but then Southampton gave me a new contract and offered the same deal," he said. "It was a very hard decision to make. There was my loyalty as a Spurs fan but by this time I had settled in the Southampton area. I love the club and the people and that was enough to keep me here."

Le Tissier scribbled his signature on a three-year contract tying him to The Dell until the summer of 1993. His awards were a key factor in his decision to stay and he said: "I'm very happy with the deal."

It was the closest the player ever came to leaving but his loyalty would force him to field jibes for the rest of his career about being happy as a big fish in a smaller pool. Even his team-mates were not sure whether he might have been better advised to move on and test his talents and mentality at one of England's top three clubs.

Horne added: "The fact he never left is why he is held in such high regard along with Ted Bates. He could have gone to other clubs and I know he was severely tempted by Spurs. The fact he didn't go says something about Matt but I'm not quite sure what that is. A lot of people have accused him of lacking ambition but I know he had a strong competitive streak. He wanted to win anything he tried and win every game.

"The other side of the coin is you could say it was a commendable old-fashioned virtue that he was happy to stay where he was and wanted to win something with Southampton."

A winner's medal is something Le Tissier never achieved but, as Flowers points out, he can look back on a career full of personal happiness. "Whatever happened, he had a good career and I'm sure he doesn't look back on it with any regrets," the keeper says. "He was happy with his lot. He had his chances to move. Spurs and Chelsea were options and I'm sure other big clubs had a look.

"I can see why he stayed, though. He was a darling with the fans and was a big fish. He was adored down there and played some super football. Plus Southampton are a fantastic club and it's a great place to live. So he didn't do too badly, did he?"

1990-91

England Agonies

BOBBY Robson's exit following England's emotion-charged run to the World Cup semi-finals gave Le Tissier two targets in the second half of 1990. UEFA had lifted the ban on English clubs competing in Europe following the Heysel disaster, so Saints, having finished seventh the previous spring, had high hopes of going a step further and taking the glory nights of the early 80s back to The Dell.

Also, Graham Taylor's appointment as national boss gave Le Tissier hope that his England career was not over before it had really begun. As ever, when there was a chance to stake a claim, he was quick to seize it. It took him just seven minutes of the new campaign to pick up the thread, ironically away to Taylor's former club Villa. He left Paul McGrath spellbound with a neat sidestep and slid the ball past Nigel Spink.

His faultless finishing was good enough for an opening-day point and he said: "It was very nice to get off the mark so early. Last season, I had to wait eight games for my first goal. That might shut a few people up and show that last season was no fluke. With the new England manager, it should have kept me in the public eye. I would love to think this would be the season I get a call-up to the full England squad."

A home win over Norwich was sealed by John Polston's own goal, only for Saints to then lose against visiting Luton. Le Tissier's slanted ball across goal was touched home at the far post by Paul Rideout but his side were two down by then and there was to be no miracle comeback.

That defeat was followed up with the depressing news that he had once again missed out on selection for an England squad. And he must have felt the world was conspiring against him when even selection for an under-21 friendly against Hungary, ironically to be played at The Dell later in the week, eluded him. This time the barrier was a UEFA rule change barring the use of over-age players.

It meant Le Tissier, amazingly, would never win a cap at that age group. He would turn 22 just a few weeks later and he said of the hole in his CV: "Obviously, I am disappointed because I really thought I would be in the running this time but I have

Are you watching, Graham Taylor? Leaving Paul McGrath spellbound and kicking off the new campaign with a goal at the England manager's former club.

plenty of time for an international career. I'll just have to carry on as I am, playing my best for Southampton."

As Saints posted an impressive £734,761 profit, results on the pitch were not so notable. Most of the cash had come from the sale of Danny Wallace and it was clear Le Tissier was lacking his pal's spark around the area. He failed to make an impact in a 3-1 defeat at Nottingham Forest but notched in the opening minutes as Sheffield United were beaten 2-0. He drove to the touchline and, with apparently nowhere to go, tricked his way back on to his right foot before cracking home a vicious shot from the angle of the six-yard box.

Saints put on their usual brave display against one of the big boys in losing at Manchester United - a 3-2 defeat followed by a more emphatic loss at Everton. Le Tissier did not impress in either, although he set up goals for Alan Shearer and Neil Ruddock in a 5-0 Rumbelows Cup thrashing of Rochdale in between.

He carried on in the creative vein in the 3-3 home draw with Chelsea by arrowing in a corner for Ruddock to head home and left Coventry manager John Sillett admitting he hated coming up against his genius as Saints were inspired to a narrow victory at Highfield Road in early autumn.

Peter Billing deflected in a cross by Le Tissier, who had shuffled past two men on the right, and although Coventry levelled with David Burrows' penalty, a free-kick at the other end brought the winner. Jimmy Case stood over the ball before Le Tissier put a training-ground routine into operation, receiving the ball via Case and Barry Horne to delicately chip Steve Ogrizovic, the keeper embarrassingly 'second-guessing' and moving early in the wrong direction

"As soon as the free-kick was given, I decided to have a go," Le Tissier said. "It was just my range. That's the first time this season I've had a go from that kind of position. I practise them in training but had not previously had the opportunity in a match. As I lined it up, I noticed the keeper was trying to read it. He was standing yards over to his left, which was where I was going to hit it.

"I went for it and it was great to see it go in. I needed that goal as I have been playing a bit deeper lately and the goals have not been as frequent. But it is still up to me to make runs and get into scoring positions. I know if I keep plugging away, the goals will come."

Skipper Case, who has also been known to hit a mean free-kick, emphasised it was not pure power that made Le Tissier so effective from dead-ball situations - but his unswerving accuracy. "Matt is a very deceptive player," he said. "He can hit the ball either side of the goal and he only decided at the last second to clip it that way. It was not a particularly powerful shot but, with his accuracy, it didn't need to be."

He may have been a saviour on the pitch but he apparently failed to make the grade as a room-mate. Tim Flowers said: "I used to room with Matt but had to sack him for snoring and turning the telly off too late. He would watch anything until three in the morning and kept it on until the dot went off and the national anthem was playing!"

Horne took over from Flowers and, luckily, shared Le Tissier's nocturnal habits. He said: "He was a great room-mate. Neither of us were great sleepers and he was a clever lad, so we sat up a lot and talked. He has a dry wit. He is very quick and a typical footballer in his sense of humour - but quicker than most. Ruddock, Shearer and him were always messing around. Being a bit older, I didn't tend to get involved."

The team spirit Nicholl had developed saw the likes of Le Tissier and Ruddock enjoy their share of late nights. The inner sanctum of Saints' dressing room were also combining well on the pitch. Le Tissier reacted sharply to latch on to a rebound from Shearer's shot and net the first goal in a 2-0 Rumbelows Cup win over Ipswich at the end of October.

Then he struck in familiar fashion against Wimbledon. The Dons were one up with ten minutes left when Roger Joseph caught Shearer in the box. Saints had showed plenty of bottle in standing up to the unique Plough Lane challenge but the pressure was on Le Tissier as he faced Hans Segers from the spot for the third time. Yet again, though, the Dutchman was left bamboozled by a coolly-stroked point-saver.

It was dead-ball heaven once more for the Saints play-maker as QPR fell foul of his ever-growing confidence. This time, his deadly accuracy from a free-kick did the trick as the ball curled into the left-hand corner and set up a 3-1 win.

Le Tissier's next test was to transfer his fantastic club form to the international stage as a member of a Barclays League XI, who, to all intents and purposes, were an England B team. Wigan boss Bryan Hamilton was the figurehead, although it was clear Graham Taylor was pulling the strings, the Irishman saying: "We have included a lot of quality players who could be very close to the full international side and Matthew Le Tissier is one of them.

"He is a very talented young man and if he uses this game properly, it can be a springboard for him towards the England side. We are treating this as a top-level representative match and the idea is to see which of the players can perform at the highest level."

If Le Tissier needed a calming influence alongside him against the Irish League - and that was unlikely - he could not have wished for a better man to be geeing him along than his Saints team-mate Case. The wise old head had been asked along to influence some of the younger boys with his experience and Le Tissier said: "I'm delighted about his inclusion, both from his point of view and my own.

"If he is out there with me, it will make life easier because he knows the way I play. The England manager has had a big say in the side and I know reports of the game will be sent back to him. A good performance, and perhaps a goal, will keep me in the spotlight. Graham Taylor has been putting younger players on stand-by for the full squad, so I am hoping to be one of them. If I keep knocking the goals in, then if someone drops out through injury, who knows?"

But in a game that ended 1-1, Hamilton was not overly impressed with Le Tissier's contribution. "One or two players helped their cause but one or two didn't," he said. "Matthew Le Tissier found that he needs to step up a gear at this level. He played well in fits and starts and did not let himself down but he needs to get involved more. He is a very talented individual but he has to make that talent count."

On the home front, Saints hit a slump in the League, beginning with a 4-0 defeat at Arsenal in mid-November, although they were still flying in the cups. They tucked into a lifeless QPR to record a 4-0 Zenith Data Systems Cup win but Le Tissier was ineffective again in the high-scoring home League defeat by Crystal Palace.

Ironically, Saints knocked Palace out of the Rumbelows Cup three days later with Le Tissier capping a sweet passing move by netting the opener. Case's penetrating pass allowed Rideout to gallop through and cross for him to rifle home. He then delivered a corner for Shearer to complete a 2-0 win.

Back in the League, he produced a teasing cross for Rideout to power in a header at Leeds, only for Saints to crash again. Le Tissier and his colleagues were criticised by Nicholl for running scared in the first half as a fanatical crowd urged their side into a 2-0 lead inside ten minutes and the visitors couldn't repair the damage.

The dressing-room fireworks had an impact. At Norwich a week later, Le Tissier scored early for the third time in the season, Bryan Gunn getting a hand to his shot, which still trickled slowly over the line in the snow. The goal failed to produce a turnaround in the team's fortunes in a 3-1 defeat but provided a personal confidence booster ahead of his next England B cap.

At least it should have been his next cap. Instead, an embarrassing mix-up with the England hierarchy saw him put his international future in doubt when he dropped out of the trip to Algeria. Suffering with flu, Le Tissier left it late before informing the travelling party, through bouts of coughs and sneezes, that his aching limbs made it impossible to raise himself from his bed.

Delaying a decision might have been seen as an act of determination to play for his country - but was viewed differently by the men who mattered. He was astonished to hear criticism from the England camp of his refusal to join up and undergo a rigorous examination. Taylor and his no 2 Lawrie McMenemy were angry that he left it until an hour before the squad were due to meet to announce his withdrawal.

And, in a weekend of blizzards, they pointed out that Wolves keeper Mike Stowell had even enlisted the help of a snow-plough to ensure that he picked up his boots from Molineux before heading for the airport. The backlash left the shocked Southampton star making a series of hurried phone calls to smooth the waters.

He was led to believe he was in the clear when he was summoned for duty in the England XI in Peter Shilton's testimonial in mid-December. He made the most of his chance as a substitute in that game with a goal on a freezing night at White Hart Lane - although he had spent the previous evening sinking more than a few jars at the Saints players' Christmas party.

Le Tissier left London without any worries about his England career and said: "It was all a misunderstanding. I have spoken to Graham Taylor and Lawrie McMenemy and the matter has been cleared up. Next time, I'll let the England doctor look at me but it was nice to know from this call-up that it will not be held against me.

"It was a great honour to be asked to play in this game alongside such talented players. It shows I am still in the picture and it was great to get a goal as well. Monday night was the players' party and I got in at around 1am. It was only then that my wife told me I'd been asked to play. Of course I was delighted to do so. It was a super tribute to Peter Shilton, who is a tremendous professional. To score was a nice bonus. I was disappointed not to get on earlier but, considering the way I felt at the end, it was probably just as well!"

Unfortunately, despite his instant recall after the debacle surrounding his illness, the Algeria incident seemed to be noted down as a black mark against his name at FA HQ; a reason perhaps why he had to push on towards even greater Southampton deeds if he was to ever make it at international level.

In between his England experiences, Le Tissier had welcomed a new team-mate at

The Dell. Alan McLoughlin was signed for £1m from Swindon in a bid to add more industrious creativity and allow him to continue to roam free. The midfielder's debut against Aston Villa on December 15 helped stop the rot after four League defeats in a row, although it wasn't the Irishman who grabbed the headlines.

The touch of class came from a familiar source, Le Tissier glancing home Micky Adams' cross as Saints dominated, only to be restricted to a point by David Platt's late penalty. The draw was nevertheless to herald a return to the player's free-scoring days of the previous season, following the brief interruption of a defeat at Liverpool.

The golden patch brought five goals in four League games, starting with a Boxing Day home clash against Manchester City. With nine minutes left, he made the most of a defensive mix-up to fire home the clincher in a 2-1 victory. And, three days later, he geared up to face one of his heroes, Paul Gascoigne, as Tottenham arrived at The Dell for a Christmas bonanza.

Gazza was consistently blamed as the main reason for Le Tissier not breaking into the England squad. The lovable Geordie was now a full-grown national icon following his tearful displays in Italia 90 and was taking everything in his stride as his football blossomed despite a media scrutiny that would have stunned even Wayne Rooney.

That kind of stress was just what Le Tissier dearly wanted to avoid in his own life. "I don't envy Gazza at all," he said. "He is under far too much pressure for a young lad. There is such a lot on the shoulders and he's done exceptionally well to cope. I'm amazed he has kept his sanity although, after speaking to him at Peter Shilton's testimonial recently, I'm not sure he has!

"The papers seem to have a different story about him every day and I admire him for the way he handles things. I like to think I could cope with that pressure but you don't know until you have it. Not being in the full England squad, I have escaped that media attention but it is nice to be compared with Gazza because I do admire him, particularly his dribbling ability.

"I love to watch him play, although I don't want him to get too much on the ball against us. He is one of the few players I would pay to go and see. I like to think I also play to entertain and attack. When I get the ball, the first thing I think about is going for goal. That is the way the game should be played."

The match was billed as a showdown between two of English football's biggest showmen and Le Tissier must have thought he proved a point by emerging on top. In the 17th minute, he twisted past two Spurs defenders before cracking a drive past Erik Thorstvedt. Then he delivered a free-kick for Ruddock to head down and Rod Wallace to sweep home. Le Tissier went full stretch to slide in and hook a long punt past the Norwegian keeper to wrap up a 3-0 win.

It was not just on the football pitch that he was proving deadly. He was also beating his team-mates on the golf course with his dead-eye putting and Flowers found out that Le Tissier could find the target in other games as well. "He loved sport and was pretty good at whatever he tried," he said. "We used to play snooker after training and he regularly beat me 10-0.

"He said to me this one day: 'I might as well buy you a pair of white gloves for Christmas because all you do is take the balls out of the pockets when we play.' But that just summed him up. Even as a kid, he was cocky. His attitude was always that he was a player. He felt that if you got the ball to him, he would make something happen and he did so on a regular basis. Sometimes, it looked like you were out of a game and Matty would turn it round for you. He was a top player."

The follow-up to the Spurs match was less than inspiring as Saints suffered an off day away to Sunderland and lost to a penalty by Kevin Ball. But Le Tissier was then the match-winner as the side beat Ipswich on FA Cup third-round day. His measured corner set up an equaliser for Shearer, who returned the favour by heading down for the no 7 to lash home a rocket of a drive.

He needed two bites of the cherry to make the tie safe in the second half, with Rod Wallace and McLoughlin combining to send Micky Adams galloping away for a cross that Craig Forrest blocked. The rebound fell to Le Tissier, though, and he completed the job from a yard out.

The star man was in dominant form once again in a stunning win at Luton. With Saints 2-1 down, he got to work by latching on to a penetrating pass by Alex Cherednik, which was cleverly dummied by Wallace, and drilled in the equaliser. A sharp turn at the far post then gave him space to fire an accurate shot across the keeper to edge his team ahead before Wallace converted a centre by Shearer to clinch a 4-3 success.

Le Tissier was not able

Not just a winner on the pitch - as Neil Ruddock found out.

to conjure up a similar performance at home to Manchester United in a Rumbelows Cup fifth-round draw in which Shearer scored. But he shone as Shearer bundled Mark Crossley into the net for a controversial opener as the points were shared with Nottingham Forest in mid-January.

His progress was subsequently hampered by a hamstring injury suffered when Saints went out 3-2 in their replay at Manchester United. He struggled through some games while missing others, the side being thrashed 4-1 at Sheffield United and finally overcoming Coventry in the FA Cup fourth round with a 2-0 replay win at Highfield Road - fast becoming a lucky ground for them.

Although his dodgy hamstring continued to plague him, he was able to get through a 2-1 defeat at QPR and net his tenth penalty in the process. He also teed up Ruddock for an early headed goal in the FA Cup clash with Forest, who still hit back for a draw. Le Tissier was later subbed, though, and was left on the bench when Leeds lost at The Dell in early March.

He was back in the starting line-up in the Monday night replay at Forest, only to remain a peripheral figure in a 3-1 crash, his one sparky moment coming when he clipped the bar with a chip. Southampton's season was falling apart as he sat on the sidelines, injury forcing him to miss the defeat at Palace. Even when recalled for the visit of Manchester United, the club's talisman was far from sharp in a 1-1 draw earned by Ruddock's goal.

Le Tissier did finish the season with a flourish, though, with six goals in nine matches after missing the dramatic 4-3 home defeat by Everton. He needed to. Saints had dropped alarmingly into relegation danger but pulled clear with one of their characteristic recoveries, starting with a 2-0 win at Chelsea and continuing with a 3-3 draw at Manchester City.

McLoughlin was chopped down by keeper Dave Beasant at Stamford Bridge and Le Tissier ensured the chance from the penalty spot did not go to waste. Then he raced on to a long pass from Kevin Moore to crash Saints ahead at Maine Road. "The injury kept me out for four weeks and it probably took me another two or three to get fully fit," he said. "Even before the injury, I was not playing that well but the goals came."

The two results lifted the gloom and Le Tissier banished any fears of the drop with the only goal at home to second-placed Liverpool, enjoying a touch of fortune as his fourth minute long-range shot flew past Mike Hooper with the aid of a deflection.

The hero of that game was dragged off in the next as Spurs took White Hart Lane revenge for their mid-season defeat, with Gary Lineker scoring twice and having a penalty saved by Flowers. But his roller-coaster run-in continued three days later when Nicholl acclaimed his best performance of the season as he salvaged an unlikely point at home to eventual champions Arsenal.

After tracking back manfully throughout the game to keep a check on the Gunners, he popped up in the 79th minute to equalise. Adams, whose own goal five minutes earlier had put Arsenal ahead, fired in a cross from which the Gunners defence inevitably appealed for offside. Le Tissier ignored the screams and rammed home his 17th League goal of the season.

It was a fantastic all-round performance, containing the leg-work to tame Arsenal's talented runners and the energy to turn up in spots that could hurt a team set to win the title for the second time in three years. "He did his best to do the side of the game that involved getting back," Flowers said. "It didn't come naturally because, when we were defending, he liked to float into a position where he could best spring an attack.

"Today, there are plenty of those players in the Premiership because the game has evolved. He certainly didn't ignore his duties, though. It wasn't like he was a wrong 'un and didn't try and do his bit. It just wasn't his forte. Getting into the last third and making things happen was what he was all about."

Le Tissier was spot-on again when his 81st minute penalty edged Saints ahead for the first time in a home game against Sunderland that they eventually won 3-1. And his piledriver was too hot for Steve Ogrizovic, allowing Rod Wallace to nip in for his second of the game, as Coventry were also beaten at The Dell. His club form was back on track but still didn't spare him more England disappointment.

He was left out of the late-season B team clash with Iceland at Watford, a stunning 22-goal haul clearly having failed to convince Graham Taylor he was worth another look. "Of course I was disappointed not to be in the squad, especially after scoring four goals in five games," he said. "All I can do is keep sticking the ball in the back of the net and hope to be picked next time."

Taylor was quick to dispel rumours that Le Tissier was being punished for not making the Algeria trip. But he did suggest that the Saints star needed to utilise his God-given talents more consistently to make that cherished step up. He was forthright in spelling out that the player's inability to win a place in the squad for the summer tour to America was down to his own failings.

And Taylor administered a massive kick up the backside by insisting Le Tissier had to move out of his comfort zone if he was to progress on the international stage. He said: "Matt ought to take a look at himself. He is very inconsistent. I'm not trying to interfere or be critical. I'm just saying what everyone knows about him. He needs to apply himself more.

"Players need to know now what they have got to do to get into the squad. It is no good me telling them in two years' time why they have not made it. It is hard enough for me to pick a team at the best of times without picking a player when I have no idea what he is going to give me. I don't need that problem. I had enough of it at club level. I cannot be wondering if this is going to be the game where he turns it on. I have to be certain what he will give me.

"People talk about his free-kicks but Barnes and Gascoigne can take free-kicks. It needs to be more than that. Players have got to ask themselves if they want it and if they want it badly enough. They must be prepared to be put out because of their desire to succeed. The next two years will be very important for the likes of Le Tissier and Shearer and Wallace.

"Some players will come through and we have already told the under-21 lads that some of them will be in the senior squad by the time of the next World Cup. At the moment, we don't know who they will be but, by then, they will be 24 and should be looking to break into the side. I would hope to have the squad for the next World Cup finals pretty well settled by 1993, although there will be chance for others to burst on to the scene at the last minute."

Taylor's comments about Le Tissier's mental approach amounted to a withering attack. The manager had picked up the vibes that the precocious front-man was letting games pass him by if things were not going right. It was a damning accusation and one Le Tissier would spend the summer brooding over once the final two League matches were out of the way.

He was one of the few players to take any joy out of the 6-2 loss at Derby - but only because he beat Shilton from the penalty spot when Shearer was impeded. Then came a draw with Wimbledon that was quickly overtaken by off-field events. Nicholl was sacked at the end of the campaign and Le Tissier was surprised.

The club thanked the popular manager for his services over six years and publicly acknowledged his 'honesty, integrity and dedication.' "It's a sad day for the club but a manager with high ideals has not produced the consistent results which his hard work deserved," said a statement from The Dell.

The former Saints and Northern Ireland defender had handled Le Tissier cleverly and was strong enough to ignore calls to over-play his rising star at too early an age. He had also brought the best out of him by employing him in such an attack-minded formation. With Rideout, Shearer and Rod Wallace, he formed the four-man spearhead that had given Saints fans some of their happiest memories.

Now Le Tissier would have to start again with a new man in charge.

1991-92

Trying Times

C HRIS Nicholl's demise was meant to herald a new dawn, with the promise of a high-profile successor who would be capable of leading Southampton's crop of starlets into unchartered territory. The next manager would be of such calibre that a regular top-six spot was being viewed by the Saints board as realistic.

Mouth-watering prospects were dangled in front of excited fans by the media, among them England under-21 coach Ray Harford. He was a strong front-runner and the future looked rosy but he was overlooked and the men upstairs instead unleashed a nightmare on Matt Le Tissier.

Ian Branfoot was well rated by Dell bosses but little known outside Reading - the club he had taken into the old Second Division in 1986 by a huge margin. His strong character and straight talking impressed in the interview process, his determination to succeed convincing the powerbrokers they had found the right man. If only they had done a little more research......

Branfoot's style was never going to be popular with supporters who had enjoyed some exhilarating times under Nicholl. And the biggest casualty was ultimately going to be the south coast darling, Le Tissier. The new gaffer's ideas did not allow for a free spirit to wander in and out of games at will, picking up loose balls and creating chances from deep.

He was from the Graham Taylor school of direct play, with defenders launching the ball to the strikers, and midfielders chasing around picking up scraps. By now, Rod Wallace had left for Leeds and, surveying his troops, Branfoot picked out the man he believed was the key to success at Southampton - and it certainly wasn't an enigmatic forward from the Channel Islands.

Branfoot had spotted Alan Shearer's emerging talents and made the future England captain the focal point of Saints' attack despite his distinctly modest return of ten goals in 61 starts. The manager had already upset the Dell faithful by letting the 37-year-old Jimmy Case depart on a free transfer to Bournemouth. With Le Tissier's role considerably toned down, there was a fear that a new era of long-ball football was being ushered in.

Le Tissier was called in a few days before pre-season training for a heart-to-heart in which he was given an explanation about the new job he would be expected to carry out. Surprisingly, after scoring 40 goals in two seasons as a right-sided striker, he was earmarked for the more disciplined task of patrolling the flanks.

Tackling back was now part of his remit as well as attacking full-backs and, after sampling the new system, he put a brave face on the part he was to play in Branfoot's world. "The new boss called me in before we resumed training," he said. "It was a very basic chat. He explained how we would be playing and how he expected me to work in a different role.

"He said he was impressed by what he had seen but that I needed a kick up the backside. Mind you, that has always been the case! Possibly, Graham Taylor felt the same, so it would be very ironic if I played this role, scored half as many goals and ended up getting in the England squad. I am not thinking about that at the moment. I'll just do what the manager asks and, if anything comes from it, so be it.

"At the moment, I'm getting used to the system and doing what is asked of me. Once I have got used to it, I can try a few different things and see how they go. It is a very different style of play from what we have been used to and it's going to take a few games in the First Division to find out whether or not it suits me.

"I certainly don't see myself scoring as many goals as I have done in the last couple of seasons but I am not worried about that as long as we win games. It is hard work but I'm enjoying life under the new manager. He seems a good honest bloke. He is straight down the middle and you always know where you stand with him. That is all you look for.

"He came across very well with us and he likes to share a beer with us, which is good. There is a much different atmosphere about the place and a bit more organisation about our play."

Branfoot knew that shackling Le Tissier's talents would not be popular with adoring Saints supporters but launched a PR exercise to explain why using the player's elegant skills in a more demanding role would create a better team man. "Le Tissier has got to help out," he said. "I can't stick him up front on his own because it would be a luxury. If Matty is so good, why has he not played for England?

"Good strikers work their legs off. Look at John Barnes and Ian Rush. They work very, very hard tackling back but are still able to do their own thing and use their great skills within the overall framework of the team. That is all I'm asking Matt and the rest of our players to do. And with the kind of money they are on, I don't think I am asking too much.

"To be fair to him, he has done extremely well for me. He has worked hard for the team. He may have to sacrifice a bit of himself but it is for the good of the side. He

Matt Le Tissier, watched by Alan Shearer (left), on the warpath in a 1991-92 match at home to Chelsea.

still has licence to do his own thing because he has great talent and I would not want him to stop doing what he is best at. It is a question of getting the balance right."

Despite the reservations of Saints fans - and presumably Le Tissier - the season could not have started better. Shearer took just two minutes to score at home to Tottenham in a game that passed Le Tissier by. But it went downhill as, for the second time in a row in the fixture, Gary Lineker scored twice and Spurs ran out 3-2 winners.

The no 7 was ineffective as Saints lost to the only goal at Notts County but notched his first of the season at Sheffield United. His corner was smashed home by Shearer before he himself used his left foot to volley home Jason Dodd's deep cross as a fine move helped secure the first victory of the campaign.

It took six games to rack up a second, although Le Tissier scored a penalty in the 2-1 defeat at Luton. The pressure-relieving win came against Wimbledon courtesy of Glenn Cockerill's low drive but muddied the waters further. It was the day Branfoot admitted his master plan for Le Tissier was not working.

The Channel Islander was taken off at half-time after being unable to get into the game from his deeper role. It was the fourth time in six games he had been dragged off and his frustration was reflected in a trio of bookings for dissent.

Rather than hand Le Tissier the free role he craved, the stubborn boss stuck to his guns and dropped him, explaining: "Matt is lacking in confidence, so he had to come off against Wimbledon. It may be that he will need a couple of reserve games to get back but that does not mean I don't rate him. When he's fit and raring to go, he is a real asset but he knows better than anyone he has not been playing well.

"He has had these patches before where he loses confidence. But there is no doubt he will be in the side as soon as he can get it back and start doing what he can. When he is on form, I have no difficulty at all fitting him into my system. I can forgive his lapses and his laziness when he's playing well but at the moment he is neither working nor producing."

A new threat to Le Tissier's place emerged when winger David Lee was snapped up from Bury for £350,000 and striker Iain Dowie arrived from West Ham in a deal worth £500,000. Lee would admit he lacked the ability to turn a match in Le Tissier's style but he was capable of delivering a teasing cross and tracking back to provide cover for his full-back. Branfoot kept him in the side at Le Tissier's expense when Micky Adams was recalled in the defeat at Sheffield Wednesday.

It was becoming clear the new manager considered the previous season's 23-goal hit-man to be a luxury his side could not afford in away games. Recalled against Scarborough in the Rumbelows Cup, Le Tissier struggled to make his usual mark against lower-division opponents, although Branfoot was relieved that a potential banana skin was sidestepped via a 3-1 first-leg win.

Next up at The Dell were Arsenal and Ian Wright once more wreaked havoc with a hat-trick in a 4-0 thrashing, with Le Tissier wondering just what the future held for him. Dropped for the second away game on the trot, he saw Saints grind out a 1-1 draw at Oldham, where Lee was again preferred. Even the honest winger now admits that he was stunned to find himself edging out one of his favourite players.

"It was a great honour for me to play instead of Matt," he said. "I went down there, young and naïve, and never thought I would push for a first-team place so soon. Then the manager said he was going to leave Matt out and put me in. I played quite a few games, thought I did all right and created a few goals. But then the pressure of the fans wanting to see Matt back in the team became too much.

"When you've got a choice of seeing David Lee or Matt Le Tissier in your team, everyone is going to choose Matt Le Tissier. Unfortunately for me, but fortunately for Matt and the supporters, they soon put him back in. And when he played, he was excellent. There was no comparison between him and myself. He was one of the best players in the country."

Le Tissier won his shirt back instantly and scored for the first time in a month by drilling home Shearer's cross in the second minute as Scarborough were polished off 5-3 on aggregate despite a 2-2 second-leg draw. Norwich's visit to the south coast produced a stalemate before Saints switched to the Zenith Data Systems Cup and travelled to Bristol City, where Le Tissier was handed a central striker's slot - and played the starring role.

He cleverly flicked on for Shearer to score and was deadly with his finish when the compliment was repaid in a 2-1 victory. "Matt did very well for a first time in that role," Branfoot said. "He scored, which was part of the exercise, and hopefully that will boost his confidence. He chased hard and still managed to get on the end of things in the penalty area. It was very promising."

Letting Le Tissier take his frustrations out on lower-League opposition was a clever stroke by Branfoot, who reaped further reward as the beaming star took apart Nottingham Forest at the City Ground in late October. His two goals and an assist inspired Saints to only their third win of the First Division season.

He was at his acrobatic best to volley home the opener from Lee's cross and was as accurate as ever from the spot when Shearer tangled with Carl Tiler. Soon after, he spotted Shearer lurking in the box and picked him out for a simple finish with a perfectly weighted cross. It was Le Tissier at his best and he revealed the move upfield had come from yet another heart-to-heart with Branfoot.

"It was a 50-50 decision between us," he said. "I wanted to play further forward and it went well in training, so we decided to give it a go. I like it. It gives me more options whereas before I could only really go down the wing. Now I can bring others into the game or go on myself."

As quickly as the goals came, though, they dried up again and he became reliant on cup games to find the net. In a dour ZDS tie at Plymouth, he looped in a header from Barry Horne's cross to seal a 1-0 win but admits to the worst miss of his career when he hammered against the underside of the bar from an open-goal chance six yards out against Sheffield Wednesday in the Rumbelows Cup.

Le Tissier was convinced the ball had bounced down over the line - a la 1966 - and walked off the pitch arguing with referee Roger Milford, who quickly gave him some advice about his manners. "Matthew is outstanding but he has to learn to control his mouth if he wants to be an England international," Milford said. "Players react differently. Some query a decision and get on with it. Matthew carries on arguing."

Saints saw off the Owls at the second attempt but crashed out of the competition to Forest in a fourth-round Dell replay in which Scott Gemmill netted the only goal. Branfoot then moved quickly to dismiss a rumour sweeping the city that he had had a bust-up with Le Tissier after dropping him for the December 7 clash with Liverpool.

Le Tissier had disappeared in the Forest cup game, leaving Shearer taking a battering up front. The Saints boss, keen to protect what he saw as his most valuable asset in Shearer, handed Le Tissier's shirt to Iain Dowie against Liverpool and ordered him to share the workload. But he insisted: "Talk of a row is absolute nonsense. We sat down and had a reasonable chat about why I was leaving him out.

"I don't do that with all my players but I felt I owed Matty an explanation. When I started at Reading, I used to call them all in for a chat when I dropped them but found that only put me under pressure. So now I wait to see if they care enough or have the bottle to come to me. I wanted to talk to Matt, though, to help him get the best out of himself. When he's on top form, he's a great asset. He has tremendous ability but we need to see it more often."

The talent was on show when he scored his next goal in a third-round FA Cup tie against QPR at The Dell. He once again accepted Branfoot's challenge to prove he deserved his shirt. He had been dropped for the previous three games after failing to score in four starts in November, three of those matches ending in defeat.

There had been a third goal in three rounds for Le Tissier in the ZDS as he dusted himself down and scored late on from the spot in a 2-1 Southern Area semi-final defeat of West Ham in which he had also superbly made the equaliser for Shearer. But in the League, he was left on the sidelines and a reprieve in the home draw against Notts County didn't even last 90 minutes - he was dragged off in a shocking game.

But against QPR, his extravagant skills saw him curl a cross on to Steve Wood's head for the opener and net with a long-range effort to secure a 2-0 win. It was a reminder of the tricks he was capable of and he took his new-found confidence into the following League game with Sheffield United. In only the third minute, he latched on to Dowie's knock-down and despatched a left-foot drive from a tight angle, then used his dead-ball skills to set up Richard Hall for a header that made it 2-2.

Against Saints' relegation rivals, Le Tissier's influence should have been enough to wrestle a point. But the Blades showed greater desire in the final quarter of the game and won 4-2 to leave their hosts rooted to the bottom of the table.

Branfoot had no answer to the question being tossed around the football pundits as to whether Le Tissier was a genius or a liability to his side. He said: "The problem with Matthew is I never know what I'm going to get from him, although he has the skill to win games on his own. If I can guarantee a performance from him, his would be the first name on the team-sheet every week.

"If he does not reach the high standards he has set for himself, he will be left out just like any other player. But when he's doing it, he's the best there is and no-one at the club ever doubts his enormous ability. He burst on the scene with 40-odd goals in two seasons as a virtual unknown but now he has a reputation as one of the best strikers in the First Division and teams are out to stop him.

"They are not daft. They are not going to allow him the space and time he had before because they know if they do that, he will destroy them. I will allow Matthew more scope than anyone else because I know eventually he will put one in like he did against QPR. My problem is that I have to draw a line. When he ceases to become a plus to the team, I have to bring in someone who will be."

The problem, in Horne's view, was not Le Tissier's inability to perform as an industrious midfielder but Branfoot's decision to use him in such a role. "Ian Branfoot destroyed all the good work Chris Nicholl had done," Horne said. "Chris left behind a team containing Flowers, Dodd, Benali, Ruddock, Hall, myself, Rod, Shearer, Matt.

"In time, he dismantled it but, from the off, wanted us to play in a regimented, rigid and uninventive way like Palace, Cambridge and Wimbledon. It was 4-4-2, play for free-kicks, play for possession in the final third and try and score from there. Matt

Safely on the way...another penalty finds the net, this one coming at Chelsea in the area final of the Zenith Date Systems Cup. It went on to become a memorable evening.

was very often left out of the team. If he did play, he was tied down to that system. When you have a player as good as Matt, that's a waste.

"Chris gave him a free role. He did ask him to play one side or the other but he didn't ask him to chase back. Under Branfoot, he was ordered to get up the flank and then track back. Also, Branfoot had preconceptions about a player and when he decided a player couldn't do something, that was the end for him."

Despite the manager's painful deliberations, he gave Le Tissier a seven-match run - and his form returned. Although goals were hard to come by in the League, they continued to stack up in the cups, where he was enjoying a spectacular season - never more so than in the ZDS Southern Area final second leg at Chelsea.

Leading 2-0 from the first game, Saints were eyeing a Wembley final, which Le Tissier made a reality with a hat-trick of pure quality. He slotted home a penalty after Jason Cundy was sent off for chopping down Shearer, then delightfully cut in on Adams' pass, took Tom Boyd out with one touch and fizzed a drive past Kevin Hitchcock. And he stealthy sneaked in behind Chelsea's short-handed defence to smash home his third from close range.

A League victory at Tottenham was followed by a battling Monday night goalless draw with visiting Manchester United in the FA Cup fourth round. With Saints rock bottom of the table and Alex Ferguson's men one place off the top, it appeared to be an unequal struggle. But the favourites came up against a side determined not to be dominated. And Le Tissier was in top form.

"We were a tight team down there," Flowers added. "We had a lot of adversity. We were regularly in relegation fights but always got out of it because we stuck together. We might not have been the best team technically but we had a backbone and were willing to have a go. Sometimes you could roll teams over if you did that. We fought hard for each other."

That desire was evident against United as twice Le Tissier sent Shearer bearing down on goal, only for Peter Schmeichel to use his huge frame to save. It was going to take something out of the ordinary to get past the great Dane and Le Tissier nearly produced it when Adams delivered a deep cross. In one fluid movement, he controlled and unleashed an arrowing volley at goal but Schmeichel flew across his line and threw out a giant glove to claw the ball to safety.

It left Saints with the disheartening prospect of an Old Trafford replay, a League defeat at Norwich in the meantime hardly serving as the ideal preparation. The omens were worrying as well. They had never won away to United in the FA Cup and their position in the First Division table did not suggest that the run was about to end, especially with the home team fielding an arsenal of attacking weapons that included Mark Hughes, Ryan Giggs and Andrei Kanchelskis.

But, incredibly, Saints went two up inside 22 minutes. Stuart Gray capitalised on hesitancy between Paul Parker and Schmeichel to nip in and roll the ball home from outside the area and, following an infringement on Adams, Le Tissier quickly whipped in a free-kick for Shearer to power home a header. Now could they hold out?

They suffered a body blow just before half-time when Giggs burst into the area to be upended by Flowers, Kanchelskis following up to net. Neil Ruddock commanded a brave defensive scrap for the entire second half and, with seconds left, Le Tissier was eyeing the fifth round. But it's never that easy with Saints…..

Giggs' cross was easily gobbled up by Ruddock, whose firm header should have gone out for a corner. Unfortunately, Jeff Kenna was in the way and the ball smacked into him and bounced back into play. Brian McClair was quickest to spot the potential of the moment and darted in to equalise. It was a sickener for Saints, whose players looked on in shock.

Surely, United would now steamroller Branfoot's leg-weary side, who were by this time suffering the exertions of three games in eight days. It looked all over when Bryan Robson bundled home at the far post in a scramble, the ball crossing the line by several inches before being quickly hacked away by Saints' desperate defence. To United's astonishment, David Elleray waved play on and the tie went to penalties.

In shoot-outs, one man in a side can generally be counted on to score. Saints had two. Shearer was given the frightening task time and again for England in the latter part of his career while Le Tissier was another who seemed certain to net from the spot. Most teams also send their top man up first, which is why Schmeichel must have been shocked to see Ruddock strutting up to take Saints' opening kick.

Flowers explained: "Branfoot got us into the centre circle and said: 'Right, these are my five takers. Tiss, you go first to get us off to a good start.' But Tiss just said: 'Get lost, I want to go last when the pressure is on.' That was his attitude and I have no doubt whatsoever he would have smashed it in the top corner. He would never have missed. As it happened, he didn't even get to take one."

That was because Ruddock, Shearer, Horne and Adams all converted. Neil Webb missed United's first, Lee Sharpe and Denis Irwin scored, and it was do or die for the teenage Giggs. He aimed to Flowers' left and the keeper flung himself to the turf to glove the ball away and set off on a length-of-the-field charge to celebrate in front of Saints' fans. It was a glory sprint that earned him a place in Southampton folklore.

Le Tissier had envisaged playing the decisive role himself but was still on a high, his joy increasing five days later when he received a shock call-up to Graham Taylor's 31-man squad for the senior and B games against France - the first time he had been involved at international level since the upset caused by pulling out of a B team game against Algeria 14 months earlier.

"It's funny how things work out," he said. "I couldn't even get in the 13 at The Dell. Now, here I am in the England squad. The last six weeks have gone brilliantly for me. I have been playing well and the goals have been going in but this call-up is still a bit quick. It came right out of the blue but is a great chance. I mean to make the most of it. I knew I'd have to do that little bit more to get back in with England."

The pat on the back that the selection gave him saw Le Tissier's confidence spiral. One of his trademark passes opened Chelsea's defence for Horne to score in a 1-1 draw. That one ball was a message to Taylor and Lawrie McMenemy as to just what his vision could bring to England. Gary Lineker had already announced plans to retire after the 1992 European Championship finals and the thought of Le Tissier making his debut at the same time as Shearer was causing a real stir on the south coast.

Taylor admitted: "I see Le Tissier very much as a forward. I would not put him on as a winger. He has the ability to link in and move around. And there's a chance for him to get a game. It's no good me waiting until Lineker retires and then starting to look to replace him. Any sensible employer, knowing that he was losing a key man, would immediately start looking for someone and I'm no different."

For Shearer, just seeing his pal and club colleague on the same England training ground was a cause for satisfaction. "I'm pleased for Matt because he has had a bad time this season and has come back well after being dropped," he said. "He has got his just reward for scoring goals and playing well. It would be a real bonus if Matty played alongside me because I know him well."

It was ironic Le Tissier had been brought in against the French, a year after Michel Platini had tried to poach him. "My father had quite a few phone calls from French representatives asking about me," he revealed. "There is a French connection in my family going back generations but not reason enough to qualify me even if I wanted to play for them. There was never any chance I'd choose them ahead of England.

"Platini was my idol along with Glenn Hoddle when I was a youngster. I have achieved a major ambition by playing against Hoddle and it would be nice to complete the double, although Platini would now be a manager. Everyone loves the French team of the early 80s when Platini was at his peak and that style of play would probably suit me because the pace is slower.

"I also watched Hoddle's career with great interest when I was at school. People criticise him for his lack of workrate and I stuck up for him. Now I'm in the same boat. Players like us don't charge around for 90 minutes and I've had to live with that criticism all my career. But people don't notice the workrate if you're scoring goals. I was very surprised to be selected and whichever game I am involved in, it is just great to be part of the international scene."

Unfortunately for Le Tissier, the chance was fleeting as his run-out in the B match at Loftus Road was restricted to 14 minutes. That was his opportunity to impress and, understandably, he failed to make the kind of impact needed to compel Taylor to hand him a full start in the near future.

But, to the manager's muddled way of thinking, the Saints star *was* given a second chance by being asked to sit on the subs' bench for the full international the following evening as Shearer marked his England debut with a goal. Le Tissier was sent home with something of a flea in his ear, Taylor effectively telling him: "I've done my part. Now it's up to you to show me through your workrate that you have to be included."

Taylor said: "We all know about Matthew's talents but my feeling has been that

Matt Le Tissier and Alan Shearer find time for fun in the build-up to England's double header against France in February, 1992. While Shearer was all smiles after a goal in the senior international, his club-mate was less fulfilled by events.

talent alone is not enough. That usually gets you the runners-up spot but applied talent gives you the chance of being first past the post. Matt may feel people don't understand him but I hope that, by selecting him, I've given him a little bit of love and shown him that he is involved.

"He may have felt he was not part of my plans in the build-up to Sweden. If he did, he was wrong and I hope this shows that. I know what he's like. I have watched him at times and wondered: How can I justify picking him? Sometimes his attitude on the pitch in terms of applying his talent has raised that question. The game is littered, right through history, with people who should have won more caps. Nobody ever says it's their fault. It's always somebody else's fault. It really is up to him now."

Horne, Le Tissier's room-mate at Southampton, was hardly shocked by the words and now believes the England coach belonged in the same boat as Branfoot; a manager who put workrate above ability. Taylor selected Carlton Palmer, and Horne said: "You look at some of the players Graham Taylor capped and you can understand why he didn't like Matt," he said.

"If you look at his style of play, right through his career, he wasn't the type of manager who could use Matt. But Matt was a match-winner whenever he stepped on the pitch, so someone wasn't getting the best out of him."

Le Tissier took Taylor's advice on board as Saints went to Third Division Bolton in the FA Cup. He gave a stylish and effective performance and turned the first half into a dream for Richard Hall. Twice in two minutes, the defender benefited from his team-mate's superb corners to score but, from cruising to victory, Saints were caught cold, first when a failed offside trap left Andy Walker free to score, then when Scott Green headed an equaliser with four minutes left.

After drawing 0-0 at home to Coventry, Saints seemed sure to take care of the unfinished business against Bolton. But Flowers was in rare jittery form and they went close to major embarrassment as the keeper's gaffe allowed Walker to level Shearer's opener in a tie that remained equal until all hell broke loose in the final minute.

Following a hurried Flowers clearance, Julian Darby latched on to a throw-in and crashed in a long-range drive. Straight from the kick-off, Le Tissier, using his brain in search of a dramatic reprieve, spotted David Felgate off his line and tried an audacious shot from the centre circle which had the panicking keeper dashing back to save.

For once, it was not Le Tissier who saved the day - but Horne. Hardly a prolific scorer during his time at Southampton, the midfielder cracked in a screamer from fully 30 yards to equalise and underlined his hero's status for the evening when he was on hand again to net a dramatic extra-time winner with a deflected shot.

The heroics had a positive effect on Saints' League form and Branfoot finally saw his side find the edge needed to stay up. A precious point was ground out at Liverpool before Dowie scored in a win at home to West Ham and Le Tissier smashed home Shearer's cross on the volley for the only goal in the defeat of Palace.

In between, Saints were held at The Dell by Norwich in the FA Cup sixth round with Le Tissier looking a pale shadow of himself, then he was dropped for the win at Manchester City before being guilty of falling for Robert Fleck's antagonism in the replay at Carrow Road.

The game started well with Le Tissier finding Ruddock's head from a corner to earn a half-time lead. But, goaded by Fleck's nasty kick at him off the ball, Le Tissier lost his cool and aimed an angry right foot at the Norwich man close to the referee. There were no complaints from the Saints star as he was sent off; only regrets as he watched his team-mates lose 2-1 in extra-time. "We had Sunderland waiting for us in the semis and had a really good chance of reaching Wembley," he admitted. "I have to take the blame. I lost my cool, retaliated and that was it. The referee had little choice."

Branfoot had returned to his former club Reading to agree a loan deal for Michael Gilkes, who, with Le Tissier suspended, had a chance to impress. The flying winger played his part as wins over Luton, Everton and QPR took Saints to a season's best run of six League victories on the trot and lifted them to 17th.

Le Tissier may have been sidelined for that trio of successes but there was no way he was going to miss the March 29 LDV final against Nottingham Forest. Saints were at Wembley for the first time since the League Cup defeat by Brian Clough's team in 1979 and the city was gripped by the occasion despite the trophy's minor status.

Fans, faces painted in blue to reflect the strip to be worn on the day, crowded into the stadium fully expecting their side to win. But, by half-time, the 32,000 followers were crestfallen as Scott Gemmill crashed home a volley against the run of play and, seconds before the break, set up Kingsley Black for a second.

Branfoot tore into his troops at half-time but his roasting seemed to fall on deaf ears as Forest ran the show until 26 minutes from time. Then Le Tissier put Saints back in the game in unexpected fashion. Ruddock's throw was nodded clear to Terry Hurlock, who swung it back for Ruddock to this time deliver a peach of a cross. As Des Walker struggled to get airborne, Le Tissier powered in to thump home a header.

Just four minutes later, the Channel Islander turned provider with a pinpoint corner that Kevin Moore, towering over keeper Andy Marriott's attempted punch, headed home fiercely off the underside of the bar. Now Forest were on the rack as Dowie headed just wide and Hurlock saw a piledriver acrobatically tipped away before the game edged into extra-time.

Even then, it was all Saints as Le Tissier bent a shot just wide and found Dowie with two corners to force Marriott into more action. But their hearts were broken in the 112th minute when Gary Charles' right-wing cross reached Gemmill at the far post and the unmarked midfielder was clinically accurate with his finish. It was a cruel ending and a dejected Le Tissier admitted: "It was a great moment to score at Wembley but would have been better if we had won."

Still missing out in the League, Le Tissier scored twice for the reserves against

A rest for those mercurial feet....this time it's a headed goal as Roy Keane and Des Walker are left as bystanders by the effort that brought Saints back into the Zenith Data Systems Cup final against Brian Clough's Nottingham Forest at Wembley.

Luton and, when recalled to the first team, found a side brimming with confidence. One defeat in ten League games had banished any fears of relegation, although a lack of goals still rankled with fans. With the freedom from survival pressure, it was hoped Le Tissier would bring the season to an entertaining conclusion. But he failed to score in the final six matches and ensured Branfoot suffered the wrath of supporters on the day he had hoped to be their hero.

Hauling Le Tissier off at half-time against Wimbledon might have gone unnoticed as the 1-0 win mathematically secured a place in the new Premiership - set to begin the following August. Anger was rising, though, and fans turned on the manager, chanting 'We hate Branfoot' and 'Branfoot out' as the players' own celebrations fell flat.

He defended his decision to take Le Tissier off but admitted the verbal attacks got to him. "The lad was absolutely knackered, just like Alan Shearer," he said. "He has played four games in seven days and run his heart out. He has worked as hard as I've seen him. I'm paid to make decisions and I had to make sure we did not concede. We had fresh legs, so I used them. I knew the fans would not like me taking off their favourite player and they have a right to their opinion. I'm not paid to be popular but of course it hurts to hear it."

Le Tissier's workrate of the previous weeks was enough to win him another vote of approval from Graham Taylor. He was included in the England squad to face the CIS, along with Shearer and, although only earning a place on the bench for the B side, made an impressive impact when replacing Lee Sharpe at half-time. Twice he delivered pinpoint crosses, with Peter Beardsley heading off target and skipper Gary Mabbutt planting his effort straight at the keeper in a 1-1 draw.

Just days later, though, Le Tissier watched another England man, Ian Wright, take Saints apart as he netted a hat-trick in a 5-1 Highbury win. It ended a disappointing campaign on low note at a time when manager and player were thought to be at odds. But there are strong indications from elsewhere that the relationship was cordial.

"There was no friction between them," Flowers said. "Ian did what he thought best and Le Tiss had his ideas what was best. But that's football. We all get left out at times and don't agree with it. Ian played a direct game and Le Tiss preferred to knock the ball around. Ian had every right to do it his way. He kept us up. We had a big centre-forward and two big centre-halves, so we threatened at set-pieces and knocked the ball in early. He had a big team ethic and people would say Tiss' workrate wasn't the best. But his argument was that if you gave him the ball, he'd win a game. It's one of those double-edged swords and it's hard to say who was right. I know he is unpopular in Southampton but I liked Ian Branfoot. He was straight and good as gold to me."

Lee also defends Branfoot's handling of the star. "To be fair to Ian, he persevered with him for quite a while but it got to a stage where he might have lost his job," he said. "That was what happened in the long run."

The thought of Branfoot heading to the exit door had crossed Le Tissier's mind. Unfortunately, outlasting him would take longer than expected. Not that Shearer minded. "I think I prospered under him," he said. "He introduced a slightly different style with an emphasis on getting the ball to me early or playing it down the channels for me to run on to. Working with him was a pleasure because I think he played to my strengths. I'm certain that's one of the reasons my goal tally increased.

"Matt had a God-given talent - a natural ability that enabled him to do things with a football which most other players could only dream about. We used to marvel at the things he did in training and, what's more, he produced them in matches as well.

"Matt, Rod Wallace and I emerged around the same time. We arrived in the team without much experience in the reserves. I suppose that was a tribute to Chris Nicholl, who was never afraid to give young players a chance if they were good enough. The three of us were different players and personalities. Matt was a one-off ball player who liked to do things off the cuff. Rod was lightening quick and a very good finisher. I was a good old-fashioned English centre-forward. We blended quite well because our styles complemented each other. We grew up together as footballers without ever socialising that much."

1992-93

A Powerful Reply

MATT Le Tissier must have wondered just how bad life under Ian Branfoot could become. Despite scoring 15 goals in 1991-92, it had gone down as his first poor season and there was worse to follow for Saints fans in a summer in which England performed dismally in his absence in the European Championships. They struggled for goals and failed to progress beyond the group stages.

Le Tissier's close pal, Alan Shearer, who was on the fringes of Graham Taylor's squad in Sweden, inevitably left The Dell once Manchester United and Blackburn had made their advances, although, surprisingly to some, he turned his back on the potential glory of Old Trafford and European football to sign up to Kenny Dalglish's Ewood Park revolution.

He was also romanced by Newcastle boss Kevin Keegan but felt that a return home, however emotionally satisfying, would not be right at that time. The one bright spot about Shearer's departure was that Le Tissier was in line to again take over the mantle of spearheading Saints' attacking threat.

There was bad news in store for him, though. Branfoot refused to budge from his tried-and-tested method of playing the ball early to a big striker and trying to pound opponents into submission. Instead of building a system round Le Tissier's undeniable skills, he splashed out nearly £1m of the £3.5m from Shearer's sale on the former Chelsea duo, David Speedie and Kerry Dixon.

Frustratingly for Le Tissier, the job he craved - a striker's role at The Dell - went to Speedie, a player who had been reluctant to quit Blackburn in the first place and head to the south coast. The main man had no choice but to accept being slotted again into a wide midfield role behind Dixon and Speedie. Branfoot had predicted 'flowing, artistic, attacking football' but the front-running pair fired blanks in the opening-day 0-0 home draw with Tottenham.

It was left to Le Tissier to become Saints' first scorer of the season - an emphatic finish in a defeat at QPR that was ultimately just as emphatic and further marred by the sending-off of Micky Adams. Their first point came in a draw at Aston Villa, although he failed to last 90 minutes and then missed the home defeat by Manchester United; four games without a win and another season of struggle was already on the agenda.

Branfoot desperately needed someone to give the club a kick-start and, unsurprisingly, it was Le Tissier who rode to his rescue. Middlesbrough arrived in town on the day Perry Groves was handed his Saints debut after signing from Arsenal for £750,000. But a youngster who grew up at the club proved the match-winner.

Having seen Paul Wilkinson open the scoring, Le Tissier levelled with a 79th minute penalty after Alan Kernaghan handled, then provided the corner for Nicky Banger to become the hero as he outjumped his markers to ram home a header. Three points were finally on the board but Branfoot's dream duo of Dixon and Speedie had yet to find the target in five games.

That poor run ended at Anfield on September 1, with Le Tissier supplying the ammunition. He used his trickery to provide a cross which Dixon clinically volleyed home. Ex-Saint Mark Wright levelled, although Branfoot's side could hold their heads high, having attacked Liverpool and given them a fright in pocketing a 1-1 draw.

The trip to Norwich pitched Saints against the surprise leaders and they were just three minutes short of a deserved point from a hard-working performance when Mark Robins netted. It meant they slumped to 18th place and their new strikers were still struggling to come to terms with life at The Dell, where it was Le Tissier on target once again in a 2-1 defeat by QPR.

Francis Benali's second minute free-kick bobbled around the box before Le Tissier took control and drilled home. But Saints fell apart after the interval with Andy Sinton and Justin Channing scoring in the Londoners' victory. Le Tissier was now the focal point of the club. Quite simply, if he failed to get on the ball, Saints failed to make an impact on a game and usually lost.

That was never more evident than in the home draw against champions Leeds, the midfielder supplying the pass for Groves' sublime finish. As usual, Saints could not hold on and there were only six minutes left when Gary Speed robbed them of a deserved win. Confidence was clearly low and was not lifted when the side were held 0-0 at Gillingham in the Rumbelows Cup second round.

Saints belatedly recorded their second win three days later after spending large periods of the game at Crystal Palace on the ropes. This time it was Dowie, one of the 1991-92 heroes forced to make way for the Dixon and Speedie show, who was recalled in search of a remedy. He scored two goals that must have felt all the sweeter when he learned that the unpopular Speedie had been transfer-listed.

While Branfoot tried to move out some of his captures, he was also keen to keep Le Tissier. As Aston Villa were added to the list of interested clubs, the board decided it was time to discuss a new deal. "We have made him what we think is a very good offer," the manager said. "We are obviously anxious to make sure he stays.

"He has not come back with an answer yet but we're in the very early stages of negotiations. Ideally, we would like to get it settled as soon as possible. When Matt is on song, he is one of the best. He has tremendous natural ability and has been working harder this season. He has tackled back and held opposing players up but he is still effective going forward and is trying hard to cut back on the dissent. He is one of our most gifted players and we don't want to let his contract expire."

For Le Tissier, the new deal was less about the financial benefits and more about playing in a side producing entertaining football and hunting the odd trophy. He said: "The manager offered me a contract a few weeks ago and I'm thinking about it. I won't rush anything but if it was about money, I'd have left a long time ago. I want to play in a successful team. I hope everything will be resolved by Christmas. The football side is more a sticking point for me, although there are encouraging signs."

Le Tissier was as much at fault as his team-mates when Saints embarrassingly crumbled once more at Sheffield United but netted twice as Gillingham were beaten in a Rumbelows run that ended at the next stage as the side failed to find the net against a revenge-fuelled Crystal Palace. In between, he was reinstated for a League defeat at Manchester City after missing out on the home draw with Wimbledon.

The football may not have been pretty but few could ignore Saints' desire to scrap for every point, although it needed touches of magic from Le Tissier to reap the full rewards. And there was a real irony in the fact that he effectively saved Branfoot from the sack with his best performance under a manager whose style left him cold.

Branfoot had needed a police escort to the tunnel when Saints were beaten by Palace and the match against Oldham on October 31 brought a sit-down protest from fans. Anger had grown so intense that he knew beating the Latics was a must if he was to survive. He bravely went for broke by giving Le Tissier a free role - and was paid back as the Channel Islander revelled in the space to spark attack after attack.

With his defence duties put on hold, he delivered an accurate centre that Richard Hall feasted on to spectacularly plant a diving header into the net and clinch Saints' third League victory. Many fans had thought Le Tissier might have served up one of his off nights, knowing that defeat would pave the way for a new manager, most likely one who would be much more sympathetic to his cause. Instead, after stirring Saints to a welcome win, he spoke up for his boss.

"You can't help but admire the guy," he said. "To walk down that touchline and put up with that amount of abuse says a lot about his strength of character. He just smiles it all off. I deliberately looked over at him before the match and he was still smiling. He didn't flinch. I was reading in the programme that every Southampton manager goes through this sort of thing. Even Lawrie McMenemy got it.

"Chris Nicholl was here for six years and had it for the last six or nine months but he went in the directors' box. Ian Branfoot is not taking that easy option. He will stand up and be counted. He will take the flak and the lads admire him for that. It doesn't come across to us players that it all affects him. He is very strong mentally. He has to be to walk up and down that touchline every game.

"Last season, when nearly everyone had given us up as dead and buried, his character came out in the team. We finished quite respectably and reached a Wembley cup final. Our style of play has been one of the main grouses and the crowd will take some winning over. In the last few weeks, we have tried to pass the ball about a bit and the signs are encouraging. It is all about confidence really."

Another painful-to-watch display garnered a point away to Ipswich, and Le Tissier's season enjoyed a mini-revival - initially at the expense of his

It wasn't only referees who got it in the neck - just ask Paul Ince! He is the sufferer in this clash at The Dell.

mate Shearer. The striker's first return to The Dell was the focus of media attention but Saints' no 7 stole the limelight by finding a hole in Blackburn's defence to crash in a rasping drive from Dowie's intelligent flick-on. It was only the side's 13th goal in 16 League games but once again the lead was squandered, with Kevin Moran equalising in a match in which Ken Monkou ensured Shearer hardly got a look-in.

Le Tissier was on target again at Nottingham Forest, this time using his head to net after being unwisely left unmarked to reach Adams' cross. The win lifted Saints to 16th and away from the drop zone for the first time in the season. Things then got even better when Arsenal were beaten 2-0 at The Dell before Le Tissier was further boosted by words from Graham Taylor.

The manager insisted he was still in his plans despite not picking him since the B international at the back end of 1991-92. "The reason Le Tissier is not in the England squad at the moment is simply because there are other players ahead of him in the reckoning," he explained. "We all know about his touch, his control and his ability. What he has to do now is keep working hard and wait for a chance.

"We don't have B games at the moment, which makes it hard to look at players who are too old for the under-21s but have not been able to force their way into the senior squad. I took Le Tissier to South America with the under-20 squad and know what he can do. I certainly would not rule out the possibility of calling him up. He scored a great goal against Blackburn and he's performing well and working hard."

By now, Branfoot's vision of seeing Dixon and Speedie recreate the double-act that had terrorised defences during their time at Chelsea was a distant memory. Dowie was the main target man and scored, along with Neil Maddison, in the win over Arsenal, the same combination finding the target in the 2-2 draw with Coventry.

Le Tissier had scored few easier goals than the one with which Saints then went into an early lead at Everton. It was a case of Christmas coming six days early when Neville Southall threw the ball straight to him and he got over his surprise to smack a shot past the Welsh keeper. But his sixth League goal of the season was undone by a Peter Beardsley penalty and a winner from recently released ex-Dell boy Paul Rideout.

After the previous season's Zenith Data Systems run to Wembley, Saints were handed a TV slot as the FA Cup third-round draw gave them chance of revenge against Nottingham Forest. Brian Clough's side must have known about Le Tissier's underrated aerial ability, having seen him score in two previous games against them with his head. But once again he was left with space in the area to nod home.

Adams and Glenn Cockerill paved the way for him to open the scoring but, seconds before the break, Saints threw the game away. Roy Keane was left unmarked to power between two defenders and head the leveller, then one-time Branfoot target Neil Webb fired Forest in front with a touch of class that Le Tissier himself would have been proud of.

Le Tissier tried his best to save the day and only Crossley's fingertips stopped him dribbling into a scoring position. When he did beat Forest's keeper, he saw a shot clip the bar and also cursed as Stuart Pearce raced back to clear off the line.

With Saints out of the Cup, their League form was coming under greater scrutiny. A Maddison header scraped a home win over Palace as the free-flowing style promised by Branfoot claimed victories on and off the pitch. After months of wrangling, Le Tissier was finally convinced he could once again shine in a Saints shirt and agreed a new contract covering two and a half years.

As if to mark the fact that Branfoot had changed his thinking over Le Tissier's deployment, Speedie agreed a two-month loan spell at West Brom on the very day pen was put to paper at The Dell. "The football aspect has always been important to me and I feel we are going the right way in terms of how we are playing," Le Tissier said.

"People who know me know money is not my main reason for playing football. I want to enjoy it and I'm doing that much more now that I'm up front. The gaffer likes his two solid rows of four to do their bit defensively and I don't quite fit into that category. So this is possibly my best role and it keeps me involved much more, which is important.

"I have been labelled as a player who drifts out of the game when playing wide right but that criticism has not been levelled much this season. Another factor was that Alan Shearer and myself both broke into the England squad last season, which shows you can get international honours without playing for one of the big clubs. That was very encouraging. I'd love to play for my country. Graham Taylor has a few out now, so I am keeping my fingers crossed.

"I have always been happy at this club. It has been my home for almost eight years and there is a sound squad. I want to help keep them in the Premier League and then help them challenge for honours next season."

Le Tissier's decision was seen as a major triumph for Branfoot. Many thought he would have little hope of clinging on to the striker after the way he banished him to the reserves in his first season in charge. "I am absolutely delighted Matty has decided to stay and that it has all been tied up so early," the manager said. "There are very few players in the game with his touch and skill on the ball.

"He can turn a game in an instant and certainly has the ability to play for England. He is one of the foundations for the future of the club and getting him signed up proves we are not prepared to see all our best players leave. It demonstrates we are having a go and also demonstrates Matty's faith in the club. He must feel there is a future here, otherwise he would not have signed.

"We still have to operate within the confines of our budget but we are prepared to go to the limit to keep our best players. Hopefully, it will also show that we appreciate skilful players who can entertain the fans. I hope he will help us be successful."

Le Tissier celebrated with a fantastic goal before his side collapsed again away to Middlesbrough in late January. He outrageously flicked over a defender and crashed home an equaliser, only for Wilkinson to find a winner with 20 minutes left. Le Tissier was then bang in form as Saints beat Aston Villa at home, coming up with a clever chip to find Banger for the opener.

He also conjured a perfect delivery for Hall to head home at Spurs as Saints' Jekyll and Hyde nature again haunted Branfoot. They went 1-0 up through Dowie but four goals in five minutes and a red card for Benali saw them slump to a 4-2 defeat that was followed by wins at home to Norwich and Liverpool - and the exit of Dixon on loan to Luton; an admission by the manager that his summer plans had failed.

Le Tissier continued on his talismanic way when his corner allowed Kevin Moore to score in the second minute to set up the defeat of Sheffield United at The Dell. And he enjoyed tormenting Wimbledon yet again as Saints won away for the first time since November, a big deflection on his left-foot shot beating Hans Segers before he stuck a ball on Moore's head for the second successive game to secure a 2-1 win.

After a deadlock at Blackburn, Le Tissier was the last-gasp hero in a crucial 4-3 win over Ipswich. He had already found Hall with an early corner for an equaliser at 1-1 and scored from the spot following Ian Stockwell's foul on Maddison. It was 3-3 going into stoppage-time when he ensured Saints' sixth straight home win by prodding home and wheeling away in celebration after Monkou's powerful header smacked against the bar.

Le Tissier's penalty-king reputation was now firmly established and he dismissed fears that his immaculate record was heaping more pressure on him every time he stepped up. "The fact I have never missed a penalty does not even go through my mind when we get one," he said. "There are a few butterflies while I wait to take it but, once I start my run-up, I don't think of anything except putting the ball in the net.

"I don't ever want to put one wide or too high. That for me would be the cardinal sin because it is basically a free shot from 12 yards and you should hit the target. The penalty helped set up a good end to the game and although we have had good results against some of the top clubs, for sheer excitement that has to be the best game the fans have seen here this season.

"The way we are playing right now, we could easily finish in the top six. The first three places are taken but, after that, it's wide open. It's just nice to be looking up rather than over our shoulders and that has shown in our performances. We have not had to scrap for the points and it's nice to be in the top half of the table after being relegation favourites. We have sorted our home form out, winning six on the trot, and 18 points like that is a hell of a lot, although we must be careful not to get over-confident."

Before the trip to Arsenal, the player was given the chance to go home as he set off with his team-mates for a friendly against a Guernsey XI. Predictably, the Le Tissier name was first on the score-sheet, although this time it was brother Kevin who neatly brought down a cross from another sibling, Carl, and fired past Tim Flowers.

With over 3,000 packed in to see their returning hero, Matt finally turned on the style by lifting the ball over the defence to allow Maddison to slam home the equaliser. Le Tissier then turned up at the far post to tap in an Adams corner and, after Maddison was hacked down, Guernsey's favourite son converted the spot-kick.

It was an enjoyable break from League football and there was still a touch of the cavalier in Saints' play when they were involved in another seven-goal thriller. On this occasion, though, they came out second best at Highbury. They were 3-1 down when Le Tissier drilled in a shot which David Seaman could not hold. Surprisingly, it was left back Adams who popped up to slam home the rebound.

Le Tissier got Saints back into the game in the 50th minute when left unmarked by Arsenal's much-praised defence with enough time to take a touch from Kenna's cross before finishing right-footed. His endeavours should have been enough to secure a point but slackness at the back was punished with winger Jimmy Carter grabbing the clincher 12 minutes from time.

Few fans thought they would ever witness 14 goals in two games under Branfoot and none expected what transpired when Nottingham Forest arrived at The Dell on March 24. Saints were a goal down thanks to Nigel Clough as Le Tissier was given a

On me 'ead, son! Le Tissier with brothers Carl (left) and Kevin when Saints flew to the family's home island of Guernsey for a friendly in March, 1993.

chance to add to his season's tally from the spot. He placed the ball in his normal confident manner and strolled up with the conviction that he was about to convert his 21st penalty out of 21. But Mark Crossley guessed right and got a hand to the ball to claw it out. It was to prove the only time in 48 attempts that the Saints no 7 missed from the spot and the shock was there for all to see when he hoofed the rebound over from six yards. That was more embarrassing than the original miss.

Le Tissier recovered his composure and pride in the 72nd minute with one of his greatest goals - a sensational effort unleashed from fully 30 yards. He turned quickly on to a pass and found himself in space on the left to smash a fierce volley past the bemused Crossley. It was a fitting way to register his 100th Saints goal in competitive games but it wasn't enough to save them from defeat against a side who would finish bottom of the table in manager Clough's last season.

A 2-0 reverse at Coventry followed and Saints were dropping back towards a relegation struggle but a home win over Chelsea, thanks to Banger's strike, then gave them breathing space that was seriously dented, along with their confidence, when Sheffield Wednesday battered them into submission at Hillsborough.

The thrashing dragged Saints into a battle to avoid the final relegation spot, with Crystal Palace, Oldham, Leeds and Coventry their major rivals. They were desperate for a win over Everton at The Dell on April 17 to ease the pressure but Neville Southall frustrated Le Tissier with a series of world-class stops in a goalless draw. The deflation of failing to win quickly turned to elation, though, when other results went for them and made the point enough to ensure top-flight status for another season.

It showed how much the Dell boys had been under the cosh all season when the overworked Flowers was named Player of the Year rather than Le Tissier before the home defeat by Manchester City. Perhaps if the voting had taken place after the final day, many would have revised their assessment as the striker went on a one-man scoring mission at Oldham.

Ironically, his second away hat-trick counted for little as Saints conceded four for the fourth time since February. He began his goal fest by directing a low volley inside the post from just inside the box but was a bystander as his side were overrun by relegation-threatened opponents who were 4-1 up just past the hour mark.

His eyes lit up, though, when Saints were awarded a free-kick 25 yards out. Rather than lifting the ball over the wall, Le Tissier showed the variety in his play by finding enough space to fizz a low shot through it and into the net. And with six minutes left, Oldham made the error of leaving him unmarked to rise at the far post and head home from Kenna's cross.

That made it 15 goals in 40 League appearances in a season in which none of his team-mates reached double figures. It was an outstanding return and triggered yet more transfer speculation. Although he had signed a contract extension only a few months earlier, there were genuine fears Le Tissier would jump ship in the summer.

Having seen Shearer sold and witnessed the debacle surrounding Dixon and Speedie, Le Tissier was left wondering whether the attention he had been attracting from bigger fish was worth investigating. It was clear that no matter how many goals he scored, Branfoot was not for turning - and the manager's rigid system, set up for hard-working players rather than mercurial talents, would not be bent to make the most of his skills.

Stubbornly, Le Tissier refused to buckle in the mind games. He was not going to be forced out by his boss and said: "The manager didn't have anything to do with the way I saw the game being played, so I decided to stick it out quietly. The way things were going, I was pretty sure it wasn't going to be for long. The fans were so agitated by the whole situation that people started deserting the stadium. That's when you see chairmen panicking and heads roll."

But, for now, Guy Askham and his board were immovable and in no mood to wield the axe the supporters were happy to sharpen.

1993-94

'Better Than Gazza'

W HEN Ian Branfoot was given the go-ahead to carry on at The Dell, there was only one option for Matt Le Tissier - grin and bear it! He didn't want to leave the club, so it came down to a simple waiting game and a question of him outlasting the unpopular manager.

He knew the goals would flow if he started games - and highlighted as much with several strikes on the pre-season tour of Sweden. But when the real action began, he was once again asked to sweat blood for the team's cause rather than given licence to use his sixth sense to find spots on the pitch where he could wreak maximum damage.

His early efforts brought no success as a first-day home defeat by Everton was followed by losses away to Ipswich and QPR. Luckily, the Premiership's whipping boys, Swindon, were up next and Le Tissier took full advantage of their outclassed defence. Full debutant Neil Bartlett set up the first with a tempting cross which he took on the half volley for an emphatic finish and the second followed as he feasted on his regular supply line of Micky Adams crosses into the box. Left unmarked, he stooped to head home and send Saints on the way to a 5-1 win.

That was followed by a defeat against Manchester United - made bearable only by Le Tissier's fantastic back-heel to send Neil Maddison charging between Steve Bruce and Roy Keane to score. But, when Saints went down 1-0 at Wimbledon, the pressure on Branfoot reached fever pitch. Three points from the opening 18 was bad enough but the dreary football was stoking up anger among fans.

After watching Saints fail to score in losing comfortably at home to Leeds and away to Sheffield Wednesday, Branfoot knew changes had to be made if he was to save his job - and Le Tissier was sacrificed. The one man capable of reversing the dire spiral was left on the sidelines as workmanlike midfielders Paul Allen and Peter Reid were brought in to add more energy to a side packed with runners but lacking in craft.

Le Tissier was sent to the reserves as punishment for refusing to put in the endless leg-work Branfoot required of his players and was not happy at the embarrassment of a four-match run in front of one man and his dog in the 'stiffs.' "Reserve team football is no good to me," he moaned. "I'm told I've been left out because of a lack of consistency, which you could say about five or six others still in the team."

The football world could not understand why his talents were being wasted - and transfer rumours began immediately. One claimed Branfoot had offered Le Tissier as bait in a bid to land Liverpool midfielder Don Hutchinson, although Reds boss Graeme Souness was more interested in taking Tim Flowers. Another insisted he was on his way to Chelsea for £500,000 plus Scottish international striker Robert Fleck.

Branfoot hit out at the speculation and pointed out that the south coast's favourite son was simply using the run-outs with the club's kids as a way of regaining his form. He said: "The idea of selling Matt is quite absurd. We have watched Fleck in the past and, with Matty currently out of the side, they have put two and two together and come up with a real flier.

"The trouble is people believe this rubbish. But I can categorically deny that Matt Le Tissier is not going to Chelsea or anywhere else right now. He is a very talented player capable of turning a match with his special skills but he has not been doing that lately, so he has been left out. There is no big deal about that. Other players drop down to the reserves to enable them to recover their form. He has been in training every afternoon and has shown a good attitude. We are all looking forward to seeing him back at his best because, on his day, he is one of the top players around."

While Le Tissier dedicated his spare time to putting in extra sessions on the training ground, Paul Moody was handed his shirt. But Saints still failed to grab a much-needed win and finally the Channel Islander was recalled from the depths of The Dell for a televised date with Newcastle. Here was the opportunity to rid himself of the pent-up anger and frustration that had built up during his demeaning spell against a bunch of wannabees, has-beens and no-hopers.

With the Sky cameras present, Le Tissier took to the pitch against a side managed by former Dell favourite Kevin Keegan, determined to show Branfoot he could still be a top-class match-winner. And, in a game he says was pivotal to his career, he did so in terrific style with two goals that rank among the greatest ever in the Premiership.

The first dazzled the nation as he collected Iain Dowie's header on the edge of the area and, within three touches, had the ball in Newcastle's net. The knockdown landed behind him but he used the outside of his left boot to instantly bring it under control before flicking it away from the approaching Barry Vension. Kevin Scott charged across to cover, only to be flat-footed as Le Tissier lifted the ball over his head to come face-to-face with Mike Hooper. There was space for a volleyed finish and, although the Saints star caught the ball with the bottom of his foot rather than the meat of the boot, he still had the right direction on his shot to roll the ball in.

It was a strike good enough to win any game but Saints were pegged back when Andy Cole scored to leave Newcastle convinced they had escaped with a draw. They had not accounted for Le Tissier's desire to cap his earlier goal with a second of equal genius. Maddison nodded the ball to him 20 yards out and, using his thigh to control, he twisted and unleashed a dipping volley before a screen of defenders had time to close him down. The ball looped over the dejected Hooper and dropped into the net.

They were two of the finest goals Sky viewers have witnessed. Le Tissier, though, is convinced he was about to be replaced by Moody before scoring his first in the 61st minute. The striker was warming up on the touchline but, immediately the ball flew in, was ordered by Branfoot to stick on his tracksuit top and return to the dug-out.

There was no mention of the enforced change of mind when the manager faced the press to embarrassingly describe why Le Tissier had been left out of previous games. "They were cracking goals," he said. "But he cannot score goals like that if he is not fit and Matty himself admits that he was not as fit as he needs to be. He has worked extremely hard since he has been out of the side and lost six or seven pounds.

"He is now back to the level of fitness we expect and need, and it shows. I'm not daft. I don't expect him to be a work-horse but I do expect him to be able to perform. As well as scoring two great goals, he also worked hard for the team and gave a much greater all-round contribution."

It often took two or three men to stop Matt Le Tissier - and it was sometimes by foul means even then. The Saints star is the meat in an Ipswich sandwich here, formed by Geraint Williams (left) and John Walk at Portman Road in December, 1993.

Le Tissier resisted the urge to use the goals as a way of sticking two fingers up to Branfoot and instead concurred with him over his earlier lack of zip. He said: "I don't think I have anything to prove to the manager. He knows what I'm capable of but I wasn't playing like that before he dropped me. The trouble is people expect something special of me now and, if it doesn't come, I get called inconsistent."

But Flowers, who watched the drama from between the Saints sticks, identifies that one game as a demonstration of just how important Le Tissier was in those years in which fighting against relegation was the norm. "I remember Newcastle were in our box for 89 minutes and absolutely battered us," he says. "But that was Tiss. The two or three times we escaped and got forward, he put two in the net.

"They must have missed eight or nine decent chances and we scored from two. It was top-drawer play and Matt had that in abundance. You would look from the back and think: 'There's no way back into this for us.' Then he would get a free-kick or something and bang! We were back in the game. He always had that in him."

Le Tissier was on a roll and used a trip to Anfield to conjure up another virtuoso strike. Saints were 2-0 down when he used his magical skills once more to lift the ball over Mark Wright and turn the ex-Southampton stopper in the opposite direction before unleashing a left-foot shot past Bruce Grobbelaar. He gave Saints a real shot at sneaking a point when bursting through and rifling home a second, only for Robbie Fowler to put the game out of reach by completing his hat-trick in a 4-2 home win.

Le Tissier said: "I couldn't believe the reaction of the Kop after I scored that first goal. The opposition fans clapped so much. I've never seen a reaction like that from supporters of a team who have had a goal scored against them. That will live with me for a long time."

He was finally enjoying his football again but was saddened to see the departure of close friend Flowers, who moved to Blackburn in a £2m British record deal for a goalkeeper. Dave Beasant had earlier been signed from Chelsea for £300,000 as his replacement but it was Ian Andrews who kept a clean sheet as Le Tissier once again provided Saints with a match-winning spark by cleverly chipping a cross from which Maddison benefited in a victory at home to Spurs.

He could not match Alan Shearer's double as Saints lost 2-0 at Blackburn, although his old team-mate would have been impressed with his poaching abilities as he tucked home two goals from close range in the win at Aston Villa in late November. That made it six in five games but the fire Branfoot had started by sending Le Tissier back to the reserves burned out quickly in defeats by West Ham, Everton, Ipswich and QPR, with Saints failing to find the net.

The boss was desperate to get him buzzing again and decided the responsibility of the captaincy might put the urgency back into his game. He took over the role for the first time at Everton on December 4 and said: "It was a total surprise. The manager came up to me in the dressing room at ten past two and told me I was skipper.

"I thought he was joking and said 'Yeah, about time too!' and walked off. He came after me, so I realised he was serious. It's a great honour. I can't even say it was always my dream to skipper the side because I never thought I would. I was chuffed to bits. I didn't feel any extra responsibility on the pitch and the boss didn't give me special instructions or tell me why I was captain. I was just happy to accept."

Branfoot declared himself pleased with the initial reaction from Le Tissier, saying: "I thought he was absolutely outstanding at Everton. He showed all the individual flair we know he possesses but used it for the good of the team. The captaincy was very well deserved and, once it had sunk in, really meant something to him. He regarded it as an honour and I thought he did an excellent job."

Le Tissier kept the armband for the Ipswich game, although his elevation did not bring the form or goals Branfoot needed. A 1-0 Dell defeat seriously hurt the board, with a paltry 9,028 turning out. The club were hit hard in the pocket and then hard on the field when they lost miserably at home to QPR and then at the only club below them, John Gorman's Swindon.

Before the killer blow was landed at the County Ground, Le Tissier put Saints level when waltzing through on to Tommy Widdrington's pass and comfortably stroking home. The goal stirred Craig Brown into action, the Scotland boss making a move to try to convince him his international career should continue north of the border. FIFA had relaxed their rulings, so players who had represented a country only in friendlies were free to turn out in the colours of another nation for whom they might qualify.

With Le Tissier born in Guernsey, he was eligible to play for any one of the home nations and Brown was quickest out of the blocks in his pursuit of the 25-year-old. He said: "I've heard Matthew could be eligible and am contacting UEFA to check if that's the case. I'd certainly be interested in bringing him in. His availability would provide me with a tremendous option." Unfortunately for Brown, the player had no desire to give up on his England dream and the idea never got off the ground.

A Christmas win at home to Chelsea lifted the gloom for a while and Saints took that form to Manchester City to grab a battling point the following day. But with Lawrie McMenemy returning to the club in a director's role, the writing was on the wall for Branfoot. His side were beaten at home by Norwich on the day Francis Benali was shown red for catching Ruel Fox in the face with a flying elbow. And the bullet finally came after Saints were outplayed by visiting Port Vale in a third-round FA Cup tie. Already smarting from a Coca-Cola Cup exit to Shrewsbury, they were spared an embarrassing defeat by Dowie's goal

It failed to save the manager from the axe and Le Tissier was not disappointed. While remaining personable with Branfoot, he had disagreed with his strategies. "We just had different opinions on how the game should be played," he said. "He wanted to go long ball while I wanted to pass it as that was what I have always been taught."

The relief around The Dell was clearly visible as Saints got back to winning ways against Coventry, with Dave Merrington and Lew Chatterley in caretaker charge. And of course it was Le Tissier who fired the winner after Dowie had been caught by Paul Williams to hand him the chance to convert from the spot.

Le Tissier and his team-mates certainly didn't provide a good advert in their replay at Second Division Vale. After falling behind to a Bernie Slaven strike, they failed to stir, their KO made worse by the sending-off of Widdrington after he had missed his side's only chance. The grim defeat spelled out the need for a manager able to inspire.

They were in freefall and the board acted by appointing former Saints player Alan Ball as new boss in the third week of January. Despite his connections with rivals Portsmouth, where he had enjoyed a successful stint as manager, Ball was quickly welcomed back. And as he studied the options available to him, he realised there was only one person capable of avoiding the humiliation of relegation.

While Branfoot had marginalised Le Tissier and striven for a team who worked judiciously hard for each other without possessing the flair to score, Ball informed his new charges he didn't have time to learn about their individual games; if he tried to, he'd run out of time and Saints would be relegated. "I told them we have a fantastic player here and told Le Tissier to stand up and stand by me," he said. "I said to the players: 'Whether you like it not, he is the best player at this club by a million miles.

"His record of making and scoring goals will keep us up. He can't run and tackle. He's useless at that. So I'm going to pick someone who can pass to him and the rest of you will have to fight like hell to retrieve it. Matt will be the main man. I told him he has the hardest job because, when he gets the ball, his job is to score or create a goal."

It worked. Ball, who also urged Dowie to put himself about robustly up front, couldn't have asked for a trickier opening than a trip to Newcastle but the rewards came immediately. The Geordies were flying high under Keegan and taking visiting teams apart, so Saints were seen as lambs to the slaughter.

Even Ball's chirpy confidence could not hide the fact he had had little time to work on his players. He had to hope his pre-match rallying call would work. And he had a dream start, with Maddison showing a goal threat from midfield that few top-flight clubs enjoy in the modern game, to head a fifth minute opener.

Just as at The Dell, Andy Cole fired an equaliser and Saints looked likely to have just a point to show for their efforts. But once again, Le Tissier embarrassed keeper Hooper to register a shock win. Any team conceding a free-kick around the edge of the penalty area was giving him a shooting chance he relished - a point he proved by striding up and whipping his shot past the bamboozled Hooper at his near post.

Ball invited Gothenburg for a friendly as he attempted to weigh up the pros and cons of his side, the game giving further credence to his decision to build his whole strategy on one man. Le Tissier scored twice. "Coaches these days seem more interested in producing teams than individual players and perhaps that is why Le Tissier has been overlooked by England," the manager said.

"We have had an exceptional talent and everything will revolve around the boy. If the players here can't do it, we will get ones who can feed this jewel. He's playing with an awful lot of confidence and responsibility right now. We are asking him to play in an area of the pitch that will get the best out of him by keeping him involved.

"We have told him how good we think he is and asked him how good he wants to be. He can achieve anything in the game. People tell me that he lacks workrate and is disinterested. If he is honest about that and can improve, he can go all the way to the top. It is nothing to do with being lazy or not wanting it. I believe if he is up the middle or wide, he switches off. Once you do that, it's very difficult to get in the game.

"I decided to put him where he has to work and where he'll be involved. He has to drop off our front two when we have the ball and work their centre-backs when we don't. He has to hunt it and, when we have possession, we have to drown him with it. In training, we give it him every third or fourth pass.

"I don't want to criticise what has gone before. I'm only trying to fly his flag because he deserves to be nominated for England by his manager. He has more to his armour than people think. He does not just score spectacular goals. Some of his passes are unbelievable, too. He has great vision and awareness. He is a treat to train. He's always the last to leave, he trains twice a day and comes back for more on his own. Hopefully, he has listened and thought: 'Yes, I'm going to have a crack at this.'"

The friendly win was perfect preparation for a trip to Oldham that was flagged up as one of the crucial games of the season. Joe Royle's team were among the strugglers as well and their defence must have suffered nightmares in the run-up to the clash after the way Le Tissier ripped them apart in the final match of the previous season with a hat-trick in a 4-3 defeat.

His frustration must have built again after he laid the foundations for a second away win on the trot. The game was 26 minutes old when he engineered space out of nothing and arrowed a rising drive into the net from some distance. But Saints couldn't even hold the lead to half-time and were left feeling bitter after Simon Charlton's goal had been disallowed to leave Oldham 2-1 winners.

The defeat may have been heartbreaking for Le Tissier as Saints wasted a chance to grab points at the expense of one of their main rivals. But his goal highlighted what he could accomplish when not shackled by the need to perform defensive duties. "I'm enjoying the new role very much," he said. "I see a lot of the ball, which is helpful. It is a position I've always fancied playing. I always thought I could do that job but never had a chance to try it in this formation. When we have the ball, I'm allowed to go where I want and when we haven't got it, I have to fill in as a central midfielder.

"Basically, though, I float around and hunt the ball, which suits me. In training, the emphasis is on one-touch and two-touch passing. Previously, it was all-in training. The emphasis was not so much on passing it, more direct style. The other big difference is the atmosphere we are playing in. Everyone is a lot more relaxed around the club."

Ball signed a new strike partner for Le Tissier by taking back Craig Maskell from Swindon but, more importantly, snapped up Jim Magilton from Oxford and ordered him to use his passing skills to keep the no 7 well fed. Both men were thrown into the deep end for debuts during the visit of Liverpool on Valentine's Day.

The Sky cameras turned up in the snow to check on The Ball and Le Tissier Show and the only people disappointed were those who settled down late in front of their TVs. Within 28 seconds, Le Tissier smashed Saints ahead on a night he could do no wrong. He was almost lethargic as he waddled on to a defensive header but there was nothing lazy about the fierce strike on the half volley past Grobbelaar.

Seven minutes later, he was in the thick of the action again as he sent over a cross for Dowie to nod towards Maskell, who headed the second. And when Maskell was hacked down by Julian Dicks, Le Tissier outfoxed the eccentric Grobbelaar from the spot to give Saints a three-goal half-time lead to cherish.

Four minutes after the interval, Le Tissier was in a new situation; working out how to beat a keeper with a penalty for the second time in a game. Mark Wright's hand-ball gave him his chance and the white coating on the ground, combined with the driving wind, made his mind up as he went for power and blasted the ball in.

The match finished in a carnival atmosphere and, although the Reds pulled two

Le Tissier is mobbed after opening the scoring in the memorable game against Liverpool on a winter wonderland of a night at The Dell - an evening when he could do no wrong.

back, the only talking-point was the intricate skill and mental strength of Le Tissier, who had scored his fifth Saints hat-trick. "It was all a bit of a blur," Magilton said. "I had signed and Alan Ball told me I was starting. I remember it snowed and they changed the ball but an unbelievable half-volley from Le Tiss got us all going.

"It was a fantastic debut for me but an even more memorable night for Matt with an incredible hat-trick. The way we played meant I was asked to play differently to usual. Neil Maddison and I were basically hod-carriers for Matt. We tried to move the ball as quickly as we could to get him in possession. We didn't mind. It worked a treat because he was that good and there would definitely be an end-product."

The attributes that excited Magilton made an impact on Southampton's director of football Lawrie McMenemy, who took up Le Tissier's cause with Terry Venables. The new England boss was deliberating over his first squad ahead of the March 9 game against Denmark at Wembley, and the ex-Dell manager was keen to make sure the Saints star was rewarded for his recent form.

"I have been keeping Terry up to date," McMenemy said. "I speak to him regularly and have told him Le Tissier has more ability than two-thirds of the present England squad. On ability, he is worth a place. While I was with England, all the reports said he had undoubted skill but questioned his application. I'm not talking about running around madly for 90 minutes but applying his skill and staying involved in games.

"From what I have seen since I've been back at the club, he is doing that. If he had been as consistent as he is now, he would undoubtedly have got in the England team in the past few years. I have told him his first priority is to keep Southampton in the Premiership and then to get in the England team. I believe he can do both."

Le Tissier heeded McMenemy's words and dug deep into his magican's hat for another trick. Poor Wimbledon copped it again as he made them pay for spending much of the game tugging and kicking at him. He got his revenge when Magilton stood over a free-kick 20 yards out and suggested a new free-kick routine the pair had been practising. The midfielder rolled the ball back and Le Tissier nonchalantly flicked it up and aimed a dipping volley over the wall and past the flailing keeper.

"Lew Chatterley and Bally had seen it somewhere in Europe and told us to have a go," Le Tissier said. "I was lining up to have a direct hit but, when Jim Magilton rolled the ball back, I flicked it up and smashed it into the keeper's top left-hand corner."

The amazing strike made it six goals for the player in four games under Ball and was all that Venables needed to persuade him: Le Tissier had to be involved against Denmark. As he was called into the squad, his club boss went as far as claiming he could be one of England's greats! "In all my years in the game, I have not seen anyone able to do some of things he does," Ball said. "That includes Pele.

"I promise you with the power and pace he can put on ball, he can do things that some of the very best can't manage. I said the first day I got here that he can go as far as he wants to in the game. And I mean right to the very top. I'm here to help him but the rest is up to him. There could be even more to come from him if he grows in stature and belief and works on his strengths."

It was characteristic Ball hyperbole, aimed at building up Le Tissier's confidence. Delighted as he was to be in the squad, though, the player quickly played down the glowing tribute. He said: "I'm not sure I would go as far as Pele but it is nice of him to say that because I'm sure he has played with a few top players. It's just nice to be included but that has happened before without me getting on, so I don't want to count any chickens.

"It means a lot to be in the new manager's first squad because that is when he lays out his ideas and hopefully the players he wants to build the team around. Terry Venables likes flair and, with the squad he has picked, it certainly looks an attractive set-up and it is great to be part of it. The hard thing is not getting in the squad but getting picked to play - but this is a start."

That was a point McMenemy, with his England experience, was keen to impress on Le Tissier. He said: "He has overcome the first hurdle and the rest is up to him. We are all delighted for him and I'm sure the supporters will be too. He has undoubted natural ability. I would like to see him playing the role we are using him in but you can't expect any favours."

Le Tissier played his part in a rugged battle that earned a point at Leeds, then joined up with the England squad and said: "When Alan Ball and Lawrie McMenemy arrived, they sat me down and talked about England. Lawrie explained why I couldn't get in the international team and said I drifted in and out of matches. The change in my position got me more involved in the middle of the field and my confidence came flooding back.

"I got more chance to shoot from long range too. When I was picked for the squad, Alan Ball told me to go with my head held high and not be a little boy lost in the corner. That is what I've set out to do."

It was another boy lost who stopped Le Tissier using the game to prove once and for all that he should be a key part of England's plans. Paul Gascoigne had reported with a rib injury that had seen him miss Lazio's derby clash with Rome. He talked Venables into believing he was fit, only to struggle his way through 68 minutes before the substitution that sent an excited shiver down all Southampton fans' backs.

Matt Le Tissier, mega-hero to a generation of Saints fans, was a senior England international at last. Ironically, his first contribution was a sliding tackle! He was on safer ground, though, moments later with a dipping volley that failed to drop enough to trouble the keeper. Then, only a last-ditch tackle by Carsten Dethlefsen denied him a goal as he homed in on David Batty's injury-time pass.

His debut was over too quickly but he remained diplomatic on two fronts; about being given his first cap at a stage in the game when players were already thinking about returning to their clubs and about the fact he was introduced just a few seconds after Gascoigne had insisted on staying on to have an unsuccessful pop at goal from a free-kick in a position he himself was so deadly from.

"It was only a few days since Gazza had been hurt and I thought he did very well to play at all," Le Tissier said. "I was asking Terry Venables to get me on before Gazza took the free-kick. I really fancied having a crack. But there was no way Gascoigne was not going to take it. He knew it was his last chance. He realised he was about to be substituted and said to the lads: 'Just let me take this, then I'm off.'

"It would have been nice to get on a minute earlier but I was just so thrilled to play that it didn't really matter. Terry Venables just told me to go out and enjoy it. It was a very special moment when I walked on. It has been a long time coming but the feeling of winning my first cap more than makes up for it. At least it will put a stop to those chants of: 'You'll never play for England.' I was getting sick of those."

Le Tissier returned to club football, satisfied he was on the path to a long England career. He landed a free-kick nicely on Ken Monkou's head to ensure a point from an instantly forgettable game at home to Sheffield Wednesday before Saints were hit by their annual Ian Wright massacre, the Arsenal striker snatching yet another hat-trick against them in a 4-0 win at The Dell.

Neil Heaney was signed from the Gunners in a £300,000 move days later to add some pace to Saints' attack and give Le Tissier more options when in possession. The pairing didn't get off to the best of starts with Saints failing to give fellow strugglers Sheffield United a single scare in a 0-0 draw. Worse was to follow when Oldham left the Dell with three points, Le Tissier carving out his side's only goal for himself by winning the ball back on the left, surging past a defender and arrowing in a low shot from 20 yards.

Ball's men looked clueless at times in a defeat at Chelsea and, when Manchester City departed from one of those gut-wrenching six-pointers with their relegation fears eased by a 1-0 win, Saints needed Le Tissier's inspiration more than ever. His goal against Oldham was their only appearance on the score sheet in 450 minutes of football and the magnificent wins against Liverpool and Newcastle were a distant memory.

But while those around him may have been having doubts, he was confidently preparing for one of the most dramatic matches in his career. Saints were in the drop zone when they travelled in early April to a Norwich side also in real trouble and could only hope the Canaries' rotten run of one win in 15 League games had left them even more fragile than themselves.

It called for the kind of performance the club reserved for annual end-of-season escape acts but worries mounted when Chris Sutton's flick allowed Mark Robins to nip past Monkou and score. There was a reprieve before the interval, though, when Maddison's shot took a defection off Robert Ullathorne and flew in.

By the 55th minute, Norwich were in control and already counting the points as Jeremy Goss and Sutton swept them 3-1 ahead. Having scored only 11 away goals all season, Saints' prospects were grim. But the drama was about to begin. Le Tissier was trying to spark a revival and, when Maddison laid off, used his left foot to fire low at goal from the edge of the area. Bryan Gunn got a glove on the ball but it rolled in anyway.

Norwich were now nervous and Saints scented a point, all the more so when Jeff Kenna burst into the box and was illegally sandwiched between Darren Eadie and Lee Crooks. Le Tissier coolly converted the penalty, only for the visitors to let things slip defensively once more after working so hard to get themselves back in the game. Within 60 seconds, Sutton lost his marker Monkou to tuck away Crook's free-kick and force Ball to abandon his five-man midfield. With the shackles off, Le Tissier used his head to complete his seventh Saints hat-trick. Allen's work-rate had driven the side on all afternoon and, when he found Kenna on the right, the full-back's deep cross was despatched by Le Tissier to level the scores at 4-4.

Still there was more to come in an amazing match, Le Tissier's superb delivery of corners paying off in stoppage-time. Norwich failed to pick up Monkou's bold run and the big Dutch defender powered in a close-range header from a right-wing kick to seal an astonishing three points.

"That was the most remarkable match," Le Tissier recalled. "We were behind three times and just kept bouncing back. To do that made it a hell of a performance. Their keeper made a bit of a boo-boo for my first goal but the penalty was blatant and I was fortunate for the third because Iain Dowie and a defender had come across me, then both missed it. All I can remember was the ball hitting my head as I closed my eyes. When I opened them, the ball was in the net

"With Ken's header, it was just a case of me sticking the ball in the right place. It was a very ordinary assist but a very important one." Le Tissier later said: "The result really gave us belief we would stay up because we had been struggling at that stage."

A hat-trick hero again, this time with the help of a penalty in a sensational and crucial 5-4 victory at fellow strugglers Norwich.

The player, then on 20 goals for the season, sometimes needed the boost of scoring to get his tail up and he kicked on superbly as Saints fought to save their Premiership skins over the final month. When they took on a Blackburn side still hoping to catch Manchester United at the top of the table, he was exceptional, chipping over a cross for Dowie to head Saints in front and then producing a smart pass for Allen to beat Tim Flowers from a tight angle.

When Flowers left The Dell several months earlier, he had told Le Tissier he would never let his old pal beat him. But that boast failed to survive its first test when he was outwitted by him from the penalty spot after Tim Sherwood handled. Once more, the star man had refused to bow to the stress and Saints were out of the bottom three, only to lose 3-0 at Tottenham in his absence and fret again about their future.

He was back for the visit of Aston Villa on April 30 and was named Saints Player of the Year in the warm-up before conjuring up six goals for his side in two games. Four came from his own boot, the other two from Maddison via his assists.

Villa were sunk 4-1, Le Tissier volleying home Kenna's cross for the first and, as at Norwich, Monkou meeting his corner to score. The Channel Islander's second was a fine example of his close control as he used his left foot to collect a long ball before skipping past Nigel Spink and rolling a shot into an unguarded net. The keeper was dismissed a minute later and Maddison headed past the stand-in, Neil Cox, for the fourth from Le Tissier's corner.

Swindon were already doomed and, with two games left, seven teams were all worrying whether the relegation bullet had their name on it. Ball's men had the added trauma of having to go to two grounds that were notoriously difficult destinations - Manchester United and West Ham.

As expected, United showed no mercy and Saints' fighting display was not enough to see them nick a point off a side about to be crowned champions for the second successive season. Andrei Kanchelskis put the Reds a goal up just after the hour but it took until stoppage-time for the game to be killed off by Mark Hughes' strike.

The season was going to the wire and Saints went to Upton Park knowing that only a victory would guarantee safety. Ironically, they were in their highest position of the season, 17th, but were just a point ahead of Everton, who occupied the last relegation spot as only goal difference separated them from Sheffield United and Ipswich.

Le Tissier, having scored 13 goals in 15 games under Ball, was determined to drag his side out of the mire and saw the perfect opportunity from a free-kick a minute before the interval. He whipped a right-foot shot over the wall with enough clout to beat the keeper, equalise Danny Williamson's opener and send Saints into the break with hope, if not confidence.

As news from elsewhere constantly left Saints fearing for their safety, Le Tissier clicked. He outwitted full-back Tim Breaker on the flank before producing a perfect cross for Maddison to head his seventh goal of the season. West Ham levelled when

Beasant failed to hold Trevor Morley's shot and Paul Allen's cousin Martin Allen followed up to score - but the Hammers remained generous at the other end.

Tony Gale flattened Dowie in the box and left Le Tissier facing the most important penalty of his career. If he missed, Southampton would be contemplating life in the First Division and the loss of millions of pounds. The tension got to everyone in Upton Park - except him. Regular as clockwork, he strode forward and beat Ludo Miklosko with his sixth successful conversion of 1993-94.

It should have been enough for Saints to seal the game and they might well have done but for some last-day mayhem. Hammers fans, desperate for an end-of-season party of their own, charged on to the pitch, forcing Ball's men to head for the tunnel and check other scores on a transistor radio in the dressing room. They craned their necks and heard the news they were craving. Sheffield United were making a pig's ear of their trip to Chelsea, and Oldham were already holding a wake.

That meant Saints would have to ship three goals in the few minutes remaining to go down and they built a defensive wall that was breached only by a nervous headed own goal by Monkou. Any worries of a fretful finale were eased when West Ham supporters poured on to the pitch again to leave referee Gerald Ashby with little choice but to blow for full-time.

The 3-3 draw booked Saints in for another Premiership campaign and Le Tissier said: "We had an early knock-back but I managed to score a free-kick when the keeper was blocked out a bit by the number of players in the wall. I struck it pretty well, so he couldn't get across, and that was a big boost just before half-time.

"In the second half, I set up Neil Maddison for a goal. I jinked on the left and the defender didn't want to come and tackle me in case he fouled me, so I got a left-foot cross in and Neil - one of the best headers I've seen - nodded it in. Once we were 3-2 in front, the crowd invasion came and we went off the pitch, got the radio on and managed to find results of the other games.

"We knew we were pretty safe really. The only way we could go down was if we conceded three goals in the final four minutes and Kenny put one in his own net just to keep us on our toes! Then the second invasion came and the ref blew the whistle, possibly a tad early. It was a great escape."

Le Tissier's 25 goals in 38 League games made him one of the division's leading scorers despite the fact he was in a struggling team. Ball knew that only one man at the club could have led his troops to safety and said of the Upton Park epic: "We started badly, deservedly went behind and were really scratching around for something. It was a monster game for the club and we did not handle it at all well to start with.

"But as so often before, the genius got us out of it. I knew as soon as we got that free-kick, we would be back in it. The lad does not disappoint you like that. He does it so often that we have come to expect it from him now. There was enormous pressure and taunts from the crowds but that did not bother him at all. The kid is bomb-proof.

You beauty! Matt Le Tissier is about to be mobbed by (from left) Simon Charlton, Tommy Widdrington and Jeff Kenna after scoring one of the two goals that earned a 3-3 draw at West Ham on the nerve-tingling last day of the 1993-94 season.

"He did everything in this game. He scored two, made the other and helped win the penalty. He has been the catalyst since I came here and did it again when it really mattered. He has the most ability in this country. I would have him ahead of Paul Gascoigne - and that is some compliment. They are both good but he has won games single-handedly. The whole club is indebted to him and the lovely thing is he wants to stay and see his contract out."

It was the kind of dramatic end to a season that regularly had Saints fans biting their nails in the early 1990s. Le Tissier had carried on his back a side badly lacking confidence and unsure where they could find a win after those three defeats around Easter. His goals inspired a run-in of three victories, a draw and two defeats and meant that relegation was avoided by a single point.

In his last five appearances, he scored eight and set up six others to prove Ball right to stick all his eggs in one basket. His reward was another pay rise as he tied his future to the club for a futher three years by signing a deal that was seen as so crucial that McMenemy postponed his family holiday to put it together.

"Some people can't understand why I have signed for Southampton again when I have the chance to go to other clubs," Le Tissier added. "But personal happiness has always been more important to me than money. If I can secure my family's future while playing football, that's great.

"But I've always played football for the love of the game, not for the love of money and I'm very happy here, especially as I've achieved my ambition to play for England. It has been well documented how much I like it here. I get on really well with the fans, I love the area and this is a fantastic club. I would not have signed if I did not believe it was going places. I really do see a lot of promise here.

"Since Lawrie McMenemy and Alan Ball returned, people have started watching matches at The Dell again. I have scored 15 goals in 16 games for them, so my own form has blossomed. There's only one way to go now and that is why I've signed."

McMenemy believed Le Tissier's picking-up of his first England cap had been a key reason behind the decision to sign a contract which would take him past a decade at the club. He said: "I'm absolutely delighted to have got it signed because he is a very special talent. It was not really a persuasion job, though. We might not be able to pay what Blackburn do but there are other important things like family happiness and his football education. He has achieved his ambition to play for England as a Southampton player, is top man in this area and can still be materially well off."

The player pointed out that Branfoot's decision to make him captain had been a massive turning point in his season. Ironically, the most hated manager in Saints history had played a part in keeping them up - and keeping their star man at The Dell.

Le Tissier said: "I was chuffed to bits when Ian Branfoot asked me to become skipper because I never thought of being considered due to the fact I don't shout that much - apart from at linesmen! But it has really helped me because it gave me a bit more responsibility, which is something I needed. Being made captain was an even bigger boost than coming back into the team and scoring twice against Newcastle. That's how highly I value the job. It means the world to me.

"Suddenly, people were looking for me to lead by example, so I felt I needed to do something in every game. Perhaps that is something to do with my scoring record in the second half of the season. I've had runs of goals before but never for so long. Not that it was just me who improved. Quite a few lads had a good second half but didn't get the credit that was due because the person scoring goals usually gets the headlines.

"Simon Charlton and Jeff Kenna have both done a terrific job on the flanks. Under the new formation, they have to motor up and down the field but they both have terrific engines and have done that magnificently. The improvement in form could not have been better timed either because of our League position. It would have broken my heart if this club had gone down because it means the world to me.

"I'm not saying other players weren't showing great commitment but it probably means more to those who've been here eight or nine years like Neil Maddison, Francis Benali and me. We all have great feeling for the club. There was also great feeling for me winning an England cap, which came down to my improved consistency.

"I got 25 goals in 38 games - a ratio of two in every three - which I'm happy about. People have always said I'm inconsistent but the likes of Alan Hansen and Andy Gray can say what they like. It's water off a duck's back to me, although, when I have a good game, it'd be nice if they acknowledged it. Apparently, no-one has scored more goals for one club in the top division over the past six seasons. That must say something.

"My game has really come on under Alan Ball. His style suits me and the position I'm now playing makes it difficult for teams to pick me up unless they put men on me all the time, which creates space for others. That's good because the team isn't just about Matthew Le Tissier. We're probably only a couple of men short of having a very good side because whether we could cope with four or five injuries is debatable."

Ball, his no 1 fan, remains glowing of the player and the impact on his team-mates. "In the hour of need, he was there for them," he said. "There are lots of ways people become heroes at a club and he has shown many of those qualities.. He is loyal, played some fantastic football and scored incredible goals. All that culminated in him staying in the league for three or four years when times were really tough.

"He didn't do it with blood and guts but in the hardest way - by scoring goals. That endeared him to the people. I found him easy to handle because I told him from day one what I thought of him, how good I thought he was and what was needed from him as the most talented player in the club. I believed in him."

Le Tissier was nevertheless once again used sparingly in a run of end-of-season internationals as Venables unveiled his Christmas tree formation, with Alan Shearer left as a sole striker. Against the Greeks, England had already done the hard work before Le Tissier was introduced for Southampton-born Darren Anderton. He toiled away in a deeper role and failed to make an impact in a 5-0 win, the only promising note of the night for him being the huge roar that acclaimed his arrival.

"That was nice," he said. "It gave me a real lift. Coming on as a substitute, it is hard to pick up the pace. It is always easier to play from the start and I would love to think that might happen against Norway. I played a bit deeper to try and get involved. That wasn't planned - it was just the way things worked out."

His plea for a start against Norway went unheeded, though, and he went on for Paul Ince with just 13 minutes left. Just as he had done against Greece, he looked neat and tidy without being able to summon up that one pass or long-range shot he needed to make it impossible for Venables to leave him on the substitutes' bench next time round.

Norway's five-man midfield proved too much for Le Tissier to ferret past in a 0-0 draw in which Venables lost his 100 per cent success record. "We needed a goal in the first half when we had some good pressure," Le Tissier said. "That might have opened it up. They were very defensive and often had nine or ten men behind the ball making it difficult to break them down. They will probably be happier with the result than us."

And then he ambled off for a summer break and the chance to think about just what he could do by way of a follow-up to his sensational season.

1994-95

A Burning Desire

IT'S hardly surprising Matt Le Tissier felt it was his destiny to play for England - he had been having vivid dreams of pulling on the white shirt since he was a kid. They were not fantasies fuelled, as an excitable schoolkid, when handed his first pair of boots either. His thoughts felt more like a premonition, especially as they included taking a penalty under pressure!

He said: "I had a dream we were playing Germany in the World Cup final and I was taking a penalty two minutes from time. It was going to win the cup but my mum woke me up for school just as I was about to hit the ball. I remember writing it as an essay, although I can't remember what my teacher wrote when she marked it. But I had that dream of playing for England from the age of seven onwards. I might come across as laid-back but, underneath, there's always been a burning ambition to play for England. It means a great deal to me."

Le Tissier had already proudly played for his country three times without having enough time to really impress during bit-part appearances against Denmark, Greece and Norway. Now he was being presented with a place in the spotlight against Romania as Terry Venables decided that the player had spent quite enough time adapting to international life.

After sitting out a tepid England performance in the 2-0 defeat of USA, he was told from the moment he met up with the national team party that he would start against the Eastern European side at Wembley on October 12. "I didn't want to play him too soon and then have people turn round and say he isn't good enough or find that he loses confidence," Venables said.

"Naturally, everyone wants to see him in the England team because he's such a great entertainer but it has to be a gradual transition. I've given him a taste as a substitute when we were ahead and there was space for him to play. At the start, games can be a lot tighter. But now he has been part of things for while, it is the right time to see if he can perform at the highest level.

"I'm looking for Matt to get into the game quickly and do exactly what he does for his club. I'm playing him in the same role to try and make it easy for him because it is a big step up. That is one reason why he had to wait a while. But he has got used to the set-up and now I feel the time is right to give him a game. He has the opportunity to move another notch up the ladder and I hope he sees a lot of the ball. He is a very entertaining player who I would pay to watch as a fan. You don't have to look hard to see his qualities because they are obvious."

For Le Tissier, it was time to fulfil his potential, silence the sceptics and prove exactly why he had always believed he would start for his country. He added: "I've never really doubted that I would one day play for England, although if the wait had gone on for another year or two, taking me towards 30, I might have begun to wonder if it would ever happen.

"I never thought the chance had passed me by and I always knew that if I kept playing well enough for Southampton, I would be in with a shout. I got on the bench as cover a few years ago when Alan Shearer made his debut against France. It was a bit frustrating it did not happen then but, to be fair, I wasn't playing as well then as I am now, so I didn't deserve it."

A run of 25 goals in 27 Saints games was evidence enough that Le Tissier was in the best form of his career. But, on his big night, he found he could not take Venables on his word as that free role he had been promised failed to materialise. Instead, he was shunted out wide and ordered to play far too deep to bring the best out of his passing capabilities against a side happy to rely on their superior technique.

Le Tissier still showed his talents in patches, notably when flicking the ball up with his right foot and crashing a dipping volley just over with his left. Switching flanks with Ian Wright did give him time to set up Shearer for a headed chance but it was Rob Lee who stole his thunder by arriving late to nod the equaliser in a 1-1 draw. Le Tissier had not made the impact he wanted and was left uttering his admiration for a Romanian side better suited to exploit his style. "I did enjoy it and it would have been even nicer if we had won," he said. "But at least I got in 90 minutes.

"It was very difficult because Romania played so many at the back. They are a quality side and made it hard for us to create anything. But now I have had a taste, I would like more. Hopefully, this can be the start of a run for me. If I can keep playing well for Southampton, I might get a few more games."

Le Tissier refused to point out the reasons behind his ineffective performance, leaving that to Alan Ball. The Saints manager said: "I was a bit disappointed with the way they played Matty on the left or the right of a triangle with Shearer at the tip. It might have been better the other way round because it didn't really suit him. He did not get a lot of service and, when it came, it was in the wrong areas.

"I was quite pleased with what he did, though. He passed the ball well and knocked it around nicely but did not get into the areas where we know he is dangerous.

Up in lights....the sight all Saints fans had longed to see on the occasion of an England international at Wembley. But Matt Le Tissier's big night fell flat.

He had to track back, especially in the second half, against a very talented team. But he did not look out of place on that stage. Then again, with his talent, he shouldn't. He was at ease there, did not freeze and, hopefully, he will get more opportunities.

"He is part of a very experimental squad. Terry Venables is doing exactly right by trying different things now. We still have two years before the European Championship finals, so now it is right to have a look at people and systems. Then he can choose the best team and stick with it. Hopefully, Matty will be part of that."

Le Tissier could have done no more in a 1994-95 Southampton season in which his club form was on a par with the best in the country. He started it with a 50-yard pass that opened Blackburn's defence and let Nicky Banger scurry in for a goal. Bruce Grobbelaar, now a Saints player, saved a penalty from Shearer but was beaten by the old Dell boy as the champions-to-be were held 1-1.

The post-match talk was not about Grobbelaar's heroics but that stunning strike from Banger, who said: "That's got to be the best goal I've ever scored. Matty hits passes like that for fun in training, so I read what he would do and took advantage."

Saints then went to Aston Villa, where the travelling fans saw Le Tissier net one of his most underrated goals. His side were trailing to a first-half Dean Saunders effort when he picked up the ball a minute from time in a non-threatening position - or at least it looked non-threatening. But he clipped a right-foot shot with enough bend to see it whip across the bemused Mark Bosnich and into the top corner.

It was quickly forgotten, though, as Saints were thrashed 5-1 at Newcastle, then ended August by going down at home to Liverpool. In both games, they had plenty of the ball but the strike pairing of Le Tissier and Banger had taken just three chances in the opening four games. Maybe Le Tissier was saving himself for the cameras as he turned the club's season around with a match-winning performance at Tottenham.

With Southampton looking incapable of coming back from Jurgen Klinsmann's early goal, he sent Neil Heaney scampering away to win a penalty 15 minutes from time. After Sol Campbell was sent off for the foul, Le Tissier planted the spot-kick past Ian Walker, then netted his second last-minute goal in five games. Displaying perfect technique to bring the ball under close control, he secured a surprise win by steering home when Stuart Nethercott failed to cut out Jeff Kenna's cross.

By the following Saturday, Le Tissier had a new team-mate when Ronnie Ekelund arrived from Barcelona in a hire-purchase deal that was unusual for the time. Saints would cough up a small sum to secure the Dane's loan and pay the balance in the summer if they wanted to take him permanently.

The move had been initiated during Southampton's pre-season tour of Belgium and Holland, on which they stayed in the same hotel as Johan Cruyff's Barcelona side. Cruyff was an old friend of Ball's and, when the two got into conversation, the Saints manager revealed that he was looking for a play-maker to help take some of the considerable weight off Le Tissier's shoulders.

Cruyff thought he had the perfect player for Saints and agreed to let him go as he was struggling to break into the Spanish giants' side. Ekelund impressed in friendlies and a deal was tied up in time for him to play a minor role as a sub when Saints were held at home by Nottingham Forest. Stan Collymore was on target for the Midlanders and it took another Le Tissier penalty, this time after Alfie Haaland pushed Iain Dowie, for Saints to chisel out a point.

The side were forced to soak up pressure before Le Tissier headed a last-minute goal in the Coca-Cola Cup win at Huddersfield in their next game. Heaney then made way for Ekelund for the trip to Coventry, where the newcomer produced a performance that had even his illustrious colleague licking his lips.

Saints went behind for the sixth game in a row but Le Tissier's pass allowed Dowie to escape the Sky Blues defence and flick over Steve Ogrizovic. From then on, Ekelund ran things from midfield, delivering a low cross for Dowie to launch himself and plant his header just inside the post before finishing off with the goal of the match. Ekelund's passing was surpassed only by his movement as he twice fed Jim Magilton and received the ball back before slipping it under the keeper to clinch a 3-1 win.

Saints then beat Ipswich by the same score at The Dell with Neil Maddison heading in Le Tissier's early cross before Ekelund followed up to nod home after the Channel Islander's strike hit the bar. Dowie scored the third. The new combination were producing some of the most inventive and exciting football seen at the ground in the Premiership era and poor Huddersfield suffered as Le Tissier, now playing in a free role, went on a Coca-Cola second-leg goal spree.

He slammed an early penalty into the top of the net and took the ball off Dowie to cut along the by-line and bend a shot round the keeper from the edge of the six-yard box to register his second. His hat-trick was completed by a rebound after Ekelund had rattled the post and he still had time to sweep home from Ekelund's pull-back.

It was the first time Le Tissier had scored four times in a competitive Saints game but all his good work was wasted, in the Coca-Cola Cup at least, when they performed miserably in the third round and were dumped out by Chris Bart-Williams' goal at Sheffield Wednesday. He nevertheless said: "This is probably the best form of my career and the change in atmosphere at the club has something to do with it. I would say my free role right now is probably my best. Alan Ball wants me to get the ball in the right areas to inflict the most damage."

Everton needed Neville Southall's heroics to keep the score respectable when they were beaten at The Dell back in the League. Le Tissier's volleyed pass sent Ekelund away for the opener and Heaney's cross led to Le Tissier stroking the ball inside the post from 18 yards for the killer.

It was arguably his best display of the season so far and the one that convinced Venables to start with him against Romania. The way he took Everton apart also drew new admirers and a whisper went round at the game that Alex Ferguson was lining up a £5m bid. But the Saints board were warned that fans would lynch them if they let the great entertainer leave. Southampton Independent Supporters' Association spokesman Nick Illingsworth said: "Matthew Le Tissier is now revered as a virtual God by the fans. There would be uproar if he went. The change between now and a year ago is dramatic. It would be a terrible step back if he did go."

As if to emphasise the point, Le Tissier helped launch a dramatic, if unsuccessful, late comeback to give Leicester a scare in mid-October. Saints were blitzed by Nathan Blake's brace, finding themselves 3-0 down in the first 53 minutes, with a thrashing on the cards. Dowie scored what looked like a consolation goal, especially when Franz Carr put the Foxes 4-1 in front.

There was a late resurgence, with Le Tissier latching on to Steve Walsh's poor clearance to sweep home and Dowie nodding home unchallenged in stoppage-time but Saints could not quite force a fourth goal. Ball's side were caught out at the back again as they were defeated at West Ham and, despite Maddison's volley from Le Tissier's free-kick, they were beaten 3-1 at home by Leeds at the end of October.

It took a last-minute Le Tissier penalty after a Spencer Prior hand-ball to save Saints from an embarrassing home defeat at the hands of Norwich. One point from four games had seen them drop out of the top ten and they failed to fully capitalise on Ekelund's return to goal-scoring form at Manchester City. Paul Walsh's double for the home side was matched by the Dane's brace, the latter from Le Tissier's pass. But they were undone with 11 minutes left by Peter Beagrie's goal in a 3-3 draw.

Despite the deflating way Saints had crumbled again, talk at The Dell switched to the stunning news that Bruce Grobbelaar had been accused of accepting money to fix matches. The Zimbabwean denied the charges and showed tremendous mental strength to play in Saints' next match at home to Arsenal, in which Magilton opened the scoring before the keeper's big moment came in the 66th minute. The Gunners were awarded a penalty and the pressure on Grobbelaar must have been crushing but he flew across his line to secure a 1-0 win by keeping out Paul Dickov's spot-kick.

A draw at Crystal Palace, followed by a 1-0 home defeat against Chelsea, this time with the visitors scoring in the final minutes through Paul Furlong, meant Saints were sliding down the table as they entered December. Le Tissier took it upon himself to devise some inspiration and played his full part with two goals at Blackburn - one undoubtedly the best of his career.

He had already beaten Tim Flowers with a 20-yard shot from the right of the box following David Hughes' pass and went on to produce a piece of artistry few could match. He took Tommy Widdrington's pass in his stride and weaved past Mark Atkins before cutting across Henning Berg and unleashing a swerving shot that ripped into the top of the net with unerring accuracy.

Flowers said: "It was just a very, very good shot. He had beaten three or four men with a snaky run and then just had a very quick look up. It was a fantastic strike. I saw the ball leave his foot and must have been four or five yards off my line. He put it in the stanchion and, if someone does that, you're going to have trouble. Everyone remembers that goal but what people forget is that he was clean through in the last minute and I blocked him for a hat-trick."

Flowers' claim that it was unfeasible for him to get a glove to the wonder goal is backed up by the scorer. "It's my best - and not just because it was probably the farthest out I have scored from," Le Tissier said. "The shot I hit was exactly what I was trying to do and a good friend of mine was stood between the sticks!"

For all its brilliance, the goal was not enough to prevent a 3-2 defeat and, just as frustratingly, didn't convince Venables to keep the scorer in the England starting 11 for the clash with Nigeria. Le Tissier was suffering from the same problems he had in his early years at The Dell - being asked to step off the bench to change the game.

This time it was in place of Peter Beardsley as David Platt won the friendly for England, Le Tissier's emergence seen as little more than a nod from Venables that he remained in his thoughts. The experience added to his well-founded worries that his international career was a long way from taking off.

He longed to be a fixture among England's finest and admitted: "Over the years, I have been bracketed with Marsh, Bowles and Currie. It's quite flattering to be up there with players who were my heroes as a kid. But I would like to win more caps than they did. I don't want just to win a few, then fade away. To become a great player, you have to look at winning 50 or 60. That is something I have to aim for."

The problem for Le Tissier was landing himself a run in the England side for long enough to be able to adapt. Flowers feels he was never given the kind of opportunity needed to feel settled at international level, adding: "Matt was a bit quieter to start with when he joined up with England than he was at The Dell. Sometimes, you think: 'Am I really here?' But I think he believed he should be there in that set-up.

"He was certainly England class and some of the things he did were world-class. I don't know why he didn't get a run. Football is about opinions and some people see the game differently to others. In the managers' defence, there are a lot of very, very good players in attacking positions.

"But I'm a big believer that, at England level in particular, you need a run at it. It's very difficult and, although you might be playing top-flight football at your club, the international stage is a step up because it brings more pressure and hype. Someone needs to be behind you and say: 'We will give you a run of ten or 15 matches.'

"It happens at clubs, where people go in and out and lose their place after one

Big Mac meets big star. The most successful manager in Saints' history, by now back as director of football, offers some strongly delivered words of advice.

mistake. It's the same with your country, where the games are fewer. If you don't do well in a game, managers can be loath to give you another try. Maybe he was a victim of that. I had it to a certain extent. I'd have a couple of matches, then be hooked out and be second or third choice. A season down the line, I'd get another go, then miss out. It's very hard to get a run."

Back on the domestic front, the return of the Sky cameras on December 19 brought the best out of Le Tissier yet again, with visiting Villa the victims. He whipped in a great cross for the brave Richard Hall to fling himself forward and head home. When Ray Houghton equalised with ten minutes left, it looked like a draw - until Villa erred by handing Le Tissier a shooting opportunity.

They conceded a free-kick close on 30 yards out with the

game already into injury-time and Le Tissier sent the ball over the wall and flying towards the left-hand corner. Nigel Spink got his gloves to the ball but lacked the strength in his wrists to keep it out. Alas, that was as good as it got for Saints in the search for any Christmas joy.

They were beaten at home at 3-2 by Wimbledon on Boxing Day in a game in which Le Tissier took star billing despite the scoreline. Collecting Kenna's return pass just before the interval, he juggled with the ball before unleashing a fearsome 20-yard drive that flew past the dumbfounded Hans Segers. But the ten-man Dons took all three points through Dean Holdsworth's penalty.

Ekelund had missed the game with an old back injury, having also failed to last the previous two matches. He returned to the side for two more appearances but never played 90 minutes for Saints again. It was a short stint viewed as one of the most promising by a new signing but his refusal to undergo back surgery made him too much of a risk for Ball and he was returned to Barcelona.

Ekelund's ability had been matched in recent seasons only by that of Le Tissier, who was praised by Kenna at the mid-way point of the 1994-95 season. "Over the years, a lot of people have criticised him for lack of consistency and yet over the last five or six years, he has averaged 20 goals a season," he said. "That is consistency at the highest level.

"He has unbelievable skills and tremendous ball control and, of course, he scores spectacular goals. He's a terrific striker of the ball both in dead-ball situations and open play. Even when it seems impossible to get in a shot, he hits the target. Matt is not renowned for his pace but his body movement more than makes up for that.

"He can move a hip or shoulder to get himself half a yard and he is away or shooting for goal. I've only played against him in training but he is very hard to read. He moves the ball between his feet so quickly and so well. You think you've got him and suddenly he's past you."

Kenna, showing a perception apparently missing from the make-up of Ian Branfoot, Graham Taylor and by now Venables, argued that Le Tissier was wasted doing the donkey-work that any two-bob player with plenty of energy could carry out. He said: "I think his better position is in a floating role because the way the modern game is going, wingers need to be able to track back and tackle and that is not Matty's strength. You just have to give him the ball and let him get on with it. When he does that, he's capable of destroying anyone."

It was not just with the ball at his feet that Le Tissier was proving dangerous in his finest season at The Dell. He unselfishly used his under-rated heading ability to nod down for good friend Hughes to smash home a spectacular overhead kick for his first goal on his 22nd birthday as Saints took a point home from QPR.

Hughes scored again, this time before Gary Pallister's goal with 11 minutes to go earned Manchester United an away point. Le Tissier was back on the score-sheet in the next game, netting Saints' goal from the penalty spot at Sheffield Wednesday as they recorded their third draw on the trot.

The failure to win in four games had seen the side slip to 15th and a concerned Ball shipped Dowie on to Crystal Palace for £500,000 and bought Chelsea striker Neil Shipperley for a club record £1.2m as a new target-man for Le Tissier to feed off. "I know all about Matt," Shipperley said. "He's one of the main reasons I have come down here. With his passing ability, he will pick me out when I make my runs and I'm sure that's going to help me get among the goals."

Le Tissier struck with a towering header to score the second in a 2-0 home defeat of Southend in the FA Cup third round. But it was the League where the real worries were, although Saints were now hard to beat, as proved by a stalemate at Leeds and a 1-1 draw at Arsenal. Le Tissier poked through a pass for Magilton to score at Highbury but was struggling to come up with his expected match-winning moments.

He nevertheless remained a wanted man, with Kevin Keegan reported to be interested in him as a replacement at St James's Park for Andy Cole, who had moved to Manchester United. But Le Tissier said: "There has been a lot speculation about Newcastle but that does not affect the way I feel. My head has never been turned by talk of big money and glamour clubs.

"Everyone is different and I suppose I'm more different than most. Quite honestly, I could only ever see myself leaving Southampton if they are relegated or my place in the England side is in jeopardy. There are no problems on either of those scores, so I'm happy to stay put."

Manchester City's two own goals at The Dell gifted Ball's men a point, the second coming when Le Tissier's cross from a short corner was whipped in to the near post and Nicky Summerbee sliced into the roof of the net. Three points were tantalisingly close for the first time in six weeks, only for Saints to blow it two minutes from time when Gary Flitcroft scored.

Goals were still coming Le Tissier's way in the FA Cup, though. After Shipperley had scored for the first time for the club in a 1-1 draw with Luton at Kenilworth Road, his partner was in inspired form in spectacularly seeing off the First Division side in the replay on the evening of February 8.

He fought off a cold to set up a sensational 6-0 win by stroking home the opener, then won a penalty, which he converted, by striking the ball against Mitchell Thomas' arm. His arrogant chip won a corner from which Ken Monkou scored before, with his work done, he was subbed to preserve some energy in his weary legs. Hughes replaced him and scored Saints' sixth in front of a full house.

Ball's side then surrendered a two-goal lead away to Norwich after Hall and Magilton had struck in the side's seventh League draw in a row. For a few days, though, Le Tissier had other things on his mind when Venables threw down the gauntlet ahead of England's game with Republic of Ireland by demanding he took the international scene by the scruff of the neck. "Everyone has wanted him to play, from the press to the fans," the manager said. "Now it is up to him to do the best he can. He will play in the same position he does for his club. But the pressure is on the whole team, not just Le Tissier, because this is such a high-profile game."

Just how much the match would come under the spotlight even Venables could not have predicted as the worst excesses of football hooliganism were depressingly evident in Dublin. Both sides were still feeling their way into the game when the explosion of violence broke out, with England fans raining broken seats down on the Irish supporters in a shower of terror.

As bewildered fathers and shell-shocked sons ran on to the pitch in search of safety, the referee had no option but to take the players off and abandon a game that was ironically billed as a friendly. Le Tissier's chance was gone. In a fixture in which Venables had set his team up to showcase the player's talents, a group of right-wing extremists got in the most devastating 'tackle' of his life.

"It has to go down as the biggest disappointment of my career," he said. "I still can't quite believe it. It was all set up to be a great night and for it to end up like that is just terrible. I had such high hopes from the game and they've been shattered in the most dreadful way. The rest of the players feel exactly the same. It has to be one of the all-time low points for all of us.

"Why do people behave like this? I can't call them supporters because they clearly aren't. I didn't see too much of the trouble because I was up the other end of the pitch and concentrating on the action. I was suddenly aware of some commotion at the other end and next thing I knew, the referee was taking all the players off. From the dressing room, we didn't know what was happening until we were told the match had been abandoned, so we knew it must be bad."

It was particularly bad news for Le Tissier. While the rest of the world was rightly condemning England's supporters, the manager was close to slapping a condemnation order on his international career.

In the meantime, there were other pressing matters for him back home. He had not scored since the defeat against Wimbledon on Boxing Day eight games earlier and Saints were badly missing his goals. He did supply the cross for Maddison to head home in the narrow defeat at Ipswich, which was followed by a draw with a scared Coventry side who shut up shop.

The shortage was addressed by a goal fiesta soon afterwards. Unfortunately, six of them went in at the wrong end. Another sublime FA Cup showing from Le Tissier ended with his penalty earning a 1-1 fifth-round draw at Tottenham, whose manager Gerry Francis ordered Stuart Nethercott to man-mark him in the replay. Saints revelled in the space that presented to the rest of the midfield as Shipperley diverted in Jason Dodd's shot for the first goal and Le Tissier made it two with his second penalty of the tie and third of the season past Ian Walker.

It was extravagant stuff - until Francis realised his mistake and hauled Nethercott off at the break. Ronny Rosenthal went on and one of the FA Cup's greatest comebacks sparked into life. Rosenthal's only goal of the season had been against non-Leaguers Altrincham in an earlier round but he crashed home a volley from Nick Barmby's cross, then unleashed a rasping drive past Grobbelaar to force extra-time.

Grobbelaar had flown in only on the morning of the game from a funeral in Africa and looked jet-lagged as Rosenthal secured his hat-trick with another swerving drive from long range. With Saints pushing on, Monkou's slip let Jurgen Klinsmann play Teddy Sheringham in for a fourth and Barmby twice dribbled round the sluggish keeper to complete an incredible 6-2 win.

"It was a shocker," Le Tissier admitted. "We were 2-0 up and we were really cruising before the second half all went a bit pear-shaped. Rosenthal came on and scored the most amazing hat-trick I've ever witnessed, especially from a substitute. Two of his goals were from shots right outside the area that just swerved. Bruce didn't get anywhere near them."

It was a crushing defeat at a time when a Cup run was needed to breathe some inspiration into the club's League form. A home draw with West Ham was followed by a dismal 3-0 defeat at Nottingham Forest on March 18 that saw Saints drop into the relegation zone for the first time in 1994-95.

Failing to stop his side's tumble was a sore point for the proud Le Tissier, who was dealt a double blow by the shock news that he had been jettisoned by England. Venables named his squad to face Uruguay in the late-March clash at Wembley and, amazingly, the Saints player had gone from being a starter to a non-person. They say things happen in threes and no doubt Le Tissier was hardly surprised when FIFA ruled that no caps would be awarded for the Dublin game.

It had been a bad week for the Dell star but he defiantly urged Venables to keep his television turned on before discounting his England chances permanently. "I hope Terry Venables has a satellite dish because I'm determined to get back in," he said. "Anyone would be disappointed if they had been in the previous England squad, then left out and I'm no different. It seems I haven't had a fair crack of the whip.

"Terry Venables rang me on the morning before he announced the squad to say he was leaving me out. He didn't want me to read it on Teletext first. That was good of him but I was so taken aback I forgot to ask him why. He did not make any promises about the future either, so it's up to me to do the best to force my way back in.

"I don't feel I have anything to prove to anyone. It doesn't bother me that people have a lower opinion of me than I have. It has been going on for a long time and if I let it get to me, I'll be playing in the Third Division."

Even his England team-mates expressed astonishment at Le Tissier's staggering omission. John Barnes said: "It did surprise me that he was not in the squad. I've not been following his club form, so cannot say whether he should be in the team but I thought he would have been in the party. He is my type of player. I think he has been the best in the country this year and I voted for him as my player of the season."

The fixture list had given Le Tissier a chance to make an instant impression by placing the tasty prospect of Newcastle in front of him. He had always tormented the Magpies and was planning another thriller both to boost his England claims and to help lift Saints out of the relegation mire.

"Obviously, people are going to cast their minds back to last season's match, which brings back fond memories for me," he said. "But I'll be happy scoring from two yards and getting another win. We went to Newcastle for Alan Ball and

Feeling ten feet tall as the goals just keep flying in.

Lawrie McMenemy's first game in charge and won that one. That set us on the way to safety and we could do with the same result again now.

"That win gave us a real lift and a lot of belief in ourselves and that is what we want now. We just need a break, something to go for us and then we will be moving again. Our performance at Forest was the worst we have given for a long time. It was a worse result than the Spurs defeat in the FA Cup because at least we played well for 45 minutes in that game."

Ball threw in striker Gordon Watson for his debut following a £1.2m transfer from Sheffield Wednesday as Saints hunted their first victory in 13 Premiership games. They were now locked in a battle to avoid the final relegation spot, with Ipswich and Leicester already as good as doomed. But the occasion looked set to become another nightmare for Southampton when Paul Kitson scored and the game entered the final five minutes without Newcastle's defence having been threatened.

Then the whole season turned around in one of those magical finales so often seen and savoured at The Dell. Heaney followed up the lively Watson's diving header to equalise and, with the clock showing the start of stoppage-time, the new striker - nicknamed Flash - won instant hero status. Pavel Srnicek dropped Jason Dodd's cross at his feet and he lashed home from close range.

The keeper's composure was shot and, when he failed to hold Heaney's shot,

Shipperley was perfectly placed to fire a third. Le Tissier said: "That was an absolute belter of a last five minutes. The atmosphere in the ground was unbelievable. We were up against it again, one down and with nothing really happening for us. Once we got one, the crowd went mad and the players' energy levels just went up. People were flying around the pitch."

It was one of the great Dell nights and more was to follow, with Le Tissier back to his best when Spurs arrived on April 2. His corner set up Heaney for the opener but Saints were 2-1 down until Le Tissier latched on to Shipperley's back heel to thread a shot between Walker and his near post from a tight angle.

And Shipperley was the provider again when he found Le Tissier unmarked in the box. His first touch for once was not his best and, as the ball bounced up, he needed to shift his body weight to prod past Walker with his left foot to make it 3-2. He was embarking on mazy runs and picking off defenders with killer passes as well - the only problem was that Saints were looking equally inept at the back, Sheringham proving the point by scoring his second to tie the scores.

It needed Magilton's fifth goal of the season, a power-packed drive from 18 yards, to secure the 4-3 win but clearly Le Tissier was the star. Ball said: "I was chuffed for him because he has had a tough time recently. I know how he's feeling. It happened to me as a player when I came out of the England squad. There's only one way to answer your critics and that's to play your football. That's what he did.

"He has not stopped working for us. He has got his head down and has been a pleasure to train despite his disappointment. I was very surprised by the decision. I thought he would get a squad place at least. Then Terry Venables would have had a chance to explain exactly what he wants from him. That's what happens at club level. You sit the player down, tell him why he is being left out and give him the opportunity to understand you and what you want."

The victory lifted Saints to 17th and, although they went down at Liverpool, Le Tissier raced away to score the second in an emphatic win at Chelsea on April 12. He then drove in a powerful corner for Shipperley to score in the defeat of QPR before smashing home a low drive from Watson's lay-off in the 2-0 victory over Wimbledon that took them to 11th and dispelled any fears of relegation.

It was turning into a one-in-a-million campaign for Le Tissier and even Magilton was struggling to comprehend just how good he was. "Matt scored unbelievable goals that season from all over the place and from nothing," he said. "He whipped in shots from 25 yards and keepers could not get anywhere near them.

"Because he played a free role in that little hole, defenders couldn't mark him, midfielders let him go and he would find the space he needed. And that was dangerous because he had such great feet, he was a great finisher. It was such a fantastic all-round season and it was a real privilege to be part of it."

After a goalless draw with Sheffield Wednesday, Le Tissier turned on the style to score twice as lowly Crystal Palace were well beaten at The Dell. Keeper Chris Wilmot embarrassingly missed his high, hopeful centre in the opening seconds and the ball dropped in at the far post. He then sent over a corner for Watson to put Saints two ahead with just nine minutes on the clock.

Gareth Southgate pulled a goal back in a crazy opening 26 minutes but Le Tissier made sure there would be no late drama with a stunning goal. He galloped on to a long ball, dropped his shoulder and moved his feet quickly to gain a yard of space and crash a low drive just inside the far post.

Watson's strike was his third since joining Saints and it had not taken him long to realise who the main man was. "I was a piano carrier and Matt was a piano player," he said. "We all were carriers really. We knew what our roles in the team were. We could do a bit more but our main job was getting the ball to Matt and then working off him. No-one resented him because of his role. In my first few weeks, any goals I got were from the creativity of Matt's boots.

"He was the one that put me through all the time, so I was just happy to be in the same team as him. To be honest, I don't think Matty knew exactly how good he was, even though there was a confidence about him. He would say: 'Give it to me and I will stick it in the top corner from 40 yards.' And he could do that. All the time.

"When Ball was there, that was the best he ever played. He was given freedom to go and do what he does. There probably haven't been many talents in the country like his on the ball. Other managers looked at the negatives, not the positives. Bally was one of those who concentrated on the positives. He would say to Matt: 'Go and do the eight things you do right and don't worry about the two things you do wrong.'

"Other managers came in and were negative because they were not as confident in the job. If something went wrong, they went hunting for a reason for it and often the blame was placed on Matt. With Bally, he would just tell us to keep playing and it would come right in the end. It was great man-management."

A sore heel forced Le Tissier to sit out the 0-0 draw with Everton - the only game he missed all season. He returned as Saints went down 2-1 at Manchester United, where, incredibly, Simon Charlton had the satisfaction of becoming the first player to score against Peter Schmeichel at Old Trafford in the League that season.

Inevitably, Le Tissier was named Player of the Year before the final game of the season - a 2-2 home draw with Leicester. It was an occasion he was determined to mark with a goal and his big moment came in the 56th minute. Having lost possession on the left touchline, he harried Simon Grayson into giving up possession to Shipperley. The striker spotted his colleague's run and threaded a pass through for him to neatly roll the ball under Kevin Poole's dive.

It was his 20th League goal of what was becoming another tremendous personal campaign - at club level at least. A further ten goals had come his way in the cups, five of them in the FA Cup, and there were more strikes to come, including an emotional one against a Guernsey FA side in a friendly organised to mark the Channel Islands' liberation from German occupation.

Le Tissier also smashed a hat-trick against Yeovil in a testimonial for strikers Paul Wilson and Micky Spencer. The opposition may not have been top-class but what made the goals all the more remarkable was the fact he was playing almost on one leg. His heel injury was so bad, he was worried it may rule him out of featuring for England in the end-of-season Umbro Cup games against Brazil, Sweden and Japan.

Venables had sent scout Ted Buxton to check on Le Tissier in Southampton's final two home games as he destroyed Palace and scored his classy goal against Leicester. That was proof that the England boss was having second thoughts on his hasty ditching of the Saints goal machine.

And Le Tissier said: "The heel has been sore but it should not put me out of the tournament. A week of rest should set it right. If I'm selected, I am sure I will be ready and determined to do my best. Everyone knows how much playing for England means to me and naturally I would love to be included next week and to know I'm part of the manager's plans. I would not want him to leave me out because of the injury. Even if I did have to pull out, like any player, I would at least like to be picked."

Venables did not give Le Tissier the chance to pull out. He sent a clear message to the Dell hero by ignoring his seven goals in nine appearances and leaving him out of his squad. His rejection prompted new calls nationally for the player to move on from Southampton to rescue his international career. Chelsea were so strongly linked that several papers even claimed he had met the club's benefactor, Matthew Harding.

But refreshingly, Le Tissier insisted he preferred to put personal happiness in front of pound signs - and keep saving Saints from the drop. For the first time, he showed frustration at the constant rumour-mongering linking him with English football's big five clubs. "For nine years, I've been telling people I am happy and don't intend going anywhere," he said. "But for nine years, nobody's believed me.

"They can't understand why I'm content to stay with a small club when I could quite easily be at one of the giants. I accept that people have difficulty comprehending it but now things have got ridiculous. I can't walk down the street without dozens of people asking me when I'm going to Chelsea. I'm getting sick of it.

"Why can't people just accept the truth? That is that I'm not interested in the glamour. I don't waste money on a superstar lifestyle, so what the hell do I want £15,000 a week for? People say I have a screw loose, that I have lost it, but perhaps it's just that I'm in that 0.1 per cent of footballers who don't give a toss about unlimited money. I didn't come into football just for the money. I came into it wanting to play for my country.

"Now people say I lack ambition. I have argued that there isn't a higher ambition than wanting to play for England. All I want to do is live a comfortable lifestyle and play football. If I continue to play for Southampton on less money than the big clubs can pay me until I am 35, the chances are I'd never have to work again. More money won't improve that situation, though, because my prospects are a damn sight better already than many people's.

"I have a nice, modest four-bedroom house in Southampton, where I can relax away from the game. So why the hell do I need more? Even close friends are phoning me up and saying: 'Okay, then, when is the Chelsea deal going to be announced?' I'm tearing my hair out here because I've never even met Matthew Harding.

"Harding went on the TV recently and was more

"How many times do I have to say it?" Le Tissier and Lawrie McMenemy spell the message out yet again.

than a little cagey when asked if I was going to join Chelsea, so that didn't exactly help things. But I was supposed to have been at his house two weeks ago. Unless he's got a place in Menorca that I don't know about, that was impossible because I was over there on holiday at the time."

Le Tissier was having trouble convincing the high-powered newspaper executives in London that his background was totally alien to theirs - and that he was happy to let slip through his fingers the gold pieces they dream of holding in their palms. "There is definitely a different outlook on life when you're born on Guernsey," he said. "It's a laid-back lifestyle that doesn't see you strive for material goods and money.

"You can call it blinkered or lackadaisical if you like but I tend to think that it is perhaps the most important thing in the world. It's quite probable that I could move to a big-city club tomorrow and earn buckets of money, but who's saying I'd be happy? I simply don't want to risk what I have at the moment, just for a chance that the grass is greener on the other side."

Ball recognised his character and made no attempt to change it, preferring instead to give him his head. He wasn't looking to him to beat the drum, just the keeper. "There are two types in a dressing room," he says. "There are the gung-ho sort to get people up to a pitch to go out and graft a performance. Then you have the quieter ones who only do it because they have sheer ability.

"Matt didn't lead by example but by what he could do for you. He wasn't a shouter or a teacher of players on the pitch. He would just purely and simply finish things off and create for other people. He said: 'Look at me, I'm not a toughie. I don't stop people playing. I'm not a horrible person on the pitch. I just get on with my game with class and ability.' That was his strength and it was a massive gift.

"In the dressing room, he'd be one you had to help. It's a cruel place in many ways and you have to stand up for yourself. Being the person he was, it got a little bit out of hand sometimes and he couldn't handle that banter. It could upset him. He wasn't a fighter and wouldn't argue or be nasty. He'd just say: 'Let's play football and I'll put the ball in the back of the net. That's how I answer people.'

"I'm sure he was born with those skills but he worked very hard on them. He'd be the last out on the training pitch many times bending and curving the ball into the net time after time. I remember him getting me to roll balls to him and he would flick them up and volley them over our plastic wall. I brought Bruce Grobbelaar out to face him but he knocked three out of five past him.

"The nearer he got to the penalty area, the more uncomfortable he became with his free-kicks. He wanted to be further away to get the ball up and over, and do what he liked with it. He loved his football and loved doing the lovely things in the game. He hoped someone would take the toughness out of it so he could show what he could do. He had sublime skills and was a fantastic striker of the ball but I don't think he really fulfilled everything because he didn't play on the highest stage."

Defiant as ever, Le Tissier claimed he would rather wait for Venables' England exit than leave Southampton, if that was the choice he faced to boost his international chances. "People say I should quit Southampton to further my England prospects," he said. "If that was the case, I wouldn't have played for England at all as a Saints player.

"Obviously, I'm in a difficult situation with England. I was in a similar position here with Ian Branfoot because he didn't seem to trust me or want me to play my natural way. I believe I was strong enough then to come through that even when I was dropped. I had enough self-belief to know that if I played to the top of my ability, there was no way I could continue to be left out.

"That proved to be the case with Southampton under Branfoot and I'm sure it will be the case with England under Terry Venables."

1995-96

'Skills Given by God'

M ATT Le Tissier had notched an incredible 45 goals in 65 games under Alan Ball and it could never have crossed his mind as he sat on a far-off beach during the summer of 1995 that the Dell board were about to make a monumental mistake.

Manchester City chairman Francis Lee had made an approach for the man who best knew how to make Le Tissier tick but Ball didn't want to go. He was in charge of the club he loved and was convinced he was building a team with real potential. And, in Le Tissier, he knew he had a player few managers could dream of working with.

The Saints boss had expected his paymasters to immediately put a block on any bid his old England pal made to take him to Maine Road. He was on a paltry £50,000 a year at Southampton - the lowest wage by far among managers in the Premiership - but was content to continue on similar money.

For Ball, it was not about cash. It was about moulding a team to bring the best out of Le Tissier and seeing Saints again become regular competitors on the European scene. Few, including Ball himself, expected his chairman Guy Askham to let City get anywhere near a manager who had guided Saints to tenth place in the League just a few weeks previously.

But there had been stirrings of discontent in the boardroom and, surprisingly, Lee was told to call Ball at his holiday villa in Marbella. When the manager questioned his chairman over why he was being allowed to leave, the response was blunt. "It is up to Alan Ball to make up his own mind where his loyalties lie," Askham stated.

That was enough to tell Ball he was no longer wanted at The Dell. Rather than spend a season fighting a losing battle with his superiors, he decided to take the huge pay rise on offer and head north. For Le Tissier's career, it was a disaster. Under Ball, he had hit peak form and broken into the England squad. His failings had been overlooked in the quest to maximise his rare gift to win games single-handedly.

Once again, Saints were seeking a new manager and, having grown wise to the importance of keeping Le Tissier at the forefront of their plans, looked within.

Although rumours abounded that Graeme Souness was the no 1 target, the choice they made was guaranteed to keep their star player sweet.

Le Tissier's former youth team boss and mentor Dave Merrington was handed the pivotal role, moving from the backroom to take charge of a club he had loyally served for more than a decade. And Matt said: "Bally was good for me, there is no doubt about it. But just because he had complete faith in me and trusted me, does not mean I want to quit now he has gone. I had a long chat with Lawrie McMenemy and he assured me nothing would change as far as the style of football is concerned."

There was no certainly no sense of worry about the season ahead when Saints returned for training. Supporters were so convinced the Le Tissier bandwagon would keep on rolling that they paid homage by cracking on to the latest craze of crop circles. Well-organised fans crept into a field near Winchester and flattened down a wheat field to produce an astonishing 300ft plea championing their hero's cause.

Reading 'Le Tiss for England,' with a picture of a matchstick man kicking a football and adorned with a halo, the stunning image was created just before the release of a new single by local band Valley Slags entitled 'Pick Matty' - a number aimed at twisting Terry Venables' arm.

As supporters continued to bombard the England manager with their campaigns, it was up to Merrington to get Le Tissier excelling where it really mattered. He had led the player through the club's youth system and had ensured that he stayed at The Dell when brothers Carl and Kevin finally caved in to homesickness and headed back to the sanctuary of the Channel Islands.

He knew more than most how his brain worked and, if anyone could cajole performances out of the Saints star, it was him. He had the basics right, he knew not to mess with the good work Ball had done and he never questioned for a moment who would be the centrepiece of his managerial master-plan.

"Matty will still have his free role," Merrington confirmed. "How can you tie down a genius? I don't believe in restricting any player. You have to let him express himself, albeit within a framework. You have to have a blend. You need workhorses and thoroughbreds. Then, in Matty, we have a touch of genius which has to be harnessed.

"Basically, you can't coach a player like him. You can keep his weight right and his habits right and his use of life right but I can't teach him anything on the training field. We can have him practise his passing and shooting but I could not teach the skills he has got in a million years. They are given by God.

"Although he grabs all the headlines, I don't see the team as a one-man show. There are ten others who give everything to enable him to perform in that role and they must not be overlooked. They are all good players in their own right. It is a question of getting the blend right, so they will knit together into a strong unit."

If Merrington needed convincing that he had Le Tissier's full support, it came in a strongly worded statement from Stamford Bridge. Glenn Hoddle had been watching him display the passing skills and vision he himself had mastered in his England days. Now, with money behind him as Chelsea manager, he visualised the mouth-watering prospect of sending him out in a blue shirt.

But, when the Londoners came knocking, Le Tissier quickly shut the door on any notion of leaving Merrington in the mire. The Chelsea statement read: "We approached Southampton formally and asked whether they would sit down and negotiate a deal. They said no. Le Tissier has confirmed he does not wish to leave. We totally respect the club's and player's decisions. We have never put an offer to Southampton or made any public valuation on the fee we would be prepared to pay. We have not offered or suggested players as part of a possible player exchange."

Le Tissier quickly hit the goal trail in pre-season, netting on a trip to Ireland, doing likewise in a defeat of Wycombe and snatching two against Volendam on a Dutch tour. And the appointment of Merrington looked a shrewd move as the no 7 started the season with a hat-trick at The Dell against Nottingham Forest. The only problem was that Forest scored four in reply!

Saints were already 1-0 down when Le Tissier was tripped by Steve Chettle and got up to convert the penalty. But goals by Ian Woan and Bryan Roy left Merrington's men heading for the break 3-1 behind. Le Tissier was proving to be the only real menace and, when he was bundled over in the box in the 69th minute, he brushed himself down to fire home a second spot-kick.

But Saints just couldn't get close to Forest, with Roy adding a fourth before Le Tissier enjoyed a deflection off the wall to score with a free-kick on a pleasing day for him - and a worrying one for fans. Defeat, as usual, at Everton was followed by a home draw with Leeds, then Le Tissier produced one inspirational moment as a dogged Saints side fought for a 1-0 win over visiting Newcastle.

He showed tremendous vision to find Jim Magilton with the perfect pass and the midfielder slotted past Shaka Hislop. "It was a simple tap-in but it's a lovely goal," the scorer said. "I didn't even have to take a controlling touch because of the weight and the appreciation of the pass."

The deserved win was a rare early-season bright spot as Saints then totalled only two points and four goals from six League games, Le Tissier setting up Gordon Watson and Ken Monkou for close-range finishes in a 4-2 defeat at Arsenal. While they were having little joy, there were celebrations for Captain Le Tissier when his wife Kathy gave birth to their second child, Keeley.

Unfortunately, the joy of fatherhood was not matched by the thrill of pulling on an England jersey. Le Tissier was left out of the game against Colombia and the writing was on the wall about his international future under Venables. He was firmly out of the picture and all his six full caps were from friendlies - something that still allowed him to change his allegiance to another flag if he chose.

Just in case the hint hadn't been taken, Venables made it clear Le Tissier had no

Representing his country was a fast fading memory in 1995-96. But Matt promised never to desert England's three lions.

place in his plans by refusing to block a bid from France, Scotland or Wales to spirit him away. "I don't think I will try and block it if he chooses to play for another country," the manager said. "Like all these things, it rests on the player himself and what he wants. I won't be talking to him especially. Other players are affected as well and I can't ring them all."

The papers raved about the idea of Le Tissier being handed on a plate to England's oldest rivals but the Saints star quickly dismissed the idea of him singing Scotland the Brave and wearing a blue shirt. Instead, he insisted he was willing to adopt a new, less ambitious way of playing if that's what it took to win back his England place.

"The interest from Scotland and Wales is very flattering and I've nothing against them," he said. "But it's England or nothing for me. I've considered myself English since the day I was born and am not going for the easy option just for the sake of a few caps. I've always stated that the only ambition I've ever had is to play for England.

"I have no doubts I could fit into the England team. If need be, I can adapt my style. If the manager wants me to pass it ten yards square, I can do that. It's not difficult. I have enough faith in my ability to play whatever way Terry Venables wants me to play. It is a bit frustrating to be overlooked but I am still determined to get back in."

Whether Venables took offence at the subtle dig about England's style of play is hard to tell but one thing was certain: Le Tissier was hurting. Merrington had the problem of trying to ensure that Saints didn't suffer as well and said: "Matt is not firing like we know he can, so we have to try and find a way of helping him and supporting him, and seeing him through it.

Alan Shearer seems impressed with the efforts of his former Saints team-mate - but this was by no means the only time Terry Venables chose to look elsewhere.

"He's a great player for his club and, if he is going through a bad spell, I will live with it and back him because he is quality. He has tremendous skills, awareness and finishing ability - he can do things I could not coach. We have to look for answers. If a golfer is not putting well, he goes back to the practice ground. Matt can do the same. He is a very fast learner. You tell him something and he picks it up instantly.

"We all have highs and lows and he will come through this. In my opinion, he is one of the best 22 players in the country. He is a play-maker and he can score goals. His record over the last four years speaks for itself and I don't think you can afford to leave that type of player out of the England squad. Being left out has hurt him very much. He might well be laid-back but this is a deep wound because he is so desperate to perform for England."

A lack of goals had given Venables the perfect excuse to jettison Le Tissier, who was still capable of carving out openings. But the irritation of failing to score was beginning to tell as Southampton welcomed Liverpool to The Dell on September 22, a week after Merrington's men had lost narrowly at champions Blackburn.

Anfield is a place where gifted players are always recognised and acknowledged, whether they wear the red of Liverpool or opposition colours. It is home to the football

Le Tissier relished; passing, moving, receiving and opening up defences through the ability to see a final pass. For him now, that was rarely an option. With Saints already in the relegation battle, a meeting with the Merseysiders - even when they were on the road - meant chasing back, harassing and, just occasionally, having chance to caress the ball and dream of a defence-splitting pass.

Frustrated at seeing Saints over-run once more, he attempted to fire them up by charging into tackles. Tackling was not his strong point and two late challenges brought the wrath of the referee and a 68th minute dismissal in a 3-1 defeat.

Many players of his quality might have had thoughts at this point of quitting for an easier life. Although Venables may have lost faith, there still appeared to be plenty of desperate takers - with top dollar on offer. With Chelsea already rebuffed, the spotlight shifted to a man whose millions had just bought Blackburn a Premiership crown.

Jack Walker had previously given Kenny Dalglish the go-ahead to pay Saints £6m for Alan Shearer and Tim Flowers. And he appeared ready to dig deep once again, this time for an astonishing British record £10m, to take Le Tissier to the unlikely setting of Ewood Park. But for once, money didn't talk, with the player firmly dismissing the prospect of joining his pals.

"There really isn't much I can add to what I said at the start of the season because my situation hasn't changed," he said. "I have not heard anything from Blackburn and, even if I did, I would not be interested. I am under contract and happy to stay. I have no desire to go anywhere else. That is nothing against Blackburn or Chelsea or any of the others rumoured to be interested.

"It's just that I love this club and the area and the people here, and you cannot put a price on personal happiness. I get a bit fed up with all the speculation as it falls upon me and the club to deny it all. I thought the message would have got through by now. I spelled it out quite clearly at the start of the season when Chelsea's interest came up and nothing has changed since then."

While Rovers may not have been excited by Le Tissier's League form, there was something for their scouts to report home on in the Coca-Cola Cup, where he shone against lower-division opposition once again. This time it was Cardiff who came a second-round cropper as Saints travelled to Wales and prised a 3-0 lead.

They were inevitably inspired by Le Tissier, whose first goal provided a huge confidence booster. Subtle footwork took him past three defenders before he spotted the keeper a yard too far off his line and chipped the most delicate of goals. Two minutes after the break, there was more Matty majesty as he latched on to a Tommy Widdrington pass, skipped behind the defence and outrageously hooked the ball over the advancing Williams with enough spin to bring it down just under the bar.

In the second leg, Le Tissier's corners set up Watson and Richard Hall as Saints won 5-1 on aggregate and, in the third round, he played his part in a 2-1 home defeat of West Ham to earn a fourth-round tie at Reading - a tie that should not have proved too difficult. But Saints' patchy form caught up with them and they crashed 2-1 despite Le Tissier's free-kick being headed home by Monkou.

The defeat against Liverpool convinced Saints' money-men to enter the market and Merrington spent £850,000 on Galatasaray's Barry Venison. The defender's arrival had an immediate impact in a 2-1 win at Wimbledon and a victory over QPR in Le Tissier's final game before a one-match ban. He signed off in perfect fashion with a second-half free-kick that bent over the wall and flew in from the tightest of angles.

It was his first goal in 11 League appearances but battling draws and the dogged resistance that brought the occasional victory were hardly conducive to the football the master needed in order to dominate games. And it showed. Although recognised as the side's long-time hero, he failed to make an impact throughout either November or December as Saints flirted with the drop zone once more.

Watson reckons that was down to Merrington's confidence as boss ebbing away with every point dropped. "It was his first season in management and the first time he had any pressure as such on him," he said. "Whenever someone has that, they go negative to ensure they don't get beaten, rather than say: 'Here are your two strikers, here's Matty behind them. Right, go out and win games.'

"We didn't roll many teams over. The matches we did win tended to be by the odd goal. It was a poor season. We took one step forward and then two back and were just surviving from week to week. There was a lot of pressure on Matty under Dave, who very rarely played him, me and Neil Shipperley in the same side. Matt was a luxury and you needed an extra man in midfield at the expense of a striker. Unfortunately, I was often the odd man out."

While Watson was stewing, Le Tissier was trying every angle to get his form back. And probably the most painful decision of all was his relinquishing of the captaincy before the 2-1 defeat at West Ham on December 16. As such a proud man, handing the armband to Venison was not a decision he would have taken lightly but it was a measure of the desperation he was feeling.

"We have always had a good understanding and Matt asked to see me," Merrington said. "He said he needed help because his season has not been going as well as he would have wished. He asked if he could be relieved of the captaincy to free his mind to concentrate on his own game. It was a very honest chat which was possible because of the special relationship we have forged over the years. That gave him the confidence and courage to come and see me and I reluctantly accepted it.

"Hopefully, it will be the key to spark him again. He has been under a lot of pressure, more than most people realise, and he has got frustrated with himself. But he will come through it. He says he has never been happier in the role he's playing, which has not altered from last season. He has total freedom to do his own thing and go where his brain tells him. Now he will be able to do that, unhindered by the captaincy."

The painful Premiership struggles were forgotten when Saints were drawn against

Portsmouth in a blistering FA Cup third-round tie at The Dell. Steve Moran's heroic last-minute goal in 1984 had decided the last cup meeting between the two sides and left Pompey's fans baying for revenge in this noon clash.

Le Tissier shrugged off injury worries to play, determined not to miss out against the old enemy. He showed his intent with an early long-range effort but was not involved as Magilton beat Alan Knight to net the first. The second, although scored once again by Magilton, was Le Tissier at his best. Edged out to the right, he ambled half the length of the pitch before cutting inside his marker to crash a rasping left-foot volley at goal. Knight got a glove to it, only for Magilton to follow up and score.

Le Tissier haunted the First Division visitors once again with ten minutes left by laying on a simple chance for Shipperley to stuff Portsmouth's laughable claims of being the south coast top dogs firmly down their throats.

Back in the League, Merrington's men simply couldn't get together the run they needed to improve their miserable position. Defeat at Forest saw Le Tissier hit a low point as Saints fans learned for the first time of one reason for his dip in form.

They had not known about the injury trauma that was wrecking his season. "People keep asking me about England," he said. "To be honest, I just want to concentrate on getting my club form right. I am only interested in impressing Dave Merrington and the Saints fans right now. I can't really put my finger on any real reason why things have not gone as well for me, although I have probably had more injuries than before.

"They are all related to the heel problem I had at the end of last season. It was still troubling me at the end of the summer and I had special inserts in my boots. But they have put more strain on the calf. That restricted me at Forest, which was the worst I have felt for some time, although the previous week against Portsmouth was the best I'd felt for some time."

After Saints managed a welcome home win over Middlesbrough, fellow strugglers Manchester City picked up an important point in a 1-1 Dell draw at the end of January. Saints were indebted to Le Tissier for that point as he set up Shipperley with a fantastic raking diagonal pass for the striker to chest down and fire just inside the upright.

In a run of four home matches, Saints then drew with Everton before losing to Chelsea 3-2. They even suffered the embarrassment of being held at home by Dario Gradi's Crewe in the fourth round of the FA Cup. Dave Beasant was caught out by Gareth Whalley's cross from the left for the opening goal and the cheer that saluted Le Tissier's 63rd minute equaliser was as much of relief as celebration.

The Saints striker had barely been a goal threat all season but after being handed space by the underdogs' defence, took his opportunity superbly with a swerving shot into the top of the net. The replay thankfully shaped up differently, Saints charging into a 3-0 lead at half-time and promising a rout.

But over-confidence and complacency crept in. Rob Edwards was left free to pull one back and when Ashley Westwood headed past Beasant, Saints were suddenly edgy.

Their demons were haunting them as Dele Adebola headed against the post and they even had to survive a late penalty appeal to scrape a fifth-round visit to Swindon.

Amid a break in League action, they headed to the County Ground to face a side one place ahead of Crewe, and current leaders of Division Two. Despite dominating the opening period, they fell behind to Kevin Hurlock's shot and it needed Le Tissier's intervention once again to force a replay. He delivered a pacy corner for Watson to score with a header that bounced out of the net after hitting the stanchion.

Le Tissier sat out the replay with a dose of flu that allowed Matty Oakley to step in and score in a 2-0 victory but Saints' Premiership fortunes were to hit another slump as Merrington's well-organised side contained opponents without threatening them often enough. And that was down to Le Tissier failing to shine in a set-up designed around him as the pivotal source of attacks.

Even Merrington's presence on the touchline could not lift the player out of his rut. But he did have experience of putting the sparkle back in Le Tissier's boots from his time as reserve-team boss. "When things have gone wrong with Matt in the past, managers have passed him back to me and told me to see what I can do," he said.

"There have been times when he has driven coaches nuts. Sometimes he needs an arm around him, other times a kick in the right direction. But I have never tried to run him. I tried to work him with the ball. Giving the ball to Matty is like giving a child a piece of candy. He lightens up and brightens the whole of the pitch, and that is what we intend to continue doing."

The remedial work was not having the desired effect this time and Watson believes the problems ran too deep to be resolved by an extra hour on the training pitch. He said: "I certainly feel Dave was no Alan Ball in the way he motivated players. I don't really think he was Matt's cup of tea. I think Matt probably felt he left that behind in the youth team six years earlier."

Magilton was also convinced that Le Tissier was not the kind of player Merrington required in his hour of need, saying: "Even though he knew Matty well, when you are under the microscope as Dave was, perhaps he felt he needed someone who was a lot more hard-working, a grass-roots type of player; someone with more of a work ethic.

"But we all know in the Premiership you need someone who is a bit special, who can do something to make all the difference in a tight game. We played 4-4-2 whereas under Bally we played with three at the back to accommodate Matty. He could have played off the front man but Matt's work ethic was not perhaps what it might have been. In fairness, that wasn't why he was in the side. We had others to do that job."

Saints' nerves were seriously frayed when Jason Dozzell hit a White Hart Lane winner for Tottenham to drop them back into the relegation zone and worse was to follow on two trips to Manchester. They felt referee Steve Dunn robbed them of the chance to give United an FA Cup scare by inexplicably ruling out Shipperley's header from Jason Dodd's cross just before interval when the tie was goalless.

The incident took the wind out of Southampton sails and Eric Cantona's strike was followed by a late prod home from Lee Sharpe. The quarter-final defeat ended any hopes of some silverware in what was fast becoming a depressing campaign but just as damaging was the controversial follow-up clash with Alan Ball's City.

A point was the minimum requirement against another side in the relegation battle and it seemed Matthew Robinson's injury-time effort would be enough to achieve that as Saints rallied from two down. But referee Jeff Winter disallowed it for a borderline offside decision to condemn Saints to more heartache on a day when Watson was sent off and midfielder Paul Tisdale scored his only goal for the club.

By now, the national press were digging to find out exactly why Le Tissier was so off form and blamed a rift between manager and star player. It seemed a soft option but there was fuel to fire their imagination when Radio Five arrived in town for a lively Football Forum debate. Once again, Le Tissier's glaring honesty in a business in which that commodity is sometimes in short supply, led to controversy.

Asked by a fan whether he felt he was being used to greatest effect, he said: "It is difficult for any player to tell the manager where he wants to play. I am part of the team and if I'm asked to do a job, I will do it. Given a choice, I'd like to play a bit further forward. If I was, I might get more scoring chances. But if it means benefiting the team, I'll play where I am asked. I have spoken to Dave Merrington about it, though."

Saints director of football Lawrie McMenemy was also on the panel and attempted to defuse any row. He said: "In fairness to Dave, he's tried you in different positions - up front, behind the front two and in a free role. We don't care where you play as long as you score. In fact, I was delighted to hear the announcer say you have an average of one goal every two games each season. That means you're in for a hell of a run-in!"

The knockabout discussion was picked up by the national media and flavoured the suggestion that Le Tissier had not missed the Cup game at Swindon because of flu but through being dropped by an unhappy Merrington. That led Le Tissier to speak out and put the record straight, admitting the only reason behind his lack of goals was a simple loss of form.

"There has been no bust-up with the manager and I'm not looking to leave," he insisted. "There is no doubt in anyone's mind at the club that I was too ill to play. I've always said I'm happy to stay with Saints as long as they stay in the Premiership and that has not changed. I am not unhappy with my role in the side. I played that position for the last 12 games of last season and the team went on a terrific run."

Saints were by now in a nasty dogfight and Merrington knew who was the only man capable of lifting them out of trouble. He needed a back-up plan while the star was misfiring and that meant Le Tissier having to scrap and track back when Saints all too frequently lost possession.

Merrington explained: "The role he's playing now is exactly the same as he had towards the end of last season when the team had such a good run. I have not restricted him in any way. All I ask is that when we lose the ball, he fills certain holes. But, when we have the ball, he has licence to go wherever he wants. I never asked him to defend; just to have a responsibility to the other players when we don't have possession.

"When we get it back, he can go right, left, in the middle, across the penalty area or up front - wherever his instinct tells him. He has total freedom when we have the ball and that has not altered at all from last season."

The big question was whether Le Tissier could use the scope afforded him to start winning games for his club. His corner set up Saints' first win in seven League games when Coventry were edged out at The Dell, with Dodd the surprise scorer at the far post. Despite being the instigator of so many goals, Le Tissier's own scoring record was not a patch on his previous bountiful seasons.

With the campaign in its final stretch, he had yet to score a goal from open play in the League and boasted just four Premiership strikes in 28 games. He finally notched again on April 6, though - with his 38th successful penalty - to settle a ragged display against Blackburn. Three points were welcome but there seemed little hope of more when champions-elect Manchester United arrived in their new grey change shirts.

But with United's players comically claiming they couldn't spot each other against the spectators because of their choice of attire, Saints swept into a 3-0 half-time lead with Le Tissier finally ending his awful run and being joined on the score-sheet by Monkou and Shipperley. His strike came when he latched on to a Peter Schmeichel fumble and flicked the ball over the despairing keeper to guide home a clinical finish.

After that 3-1 win, Le Tissier didn't manage his usual heroics at Newcastle, where Saints lost to Rob Lee's early effort. Then Merrington took his troops to Bahrain for a game against the national side to get some sun on their backs and ease the pressure. Le Tissier settled that friendly with a 20-yard free-kick and was the saviour once again in an agonisingly tense encounter against already relegated Bolton at Burnden Park.

Knowing Saints needed a win to stand any chance of staying up, he was quick to spot left-back Jimmy Phillips' indecisiveness and read his pass inside in the 25th minute. He intercepted and took on the keeper with a first-time effort that swung in.

It proved the only goal of the late-April clash and Le Tissier probably headed to the dressing room thinking the win had secured Premiership survival for another year. But the huge Saints contingent knew that Coventry and Manchester City had both won away to leave all three teams on 37 points going into the final Saturday.

While Saints had scored a meagre 34 times, the defensive work Merrington had slaved over was about to pay off. Their goal difference was seven better than City, who were in the final relegation place. Saints, at home to Wimbledon, knew they only had to match City's result to stay up - and Liverpool were the visitors to Maine Road. But it was ironic that Ball's side could sink a club who meant so much to him.

There was to be no last-day glory for Le Tissier this time round as he played his part in keeping the game at The Dell tight while fans bellowed on to the pitch the latest score from Manchester. The bulletins were good to begin with, Liverpool going 2-0 up against a side full of passion and desperate for goals.

But the hope that Liverpool would close the game out, as in their hey-day, quickly died as City came back to level and leave Saints on tenterhooks. There appeared no way through Wimbledon's massed defence but, luckily, City made a crucial mistake. None of their backroom staff took a radio into the dug-out and they relied instead on the fans for information.

"It was a mad afternoon," Ball recalls. "We were at two apiece when a spectator close to the tunnel shouted that Southampton had conceded a goal in the 89th minute. It meant a draw would have been good enough to keep us up. We had the ball, so I told Steve Lomas to take it to the corner flag to kill time. He was doing that when I heard that the goal had been disallowed. I found myself running down the track trying to get another message across and no doubt looking an absolute fool."

City's draw helped ensure Saints were safe with a point while Coventry drew at home to Leeds to save themselves. Merrington headed off with a satisfied smile to visit his ill wife in hospital, little knowing that his 12 years of loyal service to the club were about to come to an abrupt, rude and undignified end.

They were brilliant for each other at The Dell - now Alan Ball had helped Le Tissier again as his Manchester City went down in bizarre circumstances and kept Saints up.

1996-97

A Hoddle False Dawn

A SENSE of loss hung round the Le Tissier household during the summer of 1996 as he came to terms with two major blows. A month after seeing his good friend Dave Merrington ruthlessly dumped by the Southampton board, he had the personal agony of missing out on England's stunning march to the semi-finals of the 1996 European Championships. Going out on penalties at Wembley was the ultimate insult - can you imagine Le Tissier hitting such a weak effort as the one Gareth Southgate managed against the Germans?

The only way to cope was concentrating on the domestic front and impressing the new man at The Dell. Merrington's departure had been badly handled by the club, his years of service ignored as he was hurriedly shown the back door. Saints had bigger fish to fry, with the arrival of Graeme Souness on the cards, and treated their former boss without the respect he deserved.

The changes were not the only ones interesting Le Tissier. It was also time for Terry Venables to stand aside as England manager for Glenn Hoddle, who enjoyed the approval of a nation when he was ushered in. As 1996-97 started, the country was on a football high, with The Dell's main man baring one of the broadest smiles.

He knew he was well rated by Hoddle because the manager had tried to sign him for Chelsea just 12 months earlier. Now he sat back waiting for his England career to be revived. And it didn't take long. He was included in the new coach's first squad after showing a refreshing new spark to his play during Souness' opening matches as Saints boss.

He was used just behind Neil Shipperley in the televised 0-0 draw with Chelsea on the opening day at The Dell, with Richard Dryden stunning his critics by keeping European Cup winner Gianluca Vialli quiet.

The lights literally went out on Saints' next performance as a power cut delayed the kick-off at Leicester. But it only held up the inevitable as Southampton were destroyed by a powerful performance from a youthful Emile Heskey. The striker scored twice as Barry Venison was sent off, the only bright spot for Le Tissier being the conversion of a spot-kick.

An early sense of foreboding gathered over The Dell but the sun was shining on Le Tissier two days later when Hoddle predictably handed him a recall. There was a nationwide buzz as fans and pundits developed a taste for the mouth-watering prospect of him being given the freedom denied him by Venables.

Hoddle, of all people, would know just how to get the best out of Le Tissier on the international stage. He had suffered similar frustrations during his England days when his world-class talents were jettisoned far too frequently in favour of players with a bigger lung capacity - and barely a modicum of his talent.

It was a time of huge optimism, with golden boy Glenn hailed as the tactical genius to motivate his players and pick the right teams to ensure that England built on the Venables legacy and lived with the world's best. To do that, they needed a player capable of unlocking well-drilled international defences, just as Michel Platini had done for France in 1984.

Paul Gascoigne had been handed that task during the Venables years but, for all his scampering and willingness to carry the ball, he was rarely carving open rearguards as he had done so brilliantly in Italy in 1990. Le Tissier still had that ability despite his poor 1995-96 season and the country was now demanding that he be given a chance to establish himself at the highest level.

Even the player himself was keen to talk up his international prospects. There was no doubting that he clearly believed in the man he had idolised while growing up on the island of Guernsey and was convinced he was about to be given the opportunity he had so desired for so long.

In Hoddle, he visualised a coach who could understand his reluctance to dive into tackles, his refusal to chase back for needless causes and his objection to pointlessly covering space when bigger opportunities presented themselves once his team-mates had recovered the ball. Surely, he must have thought, Hoddle would know that a player of his ability had higher callings and was going to waste when running round snapping at the heels of opponents.

Hoddle had picked up the nickname 'Glenda' during his playing career in England and France. It was recognition of his ability to avoid the part of the game that, although crucial, he didn't consider to be beautiful. Instead, the midfielder with the technique and vision of a footballing genius had amassed 53 caps by spraying passes around for willing team-mates to capitalise on.

There was no doubting in his own mind that Le Tissier could do a similar job if handed the chance. "My burning desire to play for England has been well documented along with my admiration for Glenn Hoddle," the player said. "I had a chance under the previous manager but did not take it to the full. I hope this time I can produce my best form with a manager who, hopefully, has belief in me.

"His appointment as England manager has given me a massive lift. There could not be a bigger incentive this season than knowing the international door is open again. It is no secret I worshipped Hoddle as a player. I loved the way he played the game and the skill he had. I suppose I tried to model myself on him because he played in the centre of midfield like I did then."

Le Tissier probably already knew Hoddle would select him in his first squad and was named at an FA press conference on August 22 in the party of 22 for the trip to Moldova. But Hoddle was quick to play down the excitement building among football purists by revealing that he was not prepared to build his side around the Southampton star's magical talents.

As the pundits were swept along in the fantasia fest of just how Le Tissier's skill might make true football artists out of an England side some described as functional and others labelled as kick-and-run merchants, Hoddle was not going overboard on whether he thought the player would cut the international mustard.

"It has been noted over the past year that I was interested in him at club level but I have never really met the boy," he admitted. "I have got to talk to him and see what it is that makes him tick. He has got immense talent and has shown that to everybody in the last few seasons. In international football, I think you need highly technical players. I've watched him twice this season but it's too early to judge anybody, even if he is in superb form.

"I need to work with the guy and find out roughly what's going through his mind. I'm not going to be able to do that if I don't bring him into the squad. Obviously I'm not going to pick my team now but everyone who's in that squad has got a chance of playing. Otherwise, they wouldn't be in it."

It was a clear message to Le Tissier that he could not afford to turn up at Bisham Abbey expecting to coast through training sessions. Gazza was still occasionally able to prise open defences with a sublime pass, and the misfunctional Geordie remained daft enough to chase round the pitch to win back possession if one of his passes was to miss the target!

At The Dell, Lawrie McMenemy was hoping Le Tissier's return to the England fold following an 18-month exile would give his club career a desperately needed boost. He had sunk to his lowest point in the previous season as a collection of niggly injuries and a sense of gloom enveloped his play. "People talked about his England rejection having an adverse affect, so we must hope this call-up will have a positive effect," McMenemy said.

"A lot of people felt he was unlucky not to be in a squad after the abandoned game in Ireland and we are all delighted to see him back in. He has his foot in the door now and it's up to him to try and impress the manager. Everyone agrees that Matt has the ability. We are all biased locally but the professionals generally feel he is up there with the elite. Now he has to mix and match with the best players in the country.

"The new manager will have his own thoughts and ideas, which he will pass on. It is up to all the players to go back and work, and the good thing is that Matt is on the starting line with the rest of them."

Souness' desire for the kind of graft Le Tissier was not used to providing became ever more evident in the 2-1 defeat at West Ham. Francis Benali's red card made it two dismissals for the club in two games and put the emphasis on a hard-working system that had not always been to Le Tissier's liking in the past.

That was all forgotten for a while as he proudly joined up with England, hoping for his big opportunity to break through on the international arena. "The problem I have always encountered is that people look to me to score goals *and* create them," he said "It might have been a lot easier for managers to pick me if I had been good at one thing and crap at the other.

"But now I have got another opportunity. Some people might have suggested that it might be a bit of a risk picking me for the Moldova game but I have never lost my creative ability. I think I can create chances in every game I play, no matter who we are playing against."

The game was a real test of Hoddle's managerial mettle. It was a World Cup qualifier and defeat against the minnows would be unacceptable. Hoddle decided there was to be no risk, so Le Tissier was left on the bench as Paul Ince and Gascoigne were given the job of controlling the game on a shockingly bobbly pitch. The emerging David Beckham was on the right and the cultured left foot and defensive ability of Andy Hinchcliffe were on the opposite flank.

Once again, the role Le Tissier was desperate to occupy was handed to the bustling Nick Barmby, who was under orders to create chances for Alan Shearer. Le Tissier went on only for ten minutes in a comfortable victory as Hoddle dangled a World Cup carrot but it was a huge psychological boost considering he was emerging from his bleakest days with England.

Most galling of all had been Venables' refusal to hand him the kind of opportunity that lesser lights such as Steve Stone had enjoyed and Le Tissier admitted for the first time to wondering whether staying loyal to Saints had cost him the chance to play in a major international tournament. "At last I feel better about my future now and that's going to do wonders for my confidence," he said. "It's a lot different to how I was feeling a year ago.

"I started dreaming of what I could do in the European Championships but you can't work like that. One full match, a couple of ten-minute spells and 27 minutes in an abandoned game wasn't a fair deal, particularly when many other players got so many matches to show what they can do. I guess one of the problems is that I never moved to a fashionable club.

"I sat down with Glenn Hoddle and had a chat. I think he sees a bit of himself in me and I get the impression that, if he picks me, it is as just another member of the squad, not as a special case. He understands that, although there are some who expect me to score an incredible goal every time I walk on the pitch. It doesn't work like that.

"I know this might be my last chance and second time round is much sweeter. I feel the manager understands me more. I feel more wanted than before."

Le Tissier used his England 'high' to help Southampton take a point from a home draw with Nottingham Forest as he fired in yet another last-gasp strike after turning smartly in the box. It was a glimpse of the old Le Tissier and it was obvious to everyone around the club that the call to arms from England had provided him with a much-needed spring in his step.

While his star was rising once again, life at The Dell was proving a little trickier for manager Souness. Three successive defeats had left Southampton in the relegation zone before Le Tissier produced a moment of magic to inspire them to their first League victory of the season - at the eighth attempt.

Matty Oakley had already slotted home the opener against Middlesbrough when Le Tissier astoundingly curled a corner past the bemused Alan Miller for a goal which knocked the stuffing out of Bryan Robson's side. He followed up by outwitting the visitors' offside trap to latch on to Simon Charlton's cross to net and secure all three points - but admitted he thought the latter would be chalked off.

"I did think it was offside," he said. "When I controlled the ball, the keeper stood still and didn't make a move to close me down. I was close to just flicking the ball to him to take a free-kick. But I knew the whistle had not gone, so I put the ball in the net just to be on the safe side. Then I turned around and saw the ref running away to the centre circle. I'm glad I did as it could have been embarrassing!"

It was the perfect send-off for Le Tissier as he joined up with the England squad for the World Cup qualifier against Poland - or so he thought. For, while he was desperate to concentrate on convincing Hoddle that he should be given a run-out in a fixture perceived to be crucial to England's chances of making the finals in France, the nation's press seemed to be more interested in his diet than in his hunger for scoring and making goals.

He had already taken the unusual step of ringing David Mellor's phone-in show to put one caller right about his weight the previous season. But when the papers went to town on what they believed to be his expanding waistline, the Saints star delivered an impassioned defence of his fitness.

"It annoys me when people band about figures they know nothing about," he said. "I have been accused of putting on two stone, which is ridiculous. The fact is that my weight is no different to what it has ever been. I am 13st 11lbs - exactly what I was in the two seasons I scored 25 and 30 goals. It went down to 13st 2lbs at the start of last season and I did not have a very good campaign. Yet I had two great seasons at my current weight and feel very comfortable with it.

"I have been doing some extra work in the afternoon when I get time between games and I'm quite happy doing anything that will help me. I have only done one extra session on my own so far, so it's a bit early to tell if it has had any effect, but I certainly feel I'm getting back towards my best form.

"The game against Middlesbrough was probably my best of the season and that has given me a real lift before joining up with England. Obviously, I would love to play or go on as substitute but I'm just delighted to be involved at this stage."

Hoddle had no qualms about Le Tissier's weight and took time out to discuss how the striker could force his way into his line-up. It was a dream chat for the Channel Islander as he heard plans for a role just behind his close friend, Shearer. He said: "I had an informal chat with Glenn Hoddle which he asked me to keep private, suffice to say he gave me a few pointers in the right direction.

"He understands the position I'm in and it is up to me to make the most of any chances. If I do get in the team, it would probably be in the position in which I came on as substitute against Moldova, just behind Alan Shearer. That seems to be the role I am fighting for at the moment.

"But I am delighted to be back in the squad and to have had a taste. Now, the next job has to be to get my first start under the new manager. After that, the target will be to get my first international goal. That would really be something special - a schoolboy dream come true."

Le Tissier acknowledged that he was a different player to the one who produced some inconsistent displays in 1995-96 and put it down to Souness' training methods. "I'm not the quickest of starters to a season," he added. "Last year, I had only got six goals by Christmas and three of those were on the opening day. I think I have already scored more from open play this time round than I did in the whole of last season and consider this a better start.

"I just hope it continues for me and for the team. The essence of every career is to be successful at club level and to get the chance at international level. Things went very well for me and Alan Ball when we did lots of short sharp stuff in training and Graeme Souness is very similar. I think I'm gradually getting up to the form that I had a couple of seasons ago."

Despite his optimism, Le Tissier remained on the substitutes' bench throughout as England scraped a 2-1 win against the Poles, Shearer bravely flinging himself at the ball to edge them ahead and then crashing home a power-packed drive. But it was nervy on and off the field and, with World Cup qualification at stake, there was little hope of the Saints star making a late appearance.

Even a frustrated Le Tissier was forced to admit that Hoddle could not afford to gamble by disrupting his team just to give him a run-out. "Like any player on the bench, I was disappointed not to get on," he said. "But the way the game was going, I did not really expect to. It was so tight that, once we got ahead, it was difficult for the manager to make changes.

"The last five minutes were a bit edgy but it was good to keep our 100 per cent record. If I'm going to achieve my dream of playing in the World Cup finals, the first thing is for us to qualify. Now I have to concentrate on getting my club form right to lift Saints up the table and hopefully stay in the England squad for the game against Georgia. If I can do well for Southampton, it can only help my bid to force a way into the starting line-up."

Le Tissier was as good as his word as he went on a goal run for Souness' side, starting with a stunning effort in the televised 1-1 draw at Coventry. There was little on when he picked the ball up 30 yards out and the small section of Saints supporters jokingly yelled 'shoot!' That's exactly what he did and his rocket drive angled away from the shocked Steve Ogrizovic and into the net.

The keeper later admitted: "He made me look a fool on television. The only saving grace was that he's done that to a lot of other keepers." It was a goal good enough to win a top-flight match and that looked to be the case until injury-time, when Dion Dublin snatched a point for the Sky Blues.

The game at Highfield Road was the first time Eyal Berkovic had pulled on a Saints shirt and the Israeli provided Souness with a selection headache. Le Tissier was surprised the club had found a player even less inclined to tackle than himself! He would have to acknowledge, though, that the new boy's passing ability was of a high order - close to touching his own world-class skills.

The pair remained in tandem when Le Tissier converted from the spot again as another recent signing, Egil Ostenstad, was upended on the day a Saints line-up now boasting some real pace crushed Sunderland 3-0 at The Dell. Souness had been working on Le Tissier's mental state with a carrot-and-stick approach that seemed to be taking effect. The manager admitted it was sure to cause occasional friction but felt the tension was worth living with.

"We can all improve but Matt knows what he has to do and he is a pleasure to work with," Souness said. "He is a very honest and likeable boy, although I can perhaps see us having words from time to time. My philosophy is very simple. Every team have players to give them a lift and these are the people you want to have on the ball as much as possible.

"I had the same argument with John Barnes. He would say he was as fit as everyone else and I would argue that he needed to be fitter than them because he was going to have more of the ball. But John didn't understand the point I was making. Matt also needs to be fitter than the rest because we have to sicken him with the ball. When you do that, things happen for you.

"If I have a criticism of Matthew, it might be that he doesn't work hard enough to get on the ball. His answer would be that others don't pass as often as they should but I think he can work harder to make angles and you need fitness to do that. But that is coming and I can see an improvement in him. We have a programme which involves him coming back sometimes in the afternoon for extra work. He likes doing it, so it isn't a problem."

The sweat sessions felt well worthwhile when Le Tissier found space to make a fool out of Manchester United keeper Peter Schmeichel in Saints' best result under the Scot. His chip was the pick of the bunch as the champions were stunned 6-3.

Berkovic had put Saints ahead early on and they took charge once Roy Keane saw red. The midfielder upset Jeff Winter with some venom-filled back-chat to earn a booking and left the official with little choice but to despatch him when he crashed into Claus Lundekvam in only the 21st minute. With Nicky Butt already off injured, Le Tissier and Berkovic were gifted the space they needed to unveil their full repertoire.

Le Tissier was the first to take maximum advantage, collecting the ball from Berkovic to edge past substitute Brian McClair and lose David May before capitalising on Schmeichel's insistence on standing ten yards off his line. The keeper had a fantastic view as Le Tissier manufactured the perfect chip to send the ball spinning over him and into the net.

Schmeichel had been chipped by Newcastle's Philippe Albert in the previous game - a goal a certain player had seen on TV and taken careful note of......

United did push Southampton at one point, a wondrous free-kick from Beckham

It wasn't just on the field that Le Tissier thrilled fans. And the title of the book, The Great Marathon Football Match, could well have summed up Saints 6 Manchester United 3.

and a May effort bringing them back to 3-2 before Ostenstad scored two clinical goals either side of a sensational Berkovic volley. Le Tissier admitted: "We were helped by Roy Keane being sent off so early. I think things may have been a little different if they had had 11 men but we were one up even before the red card.

"I scored the second. I had a little dribble past Brian McClair and May. The week before, I had seen Peter Schmeichel chipped by Albert. I'd watched that on telly and it was in my mind that Schmeichel stands out from his goal a little bit, so I didn't have to look up. I immediately thought he would be off his line and just chipped it. It was pretty special. It's nice to do a bit of homework and be able to use it."

Ferguson was magnanimous about seeing his side of stars torn apart and, although pinpointing Berkovic's ability to pop up and cause chaos all over the pitch, lauded most of his praise on Le Tissier. "If we didn't have Cantona and Scholes, he could play for Manchester United," he said.

Le Tissier was then at his dead-eye best to net a penalty when the lively Ostenstad was chopped down by Ian Nolan as Saints took a point from their trip to Sheffield Wednesday. It took his tally to six goals in five League games and meant he had broken

If your side can beat Manchester United 6-3, nothing's impossible! Matt Le Tissier, in a golden spell at the time of the annihilation of Alex Ferguson's men, donned the colours of the county cricket club for a photo shot and showed that he was up for a trick or two there as well.

Welsh striker Ron Davies' 23-year-old Southampton record of scoring 134 top-flight goals. It also threw up excited talk of him making a first start for England since that ill-fated clash in Dublin.

Gascoigne was struggling to deal with the break-up of his marriage and Hoddle appreciated the toll that domestic matters were taking on England's match-winner. If he required a replacement, there appeared to be only one contender and Le Tissier was keen to reassure the England boss he was at the top of his game. "When the ball drops to me, I'm not thinking twice any more," he said. "I'm just hitting it - and that is all down to confidence.

"The turning point came at Coventry when I struck one very sweetly and it went in. Then I hit another against Lincoln and I just started spanking them again. I feel I'm getting back to my best."

With Le Tissier in golden form, there seemed every chance of a start, especially as the England coach began to talk him up ahead of the World Cup clash in Georgia in early November. "A lot of eyebrows were raised when he was brought in," Hoddle said. "But on the back of that, he has turned his form around. That is one of the reasons at least and it's given him a boost.

"He's got talent. There are no two ways about that and he can play up front or in a withdrawn position. He is certainly another you can add to the list of great strikers we have in England. He will hurt the opposition in and around their penalty area, whether it's coming from a deep position or starting up front."

Hoddle's encouraging words proved to have an empty ring, though. Despite all his eulogising, he frustrated Le Tissier once again by leaving him huddled up in his tracksuit along with the rest of the substitutes who watched England win in Tbilisi.

To make matters worse, the goals he was consistently netting for Saints began to dry up. His autumn strike rate had helped lift the side up to 14th but his good work was undone as the side lost five in a row in the Premiership and he dropped out of the team. First, there was the embarrassing 7-1 hammering at Everton, where Souness' decision to substitute the injured Simon Charlton with Neil Heaney hideously backfired.

Andrei Kanchelskis enjoyed a field day down the right as he scored twice and Gary Speed netted a hat-trick from midfield. Le Tissier was taken off, then he picked up an injury and went off again in the subsequent 2-0 home mugging by Leeds on November 23 - a game in which Aly Dia climbed off the bench to forever embarrass Souness with a performance so bad that he himself was eventually substituted.

The injury was bad enough to rule Le Tissier out of four games, the last of which - a 3-1 win over Derby - ended the losing streak. He was then stuck on the bench for the Boxing Day defeat by Spurs but made his point by going on to score. He chested down Alan Neilson's cross to lash home and give Saints hope of a point that was extinguished by a goal from the similarly named Allan Neilsen.

A narrow Dell defeat by Liverpool was followed by an embarrassing FA Cup exit

The spot-kick expertise that drove goalkeepers mad! The master safely registers yet another conversion. Goals from penalties again formed a substantial part of his 1996-97 tally and it was by this means he netted at Sheffield Wednesday to shatter Ron Davies' long-standing record.

at Reading, and a 1-0 win at Middlesbrough was watched from the bench by Le Tissier before his return to the starting line-up wrote another chapter of Matty folklore. Souness had done his homework when leaving his star among the subs. He had only to look back to the bleak days under Branfoot to know how the player could respond when his ability was questioned.

January 18 dawned with Saints fans moaning that several members of the board had become 'paper millionaires' by floating the club for £40m. And their gripes were growing louder as Les Ferdinand put Newcastle ahead and Lee Clark added a second with seven minutes left. But they were about to witness one of the classic Dell comebacks, with Le Tissier leading the charge.

Neil Maddison set up the finale in the last minute as he was alert to beat Shaka Hislop when the keeper spilled Charlton's free-kick. Saints piled forward in search of a point which had seemed impossible for the previous 90 minutes and, when the ball dropped to Le Tissier, Hislop must have known a bullet was heading his way. But even that knowledge didn't help as a volley crashed past him 110 seconds into injury-time to send the fans crazy.

Souness beamed: "It was hit with such venom, pace and accuracy that there is nothing Newcastle could have done apart from build a brick wall in front of the goal. If you look through Matt's career at The Dell, when any manager has left him out, he's come back with a reminder of just how good he is. I spoke with him last week and told him why I was leaving him on the bench. He wanted to play but he accepted it. There has not been a bust-up between us."

Rumours of an exchange between the two had stoked up renewed claims that Le Tissier was eyeing a transfer. But on the back of his wonder goal, he was quick to rubbish any such thoughts. "That is nonsense," he said. "It is just another in the long list. I've had to live with speculation about my future for ten years now and it simply fires me up even more.

"Why should I go? I love the club and this is a place I love to live in. I have always said that I would only consider leaving if we are relegated - and we have enough ability to stay up. There is no problem at all with the manager. I asked him why I was left out last week and he explained his thinking to me. Southampton won the game, so what more can I say?

"But it was nice to come back with a goal like that. I just hope Glenn Hoddle set his video because I hear he left just before. It shouldn't do my chances any harm with either club or country. People keep asking if it was my best goal but I'm not sure. It was the hardest I have hit the ball for a long time and it might scrape into my personal top ten. That's not being arrogant. I just think it was the timing as much as anything which made it seem so special."

The fightback should have preceded another glorious night when Dave Jones' Stockport turned up at The Dell for a Cola-Cup fifth-round replay. A double from Ostenstad had secured a 2-2 draw at Edgeley Park a week earlier and few expected County to put up such strong resistance second time round.

When Le Tissier found time to chest down Neilson's cross and fire his side ahead in the eighth minute, a place in the last four beckoned. But Saints just couldn't shake off Stockport's gritty fighters in a game which went a long way to earning Jones a job with them a few months later. Brett Angell equalised and Andy Mutch stunned the home crowd with a winner five minutes from the end.

It was Saints' last hope of success in 1996-97, their cup run having amounted to eight energy-sapping ties and boosted Le Tissier's goal count. He had scored with a sensational strike in the second-round demolition of Peterborough by lifting the ball over a defender and smashing home with his opposite foot. And he was on target as Lincoln were toppled before he sat out two tight games against Oxford that set up a meeting with Stockport - one underdog too many for Souness' outfit.

Back on the treadmill of the Premiership programme, Steve Basham was handed his debut in a bold team performance at Old Trafford, with Le Tissier pushed out to the left wing in an adventurous formation. The plan worked to start with as Ostenstad added substance to the theory that the best way past Schmeichel was by lifting the ball over his head. Gary Pallister wiped the lead out and an even contest was settled by Eric Cantona's 78th minute goal.

It was the start of a busy fortnight that was to shape Le Tissier's England career. He headed off for the crunch World Cup qualifier at home to Italy with talk raging about an ankle injury that left Gascoigne's chances of playing hanging in the balance. Hoddle's presence at Saints games had been another encouraging sign but the thought that the player may be given a rare start - against one of the world's best sides at that - was surely too fantastic for even Le Tissier to consider.

Maybe he himself knew better as he prepared to join up with the England party for a Wembley clash that was capturing the imagination of the nation. "I feel I am making head-way," he said. "I have been in all of Glenn Hoddle's squads to date, so he must think I am in with a chance at some stage.

"I know people are saying it depends on Gazza's fitness but I'm not sure. I don't see it as a straight choice between him and me because his role might not be the one I would play. When I went on against Moldova, it was for Nick Barmby, playing just behind Alan Shearer, so it might be that my main rival is Les Ferdinand and he did well in Georgia when Alan was injured."

Having had just a ten minute run-out under Hoddle and spent the manager's next two games eyeing the action as a substitute, Le Tissier was certainly not counting his chickens. "I don't feel frustrated," he added. "It must be harder for those who make the squad but don't get on the bench. I've been fortunate enough to be among the subs each time. At least then, you have a chance of getting on. I'd love to be involved because this is a massive game against a very good side packed with quality."

And his wish came true as he finally landed a coveted spot in England's attack, only for it all to go horribly wrong on match-night. Even his build-up was ruined in the most bizarre circumstances when one of his brothers broke the news of his inclusion on air to Radio Guernsey. Carl Le Tissier told the BBC: "He was very surprised to be named. We were very surprised as well because Matt has played a lot better than he is at the moment and never got on.

"He has a very close relationship with Glenn Hoddle - they are on the same footballing wavelength and talk to each other a lot. He has got a free role just behind Shearer. Matt and McManaman both have the freedom to roam around. He is so delighted. He's a bit nervous at the moment but he has waited so long for this opportunity and I am sure he'll do himself proud."

The interview left Matt open to derision and ridicule, although Hoddle refused to blame the broadcast for leaking his team and some pointed the finger of suspicion at another player. But Le Tissier copped the blame from one member of the FA, who privately called him an 'idiot.' It was not the kind of distraction the Saints man needed ahead of the biggest game of his career.

" I don't know enough about what has happened to say too much," Le Tissier said of the revelations from within his family. "Suffice to say I could have done without it. It was hardly an ideal way to prepare for a big game."

To add to Hoddle's problems, England were without David Seaman, who dropped out on the morning of the match, Gazza, Tony Adams and Teddy Sheringham. Despite the sideshow, Le Tissier was England's most dangerous player as he began with a neat turn, managed a blocked shot and followed up with a thumping header that flew wide. Then he was dragged off by Hoddle and slagged off by the press as they searched for a scapegoat for England's 1-0 defeat.

While the rest of the nation had swiftly swung from calling for Le Tissier's inclusion to calling for his head, the player could take solace in some soothing words from Hoddle. The manager said: "It is not the end of him at all. If you look at the first 45 minutes, our best two chances fell to him and in many ways he deserves credit for getting into the right positions.

"He started extremely brightly. I picked him because I felt the match would be tight and he is the sort who can turn it in one moment. Ironically, our two best chances fell to him but he could not quite turn them in. The first one might have put us in front and that would probably have changed everything. Instead, Italy had one shot all night and they scored from it. Then they defended very well. This is a setback for us but it's not a disaster. We're not out of it yet."

Respected England coach Don Howe pointed out how hard it had been for Le Tissier to make an impression, saying: "Fabio Cannavaro rarely pulled away from the left and Paolo Ferrara rarely from the right. It was flexible man-marking. They were intelligent enough to let each other pick up Shearer as and when - or one take Shearer and the other take Le Tissier, without it mattering which defender it was.

"But as the ball arrived, one of them arrived, too, and if they could get in front, they got in front. I would have liked to see Shearer rotate with Le Tissier a bit more. That might have made it more difficult for Italy."

When Le Tissier walked away from Wembley, the thought that his England career might be over must have been furthest from his mind. He said: "It was very quick and their defence was very tight. We did not get a lot of clear chances. I just hope I did well enough to get another chance. I'm already looking ahead to the Mexico match next month. It was a very depressing result and I was just disappointed that one of the two opportunities didn't go in.

"I thought the header was in because I knew the Italian keeper was off his line. That would have been something - scoring with a header! My only goal at Wembley was a header at that end against Forest in the ZDS Final. That went through my mind. The manager told me he took me off because he wanted to try the aerial route, so I'm not disheartened by that - just by the result. I enjoyed it overall. It was good to be in the starting line-up again and it's a platform to build on."

No, it wasn't - and, unhappily, things at The Dell didn't go to plan either. Le Tissier was spot-on again with a penalty to put Saints 2-0 up at home to Sheffield Wednesday, making the most of a Jon Newsome hand-ball to open a lead the team should have been capable of defending. But slack covering let in future Saints striker David Hurst for two goals, then Andy Booth bustled in for the winner.

After being frustrated by Wimbledon in a 0-0 draw, Le Tissier returned to haunt Newcastle just six weeks after tormenting them. With Saints working hard to keep the attacking talents of Les Ferdinand and Tino Asprilla at bay, Le Tissier found the back door unlocked as he raced on to Ulrich Van Gobbel's long punt to show his perfect technique and fire past Shaka Hislop.

The win at St James's Park failed to lift Southampton out of 19th place and draws against Everton and Leeds were followed by a home defeat by Arsenal. But Gordon Watson felt Souness was now finding it difficult to get the best out of his star turn, especially when he was included alongside another creative player in Berkovic.

"Everyone liked Souness and the way he trained and coached us but there was a lot of disruption to the team," he said. "We had Berkovic and Ostenstand, and Claus Lundekvam who came in as well. We also had Tore Andre Flo down for training, so you never knew who was going to be playing. It was another stop-start season when survival was the only thing that mattered.

"But one of the big problems for Matt was the signing of Berkovic. When they played together, you starved one of them of the ball. The way Berkovic played in those days, the more often he got the ball, the more you got out of him. It was the same with Matty. If you played two of them, you had to ask one of them to do something they were not good at - work back and close players down. Matt did a lot of work off the ball but he didn't do in terms of chasing people back. That's not him."

It's a point of view backed up by Jim Magilton, who believes Souness' problem was choosing between going with a player he believed was a game-breaker in Berkovic and keeping the Saints supporters on his side by selecting Le Tissier. "I don't think you could accommodate both Eyal and Matt," he said. "Eyal was an outstanding player, as gifted a player as I have had as a team-mate.

"He was very talented and if you wanted to play with two front men and get the ball to Eyal, he could make things happen. Tiss could play, too. He had an eye for a pass but as soon as he picked the ball up, he was thinking: 'Goal.' He was all about long-range shooting whereas Eyal was always looking for the vital pass. He and Egil Ostenstad formed a very strong partnership, so in my opinion you couldn't play both - and Souness fancied Eyal more."

To add further complications, Le Tissier was trying to battle on through foot and groin injuries in a bid to keep Saints up. His decision to fight through the pain was now putting his international future in serious doubt. England had a friendly against Mexico in late March and he reluctantly tried to talk himself out of the squad by admitting the pain was too much. But when he was left on the bench as Saints lost at Chelsea, there was intense speculation that a rift had developed between him and Souness.

Just as frustratingly, Le Tissier became embroiled in a row between his club boss and his international coach. Le Tissier said: "I have spoken with Glenn Hoddle and he wants me to join up with England but the chances are that I won't be able to play. The way I feel at the moment, I don't think I could do myself justice at international level and I would rather drop out.

"I am not bothered about the media reaction if I played and I didn't do well because it cannot be worse than it was the last time. I just feel it wouldn't be right to play if I was not fully fit. I will go up to meet up with the squad but I don't know if I'll be able to stay."

To Souness' anger, Hoddle claimed Le Tissier had told him he was fit enough to play for his club but had simply been dropped. Hoddle claimed: "He assured me he could have played at Chelsea. He said the injury had been no different to how it's been for the last six or seven games and we could chat when we get together. Whatever the

How it had all begun at senior international level in front of the Sky cameras - with a substitute appearance when he and David Batty went on for Paul Ince and Gazza. But would Matt Le Tissier ever become a regular in England's starting line-up?

reasons for Graeme not selecting him against Chelsea are not for me to comment on. If Graeme wants to speak to me, he can alert me to the situation."

That was a red rag to a bull as far as a fuming Souness was concerned. He said: "I spoke to Matty after he received a call from Glenn Hoddle. He was going to tell Glenn that he didn't feel he could do himself justice because of the injury. But Glenn has insisted on putting out a story totally different from the one Matt told me. I wonder where Saints fans would rather Le Tissier be next week.

"After Leicester, we have two weeks without a game; two weeks which could be vital in terms of what we do for the rest of the season. Our medical people say he has a problem which will develop and will eventually need surgery. It's the same old story of club versus country and it doesn't take a clever man to work it all out. Anyone with reasonable intelligence can see that England have a friendly against Mexico and we have eight important Premiership games left."

Despite Souness' obvious yearning to keep Le Tissier at The Dell with his feet up, the player did join up with England and had a pain-killing jab before giving up on his chances. He returned to the south coast and said: "It was very disappointing to miss the match because with so many other players out, it might have been a good opportunity. I had a brief chat with Glenn and he told me to wait until the Thursday before the game to judge the effect of the jab. But it was not right, so I came home."

Le Tissier was recalled for the clash with Leicester and was positive about Saints' chances of beating relegation despite the club being firmly entrenched in the relegation zone. "I am prepared to play on for the club even though I know I am not fully fit," he added. "If the manager decides he can't risk me, that's fair enough. But, if and when needed, I'll do what I can because it means so much for us to survive.

"It is not looking good but we've been in worse positions and come through. We were several points adrift under Ian Branfoot in 1992, then we won six on the spin. I remain positive and believe we can get out of trouble but we need to start soon."

Le Tissier was paired with Berkovic in a desperate bid to save Saints, both playing their part in a 2-2 draw with the Foxes. Berkovic set up Ostenstad for a difficult finish and Le Tissier floated in a corner for Van Gobbel to edge Saints ahead. But just when a crucial win looked on the cards, Steve Claridge was allowed in for an equaliser.

The failure to win dropped Saints to the bottom of the table with seven games left. It was looking dire as they headed to Forest for an Easter fixture but it was the game that made a hero out of Micky Evans. The recent signing from Plymouth used all his muscle to net a priceless double and set up a 3-1 win. Another trip to the East Midlands followed and this time Saints were lucky to pick up a point at Derby as Daryl Powell helped out by nudging the ball past his own keeper in the 89th minute at a time when Le Tissier had already been hauled off.

The season was set up for yet another Le Tissier-inspired late surge, only for Matt to find himself out of the side, with Berkovic pulling the strings. The Israeli international scored in the 2-0 home defeat of West Ham as Saints overcame the dismissal of Dodd to move clear of the relegation zone for the first time since Boxing Day and jump four places to 16th.

As the first team earned a 2-2 draw with Coventry and won 1-0 at rivals-in-distress Sunderland, Le Tissier showed he was back on the goal track by scoring in a reserve win over Ipswich on April 30. Missing out on the chance to play his part in the survival effort was painful and Magilton added: "Souness felt Matt could give more to the side all round and as much as Matt was a strong character who felt he should be in the team no matter what, and there were 20,000 who agreed with him, the manager decided he was going to leave him out. It was a battle of wills and the manager is always right, even when he is wrong."

Le Tissier climbed off the substitutes' bench to score at home to Blackburn three days later and give Southampton some breathing space with a victory that moved them up to 14th. After seeing Ostenstad take over his crown as Player of the Year, he flashed a powerful low drive across goal in the 73rd minute and watched the ball fizz into the net off Colin Hendry.

Le Tissier finished the season collecting splinters once again as Saints went into the final game, at Villa, knowing that a point would secure their safety. They lost 1-0 but results went for them anyway, with Sunderland losing at Wimbledon while Boro were only able to draw at Leeds.

The combination of scores left Saints two places above the dreaded line, safe by a point. It was an astonishing escape, even by their standards, and Souness was quick to opt out. When newly-installed chairman Rupert Lowe told him to do it all over again with just a £2m transfer budget, he headed for the exit.

He had already achieved the near-impossible without bringing the best out of Le Tissier. And despite failing to goad the maximum output from the legend's talents, he still looks back on his time at The Dell as an enjoyable chance to work with one of football's grand masters.

"He was exceptionally gifted and one of the best I have worked with," he said. "In terms of sheer ability, he was right up there with the likes of Kenny Dalglish, John Barnes and Roberto Mancini at Sampdoria. He has so much quality and was a one-man goal machine. You can criticise him for his workrate and try and get more out of him but that was always going to prove difficult.

"The good thing was that he was honest about it. He wasn't going to scurry about and make tackles. He simply wanted the ball in the final third of the pitch and then he would make things happen for you. We did try and get him running around more in training but it failed to make him any fitter.

"Like every manager, I'd be frustrated at times because he had so much ability and you wanted more and more from him. But he always gave the best he could. I didn't try to change him because you couldn't change him. His goals were phenomenal and that's all you could ask. Really, it wasn't about changing him. I thought I could get a bit more out of him - every manager probably did.

"But you have to accept the way Matty is. He's a very laid-back, nice guy and a real nice human being. What I tried to do with him was to get him to work harder. When I brought in Eyal, I thought they could work together. Matt was a goalscorer and creator, Eyal was simply a creator. Obviously, they weren't going to be chasing back but for a team who struggled all season, we were entertaining to watch. That was because they were both in the side.

"I did drop him towards the end because in certain games, I felt we had to be more dogged when chasing matches and that's not really Matt's style. But he gave me his all that season and that's all I could have asked for."

Unfortunately for Le Tissier, giving his all had taken a toll on his body and when England came calling for him for a summer tour, he was forced to stay at home. Doctors advised him he needed treatment to solve his groin and foot problems and he booked in for the necessary repairs in June to ensure he was fit for his next major task - impressing new boss Dave Jones.

1997-98

Man on a Mission

ONLY one man seemed to think Matt Le Tissier had a chance of making Glenn Hoddle's World Cup squad as Saints broke with deep-set tradition in 1997-98 and cruised to the finishing post without any threat of relegation. That was new boss Dave Jones, who had turned a nightmare start into a spectacular triumph despite being without the player for large parts of the season.

The Saints hero broke an arm during the pre-season countdown and spent the campaign battling to last 90 minutes as his fitness and form dipped and climbed. But five goals in seven games through February and March prompted Hoddle to chance his own arm with Le Tissier one last time. He named him in an England B squad to face Russia at QPR on April 21, when the implications appeared clear: If Le Tissier had the game of his life, he would be handed one of the remaining World Cup squad spots.

It had been left to Jones to reveal his player's deep hurt when there seemed no hope on the international horizon. "I have spoken with the England B coach Peter Taylor and he told me Matt will start," he said. "He has been given the lifeline he wanted and now he has to prove to the country he is worthy of a place in France.

"It means everything to him. When I brought him off against Sheffield Wednesday last week, we had a chat and he was disappointed because he desperately wants to go to France. People laughed a few weeks ago when I said Glenn Hoddle would not close the door on anyone. If there are injuries or players don't perform, Matt has a chance of getting in. It's up to him. There's no doubt that he has the ability but people have questioned his workrate. Yet he has worked as hard as anyone for us recently."

Le Tissier was a man on a mission as he travelled to West London on England duty - with the determination to see the job through. He probably felt this chance would never come, so he wasn't going to let it slip through his fingers. He knew exactly what he had to do: score goals, plenty of them. And he didn't disappoint.

Thousands of Saints fans travelled to Loftus Road to give their man a lift and it appeared the Russians were keen to help out, too. They failed to appreciate the damage he could wreak when handed too much space but they soon learned the hard way as he found oceans of it whenever he got on the ball.

In the 13th minute, Le Tissier scored his first goal in England colours, spotting the opportunity as Trevor Sinclair twisted and turned to whip in a low cross. Arriving late, he showed remarkable technique to catch the ball on the half volley and sweep home. The pride was obvious and his tail was up. All those glorious little tricks that had thrilled the Dell faithful over the years began to surface.

It wasn't showboating either because Le Tissier stood head and shoulders above all the other hopefuls with his telling passes and deadly delivery from corners. Most importantly, he was also a real threat in front of goal, curling a shot from an almost impossible angle against the bar moments before the interval.

His display was demanding respect and when the armband was up for grabs after Darren Anderton's exit, Le Tissier was cast in the role of captain. He led by example with two more goals in the final six minutes that proved his silky skills could cut open defences at international level.

With the swagger of a master, he ghosted past three defenders on a glorious run. Then he had the composure not to waste his good work when left facing keeper Mikhail Kharine, arrowing a searing effort into the bottom left-hand corner of the net. The nation were willing him on and Le Tissier went in search of a hat-trick in the first minute of injury-time when he climbed highest, only to guide his header against the outside of the post.

But with Hoddle already on his way back to the England team hotel, Le Tissier made no mistake from another opportunity deep into stoppage-time. He was picked out by David Johnson in plenty of space on the edge of the area and speared home a superb left-foot shot. It proved to be the last kick of the game and a buoyant Le Tissier admitted afterwards: "I'm absolutely delighted. Never in my wildest dreams did I dare to imagine that I would get a hat-trick.

"I would just have been pleased to get on the score-sheet. I have not done my World Cup chances any harm but, being realistic, it is still only a slim chance. There are 34 players ahead of me, so I am still an outsider. But I have never given up hope of making the 22 and I won't. I'm going to give it my best shot and at least then I can rest easy if I don't make it, although it will hurt.

"This was an important game for me and I'm just pleased it went so well. To get the captain's armband probably gave me even more pride than scoring the goals and taking home the match ball. It was great to get a hat-trick, although the one I got against Norwich a few years back was probably better in terms of quality. But this is the most precious in terms of its timing."

Peter Taylor may not have had direct input into England's final 22 but made an emphatic recommendation that the Saints star should be taken to France. He said: "Glenn will be delighted for Matt because it backs up his own judgments. I am sure

Matt's super show may have done the trick!

22/4/08

THIS GAME had been billed as Matthew Le Tissier entering Last Chance Saloon — and he walked out clutching a bottle of champagne as the Green Flag Man of the Match after a dream display for the England B side at Loftus Road.

This was the make-or-break moment for the enigmatic Saints star to prove he could transfer his sublime skills to the international arena and he responded with a breath-taking performance which far exceeded his wildest hopes.

It was almost Fantasy Football as he scored a stunning hat-trick in the 4-1 win over Russia B, hit the woodwork twice, took the captain's armband for the last nine minutes and stamped his class on the game to stake a powerful claim for a late call-up for the World Cup finals.

The three goals were all imprinted with the Le Tissier hallmark of quality but it was his overall presence on the big stage which will have given Glenn Hoddle food for thought — and immense personal pleasure.

The England coach left just seconds before Le Tissier's third goal in injury-time but he must surely already have seen enough to give another chance to a player he has long admired.

And, if the enigmatic genius can reproduce this majestic form, then he could yet achieve his dream of playing in France 98.

It seemed the whole of Loftus Road was willing him to score, not just the dozens of Saints fans who made it almost like a home game.

As it turned out, Les Ferdinand's second-minute goal from a free header was almost

TREBLE DELIGHT: Le Tissier rams in his hat-trick goal to the delight of the Saints fans at Loftus Road last night.

Surely that has to clinch a spot for the World Cup? Alas not. The heroics at QPR's Loftus Road were all in vain.

By **Graham Hiley at Loftus Road** ◆

clair superbly turned his man and crossed for Le Tissier who made great ground from the midfield to arrive unmarked and sweep home a glorious half-volley.

That gave him immense

up with telling through-balls, delivered pinpoint corners which almost produced further goals and covered vast ground to prove just how badly he wants this final chance.

With a remarkable piece of

on 83 minutes, Le Tissier had restored the two-goal advantage with trademark trickery.

The ball seemed glued to his toes as he weaved his way past three defenders before planting an emphatic shot into the bottom left corner past Mikhail Kharine, younger brother

Glenn sees a bit of Matt in himself with the way he plays. He is an outstanding talent - someone who makes and scores goals.

"The fact he scored three does not surprise me because he is very capable of getting himself in those positions. There's no doubt he has tapped Glenn on the shoulder with this performance - not just with the goals, but the way he got involved."

Hoddle piped up to reveal, no doubt with reservations about Paul Gascoigne at the back of his mind, that Le Tissier had got himself back into the running. "Matthew has done himself a lot of good with his goals and overall performance," he said. "He has not had the best of seasons but he has given me food for thought."

It had been a campaign of torment for Le Tissier, starting with pre-season training under yet another new manager. He had drifted out of Hoddle's plans following that damaging defeat against Italy, any chance of making amends then being torn from him by a succession of minor injuries that forced him out of subsequent squads.

He knew this was his last chance to sample the Holy Grail of a World Cup and was determined to force his way back in. He would be 29 when the tournament kicked off and was realistic enough to accept that by 2002 there would be a plethora of new pretenders eager to showcase their talents on the game's greatest stage.

His chances were boosted by yet another summer fall-out at The Dell, this one resulting in the departure of Graeme Souness after just one season. The manager's relationship with chairman Rupert Lowe was at a low ebb when they met to discuss transfer funds for the following season, and the upshot was that the Scot quit and headed back to Italy for a brief spell in charge at Torino.

"I came here with high hopes and expectations but it is now clear to me that I'm not able to take the club forward in the way I wanted," he said. Le Tissier, denied a place at the end of 1996-97, probably did not shed tears at the development.

Director of football Lawrie McMenemy followed the impulsive Souness out of the door, explaining that he had little choice as he had taken him to the club. Just as damaging in the eyes of Saints fans was Eyal Berkovic's decision to snub a permanent move to The Dell and head instead to West Ham.

Le Tissier was used to summer changes, be it systems or bosses. What he wasn't used to were pre-season injuries and the one he suffered in 1997 was a brutal break. The setback came in the game against Ansbach on a German tour on which he had already scored. A freak fall saw him land on his left arm with such force that the bone shattered in three painful places.

He was rushed to hospital, where surgeons had to be put off performing an immediate operation, Saints preferring the work to be carried out back home. "It is the first bone I have ever broken and I knew what had happened as soon as I did it," Le Tissier said of an injury that could not be attributed in any way to a challenge. "I turned away, stumbled and heard two clicks as I hit the ground.

"I had a horrible sinking feeling but I didn't realise how serious it was until I saw the X-rays. At that point, I just wanted to fly home and have the operation as soon as possible. It looked innocuous at the time but my arm was a hell of a mess. It's strange and annoying because it was such a nothing incident, yet it has had big repercussions. It is a real low point for me, a sickener."

A metal plate was inserted and cut his anticipated recovery time by a month. The soul-destroying news was that he would still be out for eight weeks. "It was a relief to wake up after surgery and find I could be back a bit quicker," he added. "That was a bonus. I had mentally prepared myself to be out for 12 weeks or so. That would have driven me mad because I'm not the best patient.

"There is always a positive way of looking at things and I suppose the silver lining is that at least it happened early in pre-season, so I only miss five or six weeks of the actual action. But the fact that it happened in such a meaningless match does make it all the more frustrating. That's a chance you take in these games. You play in them for year after year without getting injured, so I suppose it had to happen sometime, by the law of averages."

The searing pain Le Tissier felt was probably nothing compared to the anguish flowing through his veins when he realised he had little chance of making England's crunch World Cup qualifier in Italy on October 11. Even if he was back scoring goals by then, he would have missed the warm-up game, giving Hoddle the perfect excuse to bar him from the party hoping to send England to the finals.

The player added: "It is very frustrating because this injury will rule me out of both England games. I was really hoping to start the season well and fight my way back in. Now it is going to be very difficult. The worry is that if England qualify, the manager might stick with the lads who have got us there. All I can do is make sure that when I get back, I play well enough so he can't leave me out. But that is a long way off.

"First I have to get myself fit, get back in the Saints side and start scoring goals. And hopefully, I'll be back a little earlier than I first thought. The plaster cast will stay on for another two weeks and I have to avoid contact for five weeks after that. The good thing is that I will be able to run and do fitness work, so when I start playing again, it should not take me too long to get back."

Another worry for Matty was how the injury would affect his second love, playing golf. Some team-mates indulged in a spot of banter post-op by asking him to sell them his clubs! "When I came round from the surgery, the second question I asked was how the operation would affect my golf swing," he revealed. "The doctor says I should have enough strength to play golf.

"Apparently, that is good exercise for it; a good excuse to play even more. But a few the lads are tactfully offering to buy my clubs. Obviously football is the main thing but golf is part my life and one I want to keep doing for many years. I can play golf a lot longer than football. Even when it happened, one of the things going through my head was that we had a golf game arranged for the following morning. I was really looking forward to that as there was so little to do where we were staying."

While a return to the fairways was a long way off, Le Tissier was told to prepare for an October return to the Premiership battlefields. But with Saints in dire trouble after an appalling start, Jones was keen to see him back even sooner. The side hit rock bottom by losing five of the first six games and, without the maestro's creative talents, were struggling to trouble opposition goalkeepers.

The only victory came through Kevin Davies' goal at home to Crystal Palace as an injury-hit side suffered the ignominy of an opening-day defeat by Bolton at The Dell that set the depressing tone. With typical sense of the big occasion, Le Tissier pencilled in the September 20 visit of Liverpool for his comeback after admitting he could no longer bear to stand by and watch his beloved club falter.

"This is the longest I've ever been out of action and it is something I have had to learn to deal with," he admitted. "It is not nice watching matches. I'm not a good spectator. I find it very hard to see the lads battling without being able to help them. I've been to the home games and was going to go to Old Trafford but had a change of mind at the last minute, partly because I find it so hard to sit through a match like that.

"I actually had a bit of a 'mare watching the Arsenal game. When Neil Maddison scored the equaliser, I forgot about my injury, jumped up and down and threw my arms in the air. Everyone else was cheering and I was sitting down again, holding my arm in pain. It's just as well that the plaster was off by then - otherwise I could have knocked someone out.

"It has been a tough start for the team, with a lot of injuries. The manager has had to throw a few in at the deep end and they have not let themselves down. Beating Palace was a big result for us but the really annoying result was the Bolton one. That's the only match where I felt we should have got three points. But we'll have a few returning from injury in the next couple weeks. I know I'll be glad to start again."

Le Tissier failed to last the 90 minutes against Liverpool but his return helped halt the rot as Davies' goal earned a 1-1 draw. This time a hamstring strain forced him to limp off in the 43rd minute but by then he had been reassured that his arm would stand up to the rigours of the Premiership, Michael Thomas having clattered into him and sent him crashing on the damaged limb with the game just 28 seconds old.

"It was not a nice moment flying through the air because I knew I was going to land on it," he said. "I tried to turn around and land on the other arm but there was not time. It was not a surprise it happened so soon. I thought it probably would. It is only what anyone would do to test out an opponent they thought had a problem.

"But it was probably the best thing that could have happened because I had a slight mental thing about it and felt a lot better afterwards. I knew there wasn't much worse that could happen. It was a worrying split-second but I was fine afterwards. There were no ill-effects from the lay-off and I felt sharp. It's just a shame the hamstring did not stand up as well. I was disappointed because I was feeling good."

Once his hamstring had recovered, Le Tissier was named for his annual Coca-Cola Cup goal-fest against lower-League opposition. This time it was Brentford who felt the full frustration of his early-season agonies. He scored a typically classy opener, taking the ball on his chest and without reshaping his body, smacking it home from just inside the box. He then linked with Matt Oakley and Davies to fire an angled drive into the corner for his second in Saints' 2-0 away win that sealed an aggregate 5-1 victory.

Le Tissier may have been pleased to get his season back on track but no more than his boss. Jones had spent the early part of the campaign crying out for the creative spark and deadly finishing that were the Channel Islander's trademark, and said: "Matt had three chances, stuck two away and might well have had a hat-trick. He creates and scores and his first touch is vital in and around the box.

"The better quality Matty gives us is what we have been lacking. We asked him to give us an hour and he ran himself into the ground. He took his goals superbly and they killed the tie. We knew Brentford would throw everything at us early on and we had to be strong and stand up."

Le Tissier was back in League action for the 3-0 defeat of West Ham that finally lifted the club off the bottom of the table. And he celebrated his 29th birthday with the kind of sensational goal in the Coca-Cola Cup win at Barnsley that sent the tabloids into a fresh frenzy about his England prospects. Lifting the ball over Arjan De Zeeuw, he waited for it to drop before ramming a fierce volley past keeper Dave Watson.

He said: "Once the ball had been flicked on, it dropped nicely and I felt a surge of confidence as I went for it. I knew as soon as I hit it, it was in. I've scored better but it was nice to see it fly in. It has been frustrating on the sidelines and I just hope Glenn Hoddle has not forgotten me. While I've been out, a few players have got ahead of me in the pecking order, so I'll have to try and get a few more to convince him I am worth a place. It is up to me to fight my way back in."

Le Tissier had a month to prove to Hoddle he should figure in a Wembley friendly with Portugal and was fighting off some niggles, including a thigh strain soon after his Barnsley goal. He had a new strike partner in record signing David Hirst, the £2m buy from Sheffield Wednesday already having proved his usefulness with a brace in a 3-2 home victory over Tottenham in his second game. In the following match at Everton, Le Tissier's opener set Saints on the way to their first away win.

The televised game will rightly be remembered for Davies' coming-of-age as he picked up the ball in his own half and strode through challenge after challenge before angling home the second goal. The striker had joined Southampton from Chesterfield the previous summer after catching Souness' eye with his powerful surges during the Spirites' run to the FA Cup semi-final.

A deal was tied up before the Scot flew the nest. Davies was an astute capture and was benefiting from Le Tissier's probing passes. "It was one of my best seasons, playing with people like him, David Hirst and Carlton Palmer," Davies said. "It was me and David Hirst up front. Matt played off us and had licence to do what he wanted. He didn't do much defensively but that was fine by me.

"You don't want players like that going back hunting down tackles. You want him in positions where he is hurting opponents. If you are clever enough to make a run, he's one of those players who can put it on a plate for you. He can pick a pass. He was a big player, a legend, but at the same time was just one of the lads. The good thing about that squad was there were no egos or superstars.

"If there was a night out, he'd be there. He was a good laugh and was good to have around the dressing room. I'd like to have gone down a year or two earlier when he was putting away stupid goals. But he was still a big part of the team atmosphere. We went down Los Marinos in the Marina some Sundays and, if we'd had a result, there would be ten players down there and then off to Jumpin Jacks. It was a fun time."

Le Tissier's strike at Goodison, where he capitalised on a slow-reacting defence to head home Hirst's cross, was his first of the League season. Jones' decision to snap up Palmer, Hirst and Kevin Richardson was starting to pay off as it brought the best out of Davies and Le Tissier. And Barnsley, surprise arrivals in the top flight, suffered once more at Le Tissier's feet as he despatched an early penalty to set up a 4-1 win.

Despite the goals, Le Tissier was failing to finish matches. When he was taken off in the 2-1 defeat at Newcastle, it was the fourth Premiership game in a row he had not gone the distance. But he was making his mark, his angled pass allowing Davies to skilfully loft a shot over Kevin Hitchcock for the opener in an enthralling Coca-Cola Cup tie at Stamford Bridge, only for Chelsea to equalise and then kill off Saints with Jody Morris' 118th minute strike.

The Dell hero desperately needed to find a run of form to force his way into Hoddle's World Cup plans but a lack of fitness was evident as he was dragged off time and again. With Saints struggling and their most creative player failing to inspire, Jones admitted he thought about leaving him out altogether.

A trip to Wimbledon brought a fourth defeat in a row and the great entertainer was so ineffective that the manager sent on Egil Ostenstad in his place just ten minutes after the interval, saying: "Matt is in a bit of a rut. He's not having the best of times and things are just not coming off him. But I thought I would give him a lift by playing him. It's like every pro. He just has to keep working at his game.

"He has to do something special like score a goal or have a good game to get out of it. Players thrive on confidence and Matt's is a bit low at the moment. It's no use knocking him. We're trying to lift him and see him through this."

Le Tissier's form had slumped so badly that speculation was rife he was about to be offloaded, with Spurs and a swap deal for David Ginola highlighted as a possibility. "I don't know anything about that," he said. "The first I heard of it was on the radio but I'm still happy here. There's no desire on my part to go. Whenever I have a couple of bad games, these people try to sell me but I always bounce back and I'll do it again."

The story had worried Matt enough for him to seek a clear-the-air meeting with Jones, just to ensure the Dell chief was not thinking about cutting his losses. And the manager confirmed: "I had a long chat with Matt and there is no problem between us."

As in the past, the pep-talk had an immediate positive effect on Le Tissier as he scored one goal and created a memorable second to guide Saints to a welcome 2-1 home victory over Leicester on December 13. He showed the deftest of touches with his left foot to slot home from a tight angle in the second minute, although the side's second probably gave him greater delight.

Defender Francis Benali had come through the ranks with his more illustrious team-mate and, despite starting his career for local tyro outfit Winsor United as a lightning-quick winger with a hammer of a shot, had never scored a professional goal. That was until he made a rare trip up-field when Saints were awarded a free-kick eight minutes into the second half. He popped up on the end of a measured cross to head what proved to be the clincher.

A grateful Benali said after ending his embarrassing drought: "It was a fantastic free-kick, as only Matt can deliver. He knew exactly what was required, so all I had to do was launch my head at it and get some direction."

Le Tissier's goal against Martin O'Neill's men may have given Saints a boost - and his England chances a gentle nudge - but he was refusing to talk up his World Cup chances. "I have never done that," he said. "It isn't the way I'm made. I will do the business on the pitch. If it's good enough, it's good enough. If not, so be it. I'm happy with the games I've played and my goals from starts isn't a bad ratio.

"Now I have to show I can be consistent enough to force my way back in. This is a crucial time for me. There are only five friendlies before next summer. I don't believe in counting chickens but I do feel that if I'm playing to the best of my abilities, I'm good enough to be in the squad. I read what Glenn said in the papers about the door still being open if players perform well. I've got a great deal of confidence in my ability - it's just that sometimes other people don't share it."

No-one doubted the skills but Le Tissier wasn't putting together the kind of weekly highlights package that sends managers at the top level weak at the knees. Pressure was mounting on him as the clock ticked down and increasingly the talk surrounding him was not about whether he would inspire Saints to safety yet again, but whether his England chances had already been blown.

A mini-revival came after Christmas, with Davies scoring winners against Chelsea and Manchester United, the latter courtesy of Le Tissier's fantastic ability to land a free-kick in the place best designed to hurt the opposition. But the creator was missing as Saints won 3-2 against Liverpool, with Hirst's double strike stunning Anfield.

Le Tissier's absence capped a horrible week for him. He had been left out not only from Hoddle's top-choice 22 but also from a B squad made up of hopefuls still nursing dreams of going to France. He tried to remain positive through the disappointment and insisted he had not given up on a joyful end to a miserable season. "Time is running out but I'm not writing myself off," he said.

"Things can change very quickly and I have not lost any confidence in my own ability. I've been through spells like this before and always come back strongly. I don't see why that can't happen again now. It didn't hurt that I wasn't included in the squads because I was not expecting it. It was not a surprise but it still matters to me.

"People think because I am laid-back that I don't care. Ever since I was a little boy, it has been my ambition to play for England in the World Cup. You don't get too many chances in life and this is probably my last. It is not often you get me volunteering for extra training, so that shows how much I want to be there. I have been disappointed with my form and can't really put my finger on why it has dipped.

"I've been thinking twice about shooting, or electing to play someone else in, rather than doing things instinctively. That's down to confidence. Often when the first goal goes in, it would trigger things off. You hit one from the edge of the area, it flies in and you become the most confident player in the world again. If I can do that and start playing to the best of my ability over the last 14 matches of this season, I could still be in with a chance."

That change in fortunes finally came when he rose from the bench in the home defeat by Coventry in mid-February. It wasn't a rasping 20-yarder as he had hoped but that other staple diet of his career - a penalty, awarded after he was tripped by Roland Nilsson. The extra training was not only improving his form, it was also bringing down his weight. He lost half a stone to make him his lightest in three years.

The industry seemed to be paying off as he stamped his authority on the game at home to Blackburn in Saints' next outing. He outfoxed his markers to leave Ostenstad with a simple finish from point-blank range for the side's first. And once again he looked capable of ghosting past defenders and testing keepers, this time his old pal Tim Flowers, with powerful and accurate long-range efforts.

But the hard labour also had the gossips talking, with the papers floating the notion again that Le Tissier's time at The Dell was approaching an end. That was not the case and in a fit of anger, Jones spoke out to deny the rumours of a cut-price £2m exit. "It seems everyone wants to sell my players - except me," he stormed. "It is annoying because it is unsettling and there is no truth in it.

"Matt is a quality player and seems to have found that extra half yard, so instead of trying to beat opponents with a trick, he's powering past them. Against Blackburn, he burst through two or three times and left people standing. That was the best I've seen him play since I've been here. He has got to keep working hard and has come back for extra training as a lot of players do. He does not need to work on his technique but he does and is now reaping the rewards."

Jones was proved right as March arrived with Le Tissier in the goals. Palmer, signed as a leader the previous September, was enjoying the results and says: "Matt couldn't produce what he did without the rest of the team working hard for him. It was important everyone understood his ability. We knew if we could get Matt on the ball in the opposing half, he would cause a lot of problems.

"It took the other ten to do the work and give him the service. Did that upset some people? Well, if someone gets you a win bonus every week, you will play for him. It depends what you are like as a person as well. Matt was well liked because he was a good bloke. I suppose if he had been arrogant or had a manner that alienated people, there might have been problems. But everyone got on with him.

"At that stage, he always had a free role. That was the way to play him. He was scoring goals for many seasons, so if you give him a free role in the opposing half of the field, someone had to stay tight to him. That messed their shape up and allowed Matt to get the ball and cause most damage."

Le Tissier fired the first from the penalty spot in a 2-1 home win over Everton after Slaven Bilic was sent off for fouling Ostenstad. It was the second red card in the game, Ken Monkou having been dismissed for a professional foul that led to Don Hutchison missing a penalty for the Toffees. Ostenstad scored a second with four minutes left before Carl Tiler pulled one back.

Photographer's friend. With an 'assistant' under one arm and a hand free to see to the formalities, Le Tissier shows that he's also a natural in the field of community skills.

A trip to Barnsley, an extremely happy hunting ground for Le Tissier that season, saw him score twice, only for Saints to be sunk in a thriller. His first was a header from Jason Dodd's cross to make it 2-2 but the game was dead and buried with the visitors 4-2 down when John Beresford tapped a short free-kick into his path and he bent the ball into the top corner with characteristic deadly accuracy.

Although his efforts had been wasted at Oakwell, Le Tissier made it four goals in three games to give Saints a dramatic last-gasp win over Newcastle at The Dell on March 28. The fixture had given him reason to smile over previous years and once again he came up trumps in the dying minutes.

Stuart Pearce was the unfortunate victim as Palmer's effort bounced around the penalty area before hitting him and flying past Shay Given to cancel out Rob Lee's opener. And with just three minutes left, Le Tissier was called upon once more from the penalty spot. Of course he didn't fail his team-mates, nor spurn the opportunity to be a hero yet again.

Amazingly, the three points gave Saints hope of nicking a European place in a season they had started catastrophically. But the absence of Palmer and Oakley in the heart of midfield cost them dearly as they left Hillsborough brooding over a 1-0 defeat which effectively ended their UEFA Cup push.

For the fourth time in five starts, Le Tissier failed to see out the game and the disappointment was getting to him. After making way for Davies at Sheffield, he wore a scowl as he marched past the bench and headed straight for the tunnel. His actions suggested possible problems between irritated hero and frustrated manager, although Jones played down talk of a rift.

"Kevin Richardson did not sit on the bench when he was taken off either," he said. "If players want to sit with us, they can. If they want to go and get a shower because it is wet and cold, that's fine too. Matt watched from the tunnel, so there are no problems. People are making it into something that is not. If people are not playing well, they don't deserve to stay on but in fairness any one of ten could have come off."

With five games left, Le Tissier's turbulent season hinted at him having another free summer in which to improve his golf. Out of the blue, though, came a call from Hoddle and selection for that B team game at Loftus Road. It was the chance he believed had gone, and the excitement of seeing his World Cup adventure brought back from the dead led to an upsurge in his Saints form.

He was back at his creative best the same day as Saints were robbed of two points at Leicester, where his through ball sent Ostenstad charging away to net the first. Then he showed a quality touch to set up Hirst to fire his team into a 3-1 lead. The evening ended on a sour note, though, as his last-minute hand-ball allowed Garry Parker to score from the spot and salvage a draw for the home side.

Le Tissier was under the national spotlight again during the visit of Villa and didn't disappoint. In a depressing home defeat, he scored the pick of the goals - a long-range volley. Russia then suffered in the B game at Loftus Road as he launched his relentless pursuit of an England shirt. The chase was on! But he knew the hat-trick he smashed in while wearing the three lions had to be followed by more goals.

There was hunger in his play but Saints' season was effectively over. A mid-table place was secure, an unusual feeling for fans who had spent several years desperately checking the fixtures to see where vital end-of-season points might be gleaned.

They were 12th, a position they would remain in for the rest of the season, as they headed to West Ham on April 25. Knowing that all they had to play for was prize money, they cruised to a 4-2 victory with a style and verve that promised much for 1998-99. Le Tissier took his tally for the season into double figures by following up when his 40th minute volley came back off the post.

After a disappointing 2-0 defeat by Derby in Saints' last home game, Le Tissier was spared the prospect of sending his boyhood heroes Tottenham down in the final match. A Spurs side containing Jurgen Klinsmann had just secured their safety, so the match was little more than a showcase for his talents.

England had a friendly coming up against Saudi Arabia and he had to be in that squad if there was to be the slightest chance of him extending his season. He said: "I don't know what I would have done if Spurs had needed a point and we had got a late penalty. I might have let someone else take it - if only to protect myself.

"I would never deliberately miss but with my record, there would be all sorts of questions if I failed to score, especially as everyone knows that I supported Spurs as a child. There's no way I'd turn down a penalty tomorrow. It could be my last chance to catch the England manager's eye and, hopefully, I can force my way in against Saudi. A lot depends on the size and nature of the squad and whether Glenn Hoddle is using it to experiment. I'm hoping he does - or at least makes changes from the last game."

Le Tissier must have felt he had forced Hoddle's hand with his third goal in four games as Saints earned a White Hart Lane draw. He sat back, waiting with fingers crossed for Hoddle to name his squad but, when the manager announced his 22 on May 12, the expected changes did not include the Dell hero. Instead, another man with Southampton links earned a surprise call-up.

Tottenham midfielder Darren Anderton was elevated to the full England squad after a season beset with injury problems. He had been impressive in the B team game alongside Le Tissier but it was hard to believe his display that night could have leapfrogged him ahead of the Saints star. As Anderton celebrated, Hoddle spelled out the reasons for exiling Le Tissier to the fairways.

"Matt had had a poor season by his standards," he said. "True, he scored a hat-trick for the B team against a not very good Russian side but I think he knows just how much more we feel he should be contributing over the 90 minutes. He's got talent in abundance but we need more from him physically and mentally if he's to reach the top. I'd love to have seen him playing for Manchester United or Tottenham or Chelsea - clubs where the crowd's demands are much higher week in week out."

It was the killer blow for Le Tissier, especially as Hoddle subsequently dropped the bombshell of throwing Paul Gascoigne out of his squad. The Channel Islander could have been the perfect replacement as England's play-maker in the attempts to unlock some of the world's best defences. And a certain former Saints manager is convinced it was a mistake to repeatedly overlook him.

"The number of times I phoned Terry Venables during my time in charge, I can't tell you," said Alan Ball. "I'm absolutely mystified why he wasn't even considered. He was an international player and would have graced that stage. His abilities were up there with whoever you talk about. If you showed a tape of his goals to the Maradonas of this world, they would say: 'Wow! Who is this guy?'

"He wasn't given the chance when he was at his peak to show what he could do for his country. That will gall him for the rest of his life. He knows that he would have performed at the highest level, given the right stage."

Saints keeper Paul Jones, already an experienced Welsh international, was quick to point out that Le Tissier might have been heading to France if Hoddle had been made aware earlier of the fragile state of Gascoigne's mind. "None of us expected Gazza to be axed and maybe if that decision had been taken earlier, Le Tissier might still have been involved," he said.

"It was said he was left out because Glenn Hoddle couldn't have him and Gazza in the same side. Now he hasn't got either. Matt could certainly have filled that role."

While the people of England caught World Cup fever, Le Tissier sought familiar refuge on the golf course at the end of a troubled season in which he had still scored 14 Saints goals. His favourite other game helped take his mind off the crushing news. Hoddle's handling of the situation had deeply affected him, with exclusion coming without the courtesy of an explanatory phone call.

"Glenn hasn't spoken to me," he revealed. "His explanation in the media was that I hadn't done enough. It's his choice. He can do what he wants. I suppose if he does it for one player on the fringe, he has to do it for others. I paid the price for the stick I took in the media the day after the Italy game. People were very quick to point the finger at me when there were worse players on the pitch.

"I'm disappointed I haven't got the opportunity to play in France rather than other players who I consider to be less talented. I've been disappointed in the way that the national team has been picked, not with the 22 best players in form but on what people have done in the past. It wouldn't have hurt so much if I thought I was playing rubbish at the time but I don't think that's the case.

"There weren't many players finishing the season as well as me, scoring ten goals in the last few games. I think I deserved a place. I missed the first two months of the season through injury. From February, I was getting back to my best and thought that might have been a point in my favour. Obviously not.

"We were told to use the B international as a stepping stone and I thought I did enough to get another chance in one of the friendlies at least. But it wasn't to be. I have made two senior starts for England and that is nowhere near enough to give someone a decent chance at international level. I'm not bitter, just disappointed. I'll be 33 by the time the next World Cup comes around - and 33 stone probably."

1998-99

Chasing Channon

THE decision not to take him to France left Matt Le Tissier enduring a summer of puzzlement. And his confused state of mind was intensified by a series of changes to the personnel at Southampton as Dave Jones built on his ultimately successful first season by adding new faces to his squad.

The moves were funded by Kevin Davies' £7.25m switch to Blackburn - a figure that even in those days of crazy fees, appeared to be outrageous for a player with only one season of Premiership experience. The deal handed Jones a war-chest previously unheard of at The Dell and he was not slow in spending it.

Not all the captures were successful. Stuart Ripley and David Howells spent much of their time in the treatment room while Scott Marshall and Mark Paul were barely seen after posing with a Southampton scarf on their arrival. Mark Hughes emerged as the biggest name among the six new faces but it was the man who almost sneaked through the back door, James Beattie, who was to have the biggest influence. He was a £1m makeweight in the Davies switch and, although still raw, had the powerful talent needed to make him a renowned hit-man.

Before those deals had been done, Jones did what Saints bosses seemed to have been compelled to do throughout the 1990s - deny that Le Tissier was on his way out. Bordeaux were rumoured to be offering £4m but the manager joked: "I must have been on holiday when the call came in. It's just a load of rubbish and I have no idea where that story came from.

"I've had no contact with Bordeaux and I'm sure Matt would have told me if he'd heard from them. He hasn't been to see me at all. He knows the way I work and I would tell him if there was any truth in it. It's just yet another piece of speculation." But after more pre-season reports of Tottenham interest, Jones did add that the Dell hero could be sold if the club received an offer too good to turn down.

"Would I be prepared to sell him?" he said. "Of course I would if I felt it was right for the club. The same applies to any player here. If an offer comes in from anyone, we would have to consider it. Matt is no different from Carlton Palmer, John Beresford or anyone else.

"He is one of the best finishers I have ever worked with. He has an ability that many players would give a lot for. He also has deficiencies but is willing to listen and learn and as long as he keeps doing what I want, he will stay at this club. He has shown great loyalty in the past but that does not guarantee him a job for life. Like any player, if he stops performing to the best of his ability, decisions will have to be made."

Jones' words were a kick up the backside for Le Tissier and it was clear the Saints saviour was no longer the key man at The Dell. The manager had decided he wasn't prepared to risk the club's top-flight status on the form of any one player. And with the arrival of so many new faces, Le Tissier found himself shunted out to the left wing in the pre-season friendlies and failed to impress.

The problem was that he left Beresford exposed at full-back while not contributing his customary moments of magic in attack. Jones was obviously growing frustrated at not being able to coax the kind of performances he had seen Le Tissier produce under Alan Ball. But the player was unfazed at the threat to his first-team shirt despite the angst in the manager's office.

He was happy to welcome the new signings, who he visualised as being capable of taking some of the goal-scoring workload off him. "Sure, there will be extra pressure on me this season with the arrival of more quality forwards," he admitted. "But in a way, that also eases the pressure on me. For years, I was the one expected to score the goals to keep us up and if I was not doing it, we struggled.

"Now we have the likes of Egil Ostenstad, David Hirst and Mark Hughes, who are all capable of 15-20 goals a season. If others are scoring, it takes the pressure off me, although that isn't to say I won't be trying to score. But the summer strengthening does also increase the pressure. This is the highest number of quality forwards I can ever remember at this club.

"If one is not doing his job, he knows there are other people on the bench itching to get a game. And that will give me a new lease of life. With so many good players waiting to come in, there will be no room at all for complacency, so I'll have to keep on top of my game."

Despite a freak injury picked up by Hirst during a training run, Le Tissier began the season among the substitutes as Saints narrowly lost at home to Liverpool before being thumped 5-0 at Charlton, where Clive Mendonca ran riot. Angry supporters were mystified at his absence as Hughes partnered Ostenstad. They daubed graffiti on the Dell walls and forced Jones to qualify his earlier quotes, which were seen by some as an invitation for clubs to start the bidding.

While the controversy raged about his future, Le Tissier was sharpening his act in the reserves against Crystal Palace. He was still hoping to overhaul Mick Channon's club record of 228 goals and vowed to make a quick return and rack up the two he needed to reach 200. But he admitted he had spent the opening two weeks of the season scratching his head over his omission.

"If I'm in the team, I know I will score goals," he said. "I have been left out before but always battled my way back - and that's what I intend to do now. I still have three years of my contract left and I don't want to leave. I still love it here and want to stay long enough to break Mick Channon's record.

"I would certainly hope to do it by the end of next season, if not this. And that would mean a lot to me. Naturally I'm disappointed at being left out for the opening matches after finishing as last season's leading scorer despite missing a quarter of it through my injuries.

"I was not surprised to be left out because I'd seen it coming. The manager told me I was one of the best finishers he had ever seen, yet couldn't find room for me in the team, which I found strange. But I'm not going to make a fuss or demand a move. I'll just keep working hard to force my way back into the side."

His return soon came. He was handed a recall for the home clash with Nottingham Forest in late August and, after being tripped in the box, netted a last-minute penalty that could not conceal Saints' shortcomings in a 2-1 defeat. It was then back to the bench for the next two matches - hammerings at Leeds and Newcastle - as Jones reverted to a 4-4-2 formation in an unsuccessful attempt to shore up his side.

The boss explained the decision by claiming he needed Le Tissier to be fitter to help Saints out of their predicament. And it was hard not to notice the extra pounds the player was carrying. Jones said: "I have had a chat with Matt, which is between me and him. I honestly don't have a problem with him. We get on very well. He is a good lad and is very laid-back like me. People think he doesn't care but he does.

"Just because I said the club would consider offers for any players, people have assumed we are going to sell him. But I'm trying to build a team, not dismantle one. I won't give up on him. I want to get him fit and see him at his best. I've only seen that on videos from three or four years ago. Then he had the self-belief that he could do anything - and a fully fit Le Tissier would get in any side. He knows what he has to do and is prepared to do it. I've told him that if he's fully fit and firing, he plays."

Le Tissier put his excess baggage down to missing a chunk of the pre-season work designed to get him in shape, admitting: "I could probably do with losing a few pounds and have already started to do a few things to sort that. I didn't play enough pre-season games. That is one of the things I spoke to the manager about.

"Normally, I play six or seven warm-up games and rely on those to get match-fit. That didn't happen this year and it's one of the reasons I'm not as sharp as I should be. I put that to the manager and he agreed. That's why I played for the reserves recently and also at Bashley in pre-season. But I think it helped to have a chat with the boss. He told me what he wanted and I'm happy to go along with it. I just need to get an extra yard and hopefully get back to scoring a few goals."

Although Le Tissier was not having a major impact on matches, goals were still coming. He hit two in a reserve defeat of Barnet then Palmer's ban for a pre-season red card saw him back in the first team at home to Spurs. Advancing on to a pass by Hughes, then cleverly turning an opponent, he thundered home an effort from close range to earn Saints their first point of the season, at this, their sixth attempt.

It was his 200th goal for Saints in competitive football and, either side of it, he got a chance to build up his fitness by featuring in both legs as Southampton lost 2-1 to Fulham - then a Division Two side - in round two of the Worthington Cup.

The West Londoners were a bogey side in the cups, also beating Saints

STRIKE TWO!: Le Tissier coolly slots home his second goal against Russia last night. Picture: Paul Watts

VINTAGE MATT!

MATTHEW Le Tissier powered his way back into the frame for France with a majestic hat-trick for the England B side in their 4-1 win over Russia at Loftus Road.

The Saints star also hit the woodwork twice in a superb all-round display which could just catapult him back into the reckoning for the World Cup finals — starting with a senior international re-call against Saudi Arabia next month.

Even so Le Tissier is refusing to get carried away with his stunning success, acknowledging he still has a long way to go if he is to squeeze into the final 22-man squad to be announced in six weeks time.

He said: "I am delighted with the way it went. Never in my wildest dreams did I dare imagine I would get a hat-trick. I would just have been

By **Graham Hiley at Wembley** 22/4/98

am still an outsider.

"But I have never given up hope of making the 22 and I won't do until the final squad is announced. I am going to give it my best shot and at least then I can rest easy if I don't make it even though it will hurt.

"This was an important game for me though and I am just pleased it went so well.

Brazil 10 years ago and it was the 10th senior hat-trick of his career but the first since his treble on the opening day 4-3 home defeat by Nottingham Forest in August 1995.

He added: "In terms of quality of goals the one I got against Norwich a few years back was probably better but in terms of timing this is the most precious."

He said: "Glenn will be delighted both for Matt and because it backs up his own judgement. I'm sure that Glenn sees a bit of Matt in himself with the way he plays. He is an outstanding talent — someone who makes and scores goals.

"The fact that he scored three certainly does not surprise me because he is very capable of doing that if he gets in certain goalscoring

Flashback! It was only a few months since his name had been up in lights. Now, Saints fans were worrying whether Matt Le Tissier would hit the headlines again.

later in the season when Barry Hayles netted the winner in an FA Cup third-round tie.

Le Tissier failed to build on his goal against Spurs. Saints lost 1-0 at West Ham and 3-0 at home to Manchester United and he was again dropped to the bench. Just as he had done under Ian Branfoot, he responded in the only way he knew. When he was soon reinstated in the starting line-up, he looped in a header from Ripley's accurate cross to open the scoring at home to Coventry and supplied the low cross that enabled Ostenstad to slide home a second in a 2-1 win - Saints' first of the season.

Le Tissier was finally making an impression, his cross setting up Ken Monkou to net against visiting Middlesbrough on November 7 before he picked out Ostenstad as Saints came from behind to gain a 3-2 lead. He had been revelling in the space afforded to him by Robbie Mustoe's sending-off and must have thought his work had been done when Boro were reduced to nine men by Phil Stamp's dismissal. But the side lacked the resolve to cling on and Gianluca Festa scored in injury-time to steal a point.

It got worse. Saints were thrashed 4-1 at home by Aston Villa, although Le Tissier scored a stunner to temporarily draw them level, showing fantastic footwork and body swerves to create the space he needed to arrow home a low shot.

He then missed the 2-0 victory at Blackburn that finally saw Southampton move off the bottom and failed to score in a four-game December run back in the side that brought three defeats and one win. But he stepped from the bench to set up Ostenstad for the only bright moment in a 7-1 thumping at Liverpool before a torn hamstring in the 3-0 victory over Leeds on January 30 forced him out for several more weeks until he made a scoring return as sub at Old Trafford. Unfortunately, the game was already lost when he met Jason Dodd's free-kick to nod past Schmeichel in the last minute.

He used his head again from Matt Oakley's cross to clinch a crucial 1-0 mid-March victory over Sheffield Wednesday. The club's first win against the Owls at The Dell since 1970 was also their fifth in a row at home in a second-half-of-the-season surge that raised hope they could escape the drop once more.

Le Tissier's reward was to find himself out of the line-up for the draw at home to Arsenal, with Jones calling on him to try to adapt his game to compensate for his diminishing physical ability. The club's long-time saviour was warned that the pace of Premiership football no longer allowed him to use matches to acquire fitness. He was also picking up more injuries through playing when less than 100 per cent right.

"Matt is never going to be the player he was three of four years ago and accepts he has got to change his style," Jones said. "He's not going to burst past people with pace, so he has to find areas where he can do most damage - and that is as close to goal as possible. There's nothing to stop him being a different player but just as effective.

"He will have to work but he reaps rewards when he does that. This season, we are having problems getting him to a level of fitness because of his injuries. The Le Tissier of old would see playing matches as the way to get fit. But the game has changed and he can't get his fitness in matches now. He has to put it in on the training ground."

The main problem was that a nagging calf injury was hampering his ability to get through the training-ground work Jones was demanding. But when Saints fans needed him most, the hero answered the call to produce one final match-winning display that went a huge way to ensuring Saints would enjoy Premiership football again in the season taking them into the new Millennium.

The club were 17th and in the thick of the relegation battle when they travelled to Selhurst Park to take on Wimbledon in the penultimate game. The need for points had drawn 10,000 travelling fans to South London, many dressed up in fezzes and robes to pay homage to Saints and Morocco midfielder Hassan Kachloul.

"It was a fantastic atmosphere," Le Tissier said. "The crowd were the thing that stick in my mind. It was an incredible turn-out. It was touch and go whether I'd be fit, so I spoke to Dave Jones on the Friday night and suggested it might be best if I sat on the bench and, if need be, get 20 minutes at the end." The plan worked perfectly.

Francis Benali kept the game goalless by clearing a Robbie Earle shot off the line before Le Tissier was introduced in the 70th minute to immediate dramatic effect. He delivered a perfect free-kick for Beattie to rise majestically and head into the top corner. Then, with six minutes left, he showed the skill that for so many years had made him a match-winner, conjuring up the second direct from a corner.

"It took a glance off Robbie Earle's head," he said. "There was a big gap at the near post and I said: 'I'm going to hit it in as hard as I can. If anyone gets a touch, it goes in.' Whether the keeper would have stopped it, we'll never know but it was on target."

Blackburn, who had sold Alan Shearer to Newcastle for £15m in 1996 and had Tim Flowers lined up for a move to Leicester, drew with Manchester United and so tumbled out of the top flight with Nottingham Forest. That left Saints - at home to Everton - vying with Charlton to avoid the last relegation spot on the final day.

The nerves that had been evident on so many previous last afternoons, barely built to nail-biting proportions this time. A brace by Marian Pahars comfortably saw Saints home while the Addicks lost to Sheffield Wednesday at The Valley and went down. Dell fans had a glimpse of the future as Pahars fed off the power of Beattie amid hope that the continual relegation battles would become a thing of the past.

Beattie totally dominated in the air as he put into practice the advice Shearer had given him at Blackburn on how to outjump defenders. He was a different animal to Le Tissier, bruising and able to panic centre-halves sucked to him as they attempted to curb his power. Pahars benefitted by getting on the end of his flicks.

Against Everton, Le Tissier again failed to go the full distance and was taken off for the seventh time in 20 starts in a season in which he scored only six times. It was a year of frustration and he resorted to humour in the face of the worrying deterioration that fans and his manager had picked up on. "The gaffer has not seen the best of me," he admitted. "He says I can't go past players anymore - but I never could!"

His injury problems had denied him the chance to return to his dazzling form of the Alan Ball era. Now, more than ever, with England a fading memory, he needed a summer off and a full pre-season if he was again to be the first name on the Saints team-sheet. He had still made a good impression on Hughes, whose contribution was one goal in 36 games. They, too, were opposites; one a physical battering ram with the capacity to return the fire and finish explosively, the other inclined to operate on the periphery of the action, which he would then illuminate in spectacular fashion.

"Matt didn't play that often," Hughes recalls. "He was having problems with his calf and was struggling for fitness. But when he did make an appearance in training or in a game, you were struck by his fantastic ability. I have played with many fantastic players but Matt's finishing was probably the best I have seen.

"It was up there with the Cantonas and everyone else. He has such a short back-lift and his disguise when shooting was too much for most people. His ability to finish time and time again was astonishing. Possibly when I went there, it was at a time when the club was moving away from Matt being the main player. Maybe they felt they couldn't rely on him as much as in the past and needed to go in a new direction.

"But he was certainly an influence around the place and was a good club-man. He played a part in what we were trying to do. It wasn't one of the best years for Southampton to be honest but we finally got there and Matt, as he always did, had an impact at the end of the season. The moment I remember most was at Selhurst Park. He took a corner and it went straight in just when we needed it. That was what he was capable of. It's those things that get you out of a hole."

Hughes followed his medal-filled playing career with a successful spell as Wales boss and is uncertain why Le Tissier, who was not credited with that goal at Selhurst Park, never made it on the international stage. "I don't know why he didn't become a regular," he added. "If he was starting out now, maybe he would be recognised as a different type of player and used in a different way.

"Matt has said himself he needed the service and people to do the leg-work for him. But you knew if you got the ball to him in the right areas, he could produce. Maybe at international level, the team was never set up in a way to get the best out of Matt Le Tissier - and that is what he needed. That level was certainly not beyond him. Technically, as a skilful footballer, he was better than a lot of England players who got a steady run in the side. His ability was never in question. It was just a question of how the team would get the best out of him, and England never did."

Shearer also has a view on why Le Tissier never made it with his country. "He was given his chance by various managers without ever establishing himself," he said. "His problem was that he was never as good without the ball as with it. I'm sure he will admit he could be a bit of a luxury. At club level, there was a more tolerant attitude towards him with managers willing to let others do his running. But that was never going to happen at international level, so he didn't get a settled run.

"Matt had a very laid-back attitude that I gather is typical of the Channel Islands. He was very easy-come, easy-go. But that, in a way, was his strength because he was single-minded, unpredictable and capable of utter brilliance. My lasting memory of him was his goal against Newcastle. He took a couple of touches, lifted the ball over a defender's head and volleyed it in from 25 yards. He did it in the blink of an eye as if it was the most natural thing in the world – which to him it was."

1999-2000

Groundhog Day

IT'S hard to imagine Matt Le Tissier as a tanned Adonis, checking out the surf on Bondi Beach. But a trip Down Under was the catalyst for him to discover a new lifestyle. Ditched by Glenn Hoddle and keen to ensure that the saturation coverage of the game back home did not haunt him, he happily agreed to follow his Australian girlfriend Emily Symons for a summer break in her home country.

While he was there, he changed his diet. Fresh fish and lean meats helped him shed half a stone as he enjoyed a healthier outlook with the Home and Away soap star. And on his return, he admitted he was eyeing the start of the new season with a little less round his waist and a lot more on his plate in terms of winning back his place as one of the Premiership's top guns.

"I feel really good right now," he said. "I've had a great summer. I spent most of it in Australia and loved it. I think I signed about four autographs in a month and I just unwound. Emily got me eating sensibly and I lost around half a stone, which is good. Last season, I was living on my own and didn't cook for myself that much. It was easier to nip out for a steak or something.

"I wanted to lose some weight because that might have something to do with the injuries I picked up last season. It has been a difficult couple of years for me. I never used to pick up many knocks but it all seemed to change when I broke my arm on the pre-season tour in Germany two years ago.

"That cost me the whole of the build-up, which is something I need. I'm not the sort of player who can afford to miss the pre-season. After that, I had a lot of niggling muscle injuries and have not really had a decent run in the side. It has been stop-start. Hopefully, if I'm carrying less weight, that won't be so much of a problem."

Le Tissier had been stung into action by the number of times he was left on the bench in 1998-99, especially at the start of it. Having finished the previous season with three goals in four games, he was stunned to find himself edged out by Dave Jones' new signings - and had taken steps to make sure it did not happen again.

Kevin Davies would soon be re-signed by Saints after an unhappy year at Blackburn - in a swap deal taking Egil Ostenstad in the opposite direction - and Mark Hughes, Marian Pahars and James Beattie were still around as potential barriers to Le Tissier's hopes of a first-team place.

But his form in pre-season, which included goals against Aldershot and Reading, had given him the confidence to eye greater glories than just returning to the Saints side as a regular. "There will be a lot of competition for places this season but I don't mind that at all," he added. "It is good for everyone and I have enough confidence in my own ability to believe I am worth a place.

"My first aim is to get in the side and stay there. The second is to start scoring goals again. If those two come off, I can start to think about the third, which is to get back in the England side. I have not given up hope of that at all - but these things have to be done in the right order."

Kevin Keegan, the latest England boss, had named Le Tissier and Paul Gascoigne as the two players who could boost the nation's chances of success. The Saints star did his chances no harm by slipping a penetrating pass through for Ostenstad to net the winner in the kick-off-day victory at Coventry. The England manager's scouts would have been impressed and Dell boss Jones was delighted with the way Le Tissier contributed to his side's first opening-day win since 1988.

"I have always said there is no reason why Matt should not get back in the England team," he said. "Everyone is crying out for a man who can open up defences and he showed again here that he can do that. But it is down to him, as it has always been. He did not have the best of seasons last time but he has come back after the summer determined to put that right.

"If he stays fit, sharp and free of injury, and keeps doing what is asked of him, there's no reason why he shouldn't get the call. Matt did exactly what was asked of him here and then set up the goal with a typical piece of skill. It was a great ball but he had two players making runs for him to pick out and that was pleasing too."

Le Tissier then impressed despite Saints being beaten 3-0 at home to Leeds and was a constant thorn in Newcastle's side as Jones masterminded a 4-2 win over the Magpies. But there was a feeling of Groundhog Day for the no 7 when he finally had to succumb to an Achilles injury that had plagued him since the first pre-season match.

While the doctors gave him the good news that an operation was not needed, Le Tissier - not among the scorers in the entertaining win at The Dell - was ordered to rest just as Keegan was considering his squad for England's Euro 2000 qualifier against Luxembourg on September 4. "The scan showed there is tendonitis but it did not reveal any tear," the player said. "So there is no need for an operation at the moment.

"I have just got to let it settle so I am 100 per cent when I come back but it is hard to know how long it will take. It could be a week or three or even longer. I'd think I'll probably miss the next two games but then there's a two-week break for internationals, which is probably good timing. It will give me an extra fortnight to recover, so maybe I'll make the match at Middlesbrough.

"I've tried to play through it but I've been feeling it in every game since it happened on the tour of Norway. Now it has got to the stage where there is just too much pain to be comfortable. It's very frustrating because I can't even kick the ball until I can jog with no pain, so I'll have to do non-weight-bearing work in the gym."

Le Tissier missed his date with Boro but was back when he stepped off the bench in the Dell defeat by Arsenal in mid-September. He must have feared his run of bad luck was not over, though, when even an outing with the reserves turned into a nightmare. The idea of his appearance for the second team's clash with Chelsea was to get some match fitness under his belt. Instead, he found himself rushed to the dentist.

Neil Clement was upset at some pushing as Le Tissier tried to work space at a corner and the Chelsea defender threw a haymaker that left referee Bernard Baker with little option but to send him off. That was little consolation to Le Tissier, who was flat out on the floor with a split lip and a row of loosened teeth.

Saints reserve-team coach Dennis Rofe said: "There was a bit of jostling for position before the corner but nothing out of the ordinary to provoke that reaction. It was the usual pulling and shoving in the crowd. Next thing, the Chelsea player has turned and whacked him, which was a bit unpleasant. There was no need for it and the officials dealt with it correctly. Matt was a bit shaken but he'll be okay. I wouldn't think it will keep him out on Saturday if he was needed."

The player did recover to face Manchester United and appeared from the bench to score one of the Theatre of Dreams' most memorable goals. It wasn't the sort of magical individualistic effort that had made his name, rather a laughable daisy-cutter that ended the Old Trafford career of Italian keeper Massimo Taibi.

Saints were 2-1 down when he seized possession 25 yards out and aimed a weak shot at goal. A pub league keeper would have found it easy to flick away his cigarette and gather but that simple task was beyond Taibi. Despite getting in line with the ball, he let it slither through his midriff, trickle over his studs and creep over the line.

No-one was more surprised than Le Tissier, who followed up with a goal of pure quality to earn Saints a 3-3 draw that kept them in mid-table. Pahars had frightened United throughout, with Jaap Stam horribly caught out by the Latvian on his way to netting the game's opener in the 16th minute. This time the electric striker harassed Mikael Silvestre into giving up the ball near the corner flag and fired an accurate cross into the box for Le Tissier to angle a sweet side-foot volley into the corner.

The brace left him one short of his Premiership century and he was determined to reach the landmark in the next game, at home to Derby. The clash was being screened live by Sky and Le Tissier was relishing the chance to have his exploits registered by the watching nation.

"I'll be disappointed if I don't play after scoring those two goals at United, even if one of them was slightly fortunate," he said. "They all count! It would be nice to get to the 100 in front of the Sky cameras. It's a big milestone, which would mean a lot to me because of the good company. It would be quite an achievement, especially as most of the goals have come from midfield while the others up there are all centre-forwards.

"The good thing is I feel refreshed now. The lay-off has been good and the team have done well, so I have not had to rush back as I might have done in the past. The opposite side to the coin is that there is more competition for places and I'll have to fight my way back in. But I have plenty of confidence in my ability to score goals."

Le Tissier did start but failed to finish as Saints let a 3-1 advantage slip. He played his part in helping build the lead with a perfectly-weighted pass for Matt Oakley to fire home the second but had departed by the time Mikkel Beck notched an injury-time leveller for the Rams in the home side's second successive 3-3 draw. The match was completely overshadowed, though, by the news that Dave Jones was to face charges over a scurrilous false accusation that he had abused boys in his care while working in social services in Liverpool.

The allegations first arose in pre-season but the disclosure that Jones was to fight a court case would have dire implications for Le Tissier's season. Even in October, the worrying stop-start trend of previous campaigns was beginning to surface, although the player impressed in the Worthington Cup, playing a part in Dean Richards' winner when Saints beat Manchester City 4-3 in extra-time in a Dell thriller.

He also set up the former England under-21 captain for a crucial strike as Saints beat Liverpool 2-1 at home in the third round, only for them to crash 4-0 at Aston Villa at the next stage. But when it came to more important Premiership action, Le Tissier was either starting matches on the bench or ending them there.

He was used as a substitute at Leicester before being handed a starting role and providing the assist for Trond Egil Soltvedt in a 1-1 home draw with Liverpool. Saints were still leading when Jones withdrew him in the 53rd minute, the Dell hero shocking fans by angrily swiping a drinking bottle to the floor as he left the pitch.

"That was frustration with the decision and also with myself," he said. "I had not played brilliantly but we were winning and I set up the goal. The last two games have been frustrating for me. I'm not used to sitting on the bench. I want to be playing."

His flash of anger was a clear sign of his annoyance, although Jones was quick to clamp down on any talk that the pair had fallen out. "It was a storm in a tea-cup," he insisted. "It was frustration, nothing more. People can make of it what they like but I did not see anything untoward. He was right to be upset.

"I would not expect any player to be happy at coming off. There are no problems, though. He is part of the squad and on another day, he will play a key role. I just felt it was the right change at the time. Stuart Ripley proved it was a good one when he went on. We looked tighter and more potent going forward."

Le Tissier had no immediate chance to redress the balance. He was dropped and given a four-game run in the reserves that prompted a suggestion few Saints fans had expected. After heading the second goal in a 2-0 win over Tottenham's second string, he ventured the idea of a stint away from The Dell on loan. "I'm 31 now," he said. "I want to be playing regular first-team football. It isn't inspiring to play in front of a handful of people at St Albans.

"I don't want to leave. I've never wanted to. I want to get back in the first team here. I'm the sort of person who needs to be playing every week to get on a run of goals. I thrive on confidence, which means I try more things and they start to come off. I need a run, so it may be I'll need to go out on loan to get matches under my belt. I've not had any offers and don't know how the manager would feel about it.

"It may be a possibility. In the meantime, I'll just do my best, work hard and wait for my chance. I feel fit and ready. In fact, this is the best I've felt injury-wise for two years. That makes it all the more frustrating that I can't get a game but I understand it is hard to change the team when they are playing well."

Alan Ball, the man who made the most of Le Tissier's talents, was immediately alerted to the possibility of taking his favoured son down the road to Portsmouth, where he was now manager for the second time. The move was always unlikely because of Le Tissier's reluctance to turn out for a club viewed with hatred by Saints fans - and Jones was quick to nip in the bud any further loan talk.

He urged his player to concentrate solely on winning back his place in a red and white shirt and said: "Matt is still an integral part of the set-up here but I'm trying to build a squad. I understand the frustrations of all the players who are not getting a run of games while we are picking up results. It's hard to keep everyone happy. But if I started loaning all of them out, I would have no-one left.

"At the moment, I don't want to consider it. Matt has a great talent. He just needs to keep working hard and await his chance, as the others have done."

Ball held back on making a formal enquiry and the only official approach came from Woking, although speculation also linked the Saints star with Nottingham Forest and Crystal Palace. While Jones slammed the door on his chances of getting match fitness elsewhere, he left Le Tissier wondering what he had to do to win back a place at The Dell when he omitted him from the home draw with Coventry despite being without three first-choice midfielders.

Instead, the player laboured through an uninspiring performance in the reserves' defeat at Charlton and failed to make the squad for the FA Cup third-round victory at Ipswich. Despite not being involved on the pitch, he was using his status to put forward ideas on how Saints should play, and Davies was impressed with the way he was so positive in trying to help his team-mates while he was clearly smarting.

"If he had a feeling about something or the way we were playing or the way we could play, he would stand up and say what he felt was right for the good of the team," said Davies, who was also trying to re-invent himself. "In team meetings, watching videos or on the training pitch, if he felt something was not right, he would stop and ask the manager about possibly changing it. He was outspoken, and that's his right. He was an experienced player.

"It was a frustrating time for him. The demands were getting higher and higher and the manager felt he needed more defensive players in there. Le Tiss worked hard to get his fitness back, then spent a lot of time not playing. I think he knew what the situation was and there was talk of him going on loan. But I don't think that was really an option. He wanted to stay, otherwise he'd have gone years ago.

"He was still showing he could do it in training but I had a feeling the manager felt it was physically too demanding for him. I think Matt had the respect for other players and didn't show any anger about his situation. He wasn't sulking. When he was a sub, he came on and tried his hardest."

Le Tissier did finally return to first-team football over the festive period and set up Davies for Saints' only goal in a 2-1 Boxing Day home defeat by Chelsea, in which the Londoners made history by becoming the first English club to field a side without a British-born player in the starting 11.

But the defeat at Watford two days later came at a heavy price for Le Tissier. He was struck down with hamstring and calf injuries that were to keep him out until March - an absence during which Saints won more than they lost despite going out of the FA Cup away to Aston Villa at the first hurdle and being caned 5-0 at Newcastle.

When he did regain fitness, he was playing under a different boss - one he would hardly have welcomed. Chairman Rupert Lowe had taken the controversial decision to relieve Jones of his duties to leave him free to fight his court case and, in his place, pulled off a coup by landing ex-England boss Glenn Hoddle.

Le Tissier still blamed his one-time hero for ruining his dream of playing in the 1998 World Cup finals but tried to hide his disappointment by diplomatically claiming he had buried the hatchet. "There is no bitterness on my part," he said. "It is fair to say that I was disappointed at the time but it's all in the past. I've never been one to hold grudges and I'm looking forward to working with Glenn.

"Everyone knows he was my favourite player when I was young. I see a lot of myself in the way he played and, hopefully, he will identify with me. But like everyone, I'm in limbo until I meet him and hear what his plans are. It is a fresh start for everyone and we have to prove ourselves all over again. I would like to think he will get the best out of me but it's not just down to him. A lot lies at my door to get myself fully fit and then to perform."

The new Saints boss, now limited by a tiny transfer budget in his efforts to select creative ball players, was keen to see the England man back to full fitness. "I have always been a great admirer of Matthew Le Tissier and I brought him into the England squad," he said. "He is coming back from injury at the moment and, if we can get him 100 per cent fit, he's going to be a major asset to Southampton.

"Injuries have been a problem in the last couple of years and that was one of the reasons I did not pick him for the World Cup. I desperately wanted to look at him but he got a bad run of injuries and, in the end, it was not an option. I would love to have the opportunity to get him fully fit and, hopefully, we can address some of those problems. A couple of years ago, he was sensational. If he gets anywhere near that, he is as good as anyone in the country in my opinion."

Le Tissier's problem was just that - getting fit. It wasn't until February 23 that he ended an eight-week spell on the sidelines and returned to full training. He played a painful part in the 7-2 drubbing at Spurs on March 11 as Hoddle's homecoming turned into a nightmare on the day Mark Hughes played his last Saints game. The Welsh striker had often operated in midfield but scored only once in 25 games in 1999-2000.

Le Tissier finally pushed for a first-team start by curling home a stunning strike in a friendly run-out for the reserves against Brentford, and was upbeat as he said: "I should probably have had three but it was nice as I needed to score again. It has been a while since I got on, so it's good for the confidence to hit a goal like that. If the manager wants me, I am there. I will probably have to settle for a place on the bench at the moment. The boss wants me to take it slowly and I'm happy to do that. I'm just glad to be involved again."

As he predicted, Le Tissier was used as a sub and made the most of his brief appearance against Sunderland by finally netting his 100th Premiership goal - a big moment he had been waiting for since scoring his 99th at Manchester United way back in September. Typically, it came from the spot as he beat Thomas Sorensen in the last minute of a rare home defeat after Darren Williams handled his shot on the line.

"It is nice to have got my 100th Premiership goal but it doesn't mean much right now because we lost," he said. "I would have enjoyed the moment a lot more if it had got us some points or even come a bit sooner to give us time to equalise."

The goal earned Le Tissier a recall to the starting line-up and he helped Saints win 2-1 at struggling Bradford, then produced a cross for Pahars to score in a 2-0 defeat of relegation-bound Watford. He battled through the latter game despite a throat infection and in the knowledge that he was booked in for an end-of-season operation on a hernia problem that had first reared its head before Christmas.

He put off having the surgery after pulling his hamstring at Watford on December 28 and said: "It started to get bad just before then. I wanted to have it done after the Watford game, so the two injuries could heal at the same time. But the surgeons were on holiday for three weeks and by the time they got back, I was over the hamstring trouble. But I did not expect to then be out for three weeks with a calf injury, otherwise I'd have had the operation at that time.

"Now I need to sit down with the manager and discuss when to have it done. It will either be in the summer or the first week in May. At least there's no pressure to play right to the end of the season as we are virtually safe, so maybe I'll have it done earlier. That would give me more recovery time before we go to La Manga for a training break. I want to be 100 per cent for that, so I can build up strongly for next season."

Le Tissier did force his way through two substitute appearances as Saints were beaten 3-1 at home by a Manchester United side on the way to another title and then 2-0 at Derby. But with the side in a comfortable 15th place, he volunteered to go under the knife and concentrate on the following season.

He knew, despite all the nice words, he would have to perform above and beyond the call of duty to stay in Hoddle's plans. The question was: Would his body let him?

2000-01

Destiny of a Legend

T HE thing about legends is that they have an ability to seize the biggest occasions and make them their own. Ordinary players may pop up with wonder goals in regulation games that they later list in programme notes as their personal favourite memory. Others like Matthew Le Tissier score goals which become beloved mementos for a whole generation.

And no-one who cares for Southampton Football Club can deny that the player's fairytale strike against Arsenal in the final game at The Dell lives on in their personal recollections.

If you had listened to Le Tissier before that dramatic game, he would probably have told you he was destined to make headlines on May 19, 2001. His season had again been decimated by injuries but this was a player who knew more than any other how to kick-start an end-of-season party. And there have been few bigger in Saints' history than the day the club said goodbye to their home of 103 years.

Le Tissier had been told earlier in the week that he was in line for a place on the substitutes' bench but would be guaranteed a run-out in the charming but antiquated surroundings that had showcased his fine talents over the previous decade and a half. That was all the encouragement he needed to start building up his hopes of a starring role in what was to be an emotion-packed afternoon.

Tickets were impossible to beg, borrow or steal as Saints - safe in mid-table - set about turning the final game into a south coast event. The occasion lived well up to all expectations and was going to plan when Kevin Davies was sacrificed for Le Tissier with 17 minutes left, the contest teasingly balanced at 2-2.

Hassan Kachloul had twice pulled back an all-star Arsenal side after first Ashley Cole, then Freddie Ljungberg brought groans from a capacity 15,252 crowd desperate for a celebration. Saints fans were pleading for a hero - and in rode the old stager to orchestrate one last command performance.

Having taken up a position in the box with his back to goal, he watched the ball drop, ignored the better-placed Chris Marsden and spun on his right foot. He bent his body into an awkward shape as he twisted to make contact in such an unwieldy fashion that his effort promised to balloon into the crowd. But as his left foot flashed across the ball, the technique honed on the school fields of Guernsey was once more brought into play and he hammered his shot past the flailing Alex Manninger.

It was an incredible goal to match the best in a career typified by majestic strikes but it meant so much more than many of the football miracles he had achieved before.

The billowing net was soaking up a goal packed with the kind of emotion missing from the heat-seeking missile he guided past old pal Tim Flowers at Blackburn. That had come in a game ultimately lost. It meant more than the free-kick he crashed past the West Ham wall to ensure Southampton stayed in the top flight as at the time when his wonder goals were ten-a-penny. And it meant more than 208 others that had dumbfounded goalkeepers across the country and placed Matthew Le Tissier head and shoulders above his peers in hunting the spectacular.

Davies was for once delighted to be taken off as his departure had opened the way for the legend to strike. And he said: "Everyone could see it coming. It had to be him, didn't it? In the last minute, in the last game at The Dell - it was written for him. Everyone was estacic for Matt. We could see what it meant to him to score that goal.

Just a little bit popular! A familiar scene as the Saints' latterday legend is mobbed by fans. His status was underpinned by events on the final day of 2000-01, when no-one was remotely surprised that the scorer of the last goal at The Dell was one Matthew Le Tissier.

There was a few beers floating around and we ended up in Jumping Jacks, although I don't remember how long Matt stayed out."

Saints caretaker boss Stuart Gray also believed Le Tissier was fated to scribble the final chapter in The Dell's glorious history. "It was such a fitting way for it all to end," he said. "It had to be Matt, didn't it? It was a great moment for him and a great way to sign off. I suppose it was written in the stars somewhere that he would go on and score the winner, although that wasn't on my mind when I sent him on.

"It was not an ordinary goal but the kind we have been used to seeing from him down the years. That has made it all the more special. He showed unbelievable technique. It did not look possible for him to wrap his foot around the ball, let alone smack it with such power and accuracy. It was an unbelievable moment. It raised the roof and we were so thrilled to see it go in. The Dell deserved that kind of send-off."

Gray denied that he had sent Le Tissier on only so the player could say his own mawkish goodbye to his favourite stomping ground. "There was no sentiment on my part at all," he added. "I put Matt on because I thought he would win us the game. You can't afford to be sentimental in a game like this. We wanted to end on a winning note, so I put Matt on because he is a match-winner."

Le Tissier felt the trauma of the previous few seasons had finally been exorcised

With all hope of an England comeback now gone, it was time for reflection for Le Tissier - and at least he had some happy England memories to go with all those Saints highs.

with the goal, although he admits it took a few days and plenty of heart-felt words to make him realise just how special it had been. "When I watch the match video, I don't watch the goal itself but the reaction of the crowd," he said. "That was the nicest thing about it. I probably did not realise at the time just how much it meant to everybody.

"It only sunk in when I was reading the letters in the Echo and an article in the Pink a few days later. It sends a shiver down my spine to think about it and the happiness it has brought. So many people have come up to me to say it was exactly what they would have wanted. In many ways, it was a perfect way for it all to end. It was a very proud moment for me and not in my wildest dreams could I have imagined it would be a goal like that. I'll treasure it forever."

No-one could have denied that Le Tissier deserved his moment of glory after a wretched season ruined by a knee injury picked up in the October 23 home defeat against Manchester City. That game had been only his second start of the season and frustratingly, he tasted defeat in both of them. He earlier lasted the full 90 minutes in a 3-1 reverse against Middlesbrough at The Dell, having earned the right to start by scoring at home to Mansfield in the Worthington Cup.

Le Tissier had already set up Jo Tessem for a 35th minute opener against the Third Division side by heading down Wayne Bridge's cross for the Norwegian to pounce. And he looked in good nick when Tessem returned the compliment by nodding a ball into his path for a fizzing 16-yard shot that crashed into the bottom corner.

Le Tissier played in the second leg as Saints ran out comfortable 5-1 winners on aggregate but, by the time they were beaten by Coventry at The Dell in the next round, he was in the treatment room. A run in the reserves in February then proved to manager Glenn Hoddle that he was back in shape, especially as he tucked into his boyhood heroes Spurs to snatch two goals in a sensational 7-0 win over their second string.

His goals earned him a return to the bench for the win over Everton on March 17, although he didn't get as far as stripping off his tracksuit. Recalling him to the squad was Hoddle's last act before he walked out on Saints and proved that Tottenham, bar none, were his favourite club.

Gray was handed the manager's job on a caretaker basis and Le Tissier, a one-time team-mate of his, continued to build his fitness with matches in the reserves, bolstered by regular appearances on the seniors' substitutes bench. Ironically, in each of the four games in which he was given a run-out, he finished on the losing side.

That was all to change when Arsene Wenger arrived with his players at The Dell to discover that Matt Le Tissier can make dreams come true. Arsenal were to finish as distant runners-up to Manchester United and, while their manager may have wondered just how Le Tissier conjured up that goal, it came as no surprise to the man who was set to take on the mantle as The Dell's golden boy.

James Beattie was on his way to a season's haul of 12 goals in 42 matches and said: "I was lucky enough to play with Matt for two years at Southampton and it was an absolute privilege. In training and in games, he would do incredible things with the ball and score fantastic goals.

"It wasn't as if they were one-offs. He would just keep scoring them! So he was an inspiration to myself and the other young players at the club. Matt kept us up nearly every season with his goals and was a true super hero at Southampton."

Unfortunately, the super hero appeared to have lost his most important power - the ability to stay fit. His body was struggling to overcome a series of injuries and he was no longer considered an integral part of the Saints line-up.

The last goal at The Dell may have written his name into the history books but Le Tissier himself was determined not to be confined to the past. He still had a hunger to score Premiership goals and made a personal vow to build on the Arsenal strike. And there was the perfect reason not to let his aching bones beat him - Saints were about to hand him a whole new stage to play on.

2001-02

The Final Curtain

MARCH 19, 2002, was the date football lost another legend. Matt Le Tissier was already at the end of his tether when he decided to give his dodgy calf one last chance in a reserve fixture against Charlton at St Mary's. He was patched up for action but after only 30 minutes, he knew the game was up. A shooting pain through his lower leg immediately told him that the uphill fight was over. His body was shot and there was no way back.

Signalling to the bench, he had a look of resignation in his eye. While others may have urged him to carry on, to keep getting treatment and rest, the great man had already made up his mind. He limped to the touchline to be replaced by Brian Howard and, with shoulders slumped, struggled down the tunnel towards the dressing room.

There, he sat and contemplated a future without miracle goals or stupefying tricks, without bowing crowds and adoring Le God posters; a future without football.

Manager Gordon Strachan appeared quietly in the doorway and, acknowledging the player's disconsolate mood, sat beside him. He had suffered a loss as well - robbed of a man who he could have planned to build his team around. Both knew the outcome of the conversation they were about to have and talked candidly in an otherwise empty room about the next step for Le Tissier.

The Saints star said: "When I came off, I just knew that would be it. Gordon came into the dressing room and we were alone. He sat next to me and I said: 'You know what I'm going to say, don't you?' He simply nodded his head and said: 'I know.' That was it. I knew at that moment it was all over. Even before that game, I was 85 per cent certain I was going to retire.

"Gordon and I had a little chat and then he left me on my own in the changing room to think. He said some nice things to me about how, because of the age I had played football in, the whole of my career had been recorded on video, so I would always have something to show my children. He also told me I could be proud of what I'd achieved in the game. I had a bit of time to myself, took a bath and then left the stadium. My girlfriend was waiting for me and I took her out for a meal. She was expecting the decision, so it was no great shock."

Never one to rush things, Le Tissier took a week before calling Rupert Lowe to inform him of his monumental decision. The chairman had already worked out why the call was being made and was grateful to Le Tissier for not putting him in a difficult situation over a new contract. "In my heart, I knew I had not done enough and didn't want to put him in a position of having to say: 'I'm sorry, Matt.'"

That phone call made it official. There was no going back now and even with the reality of his situation now firmly rammed home, he refused to speculate if he may have been too hasty. In fact, it was almost a relief for him to accept the inevitable. Now he could look forward to a life without waking up fearing another niggle in his calf or wondering if he still could wriggle his way through Premiership defences.

"The last four seasons have been absolutely horrendous," he said. "It has been an uphill struggle. The problems have been ridiculous. I have had five separate calf strains and you can't carry those and expect to show any form at all. But I suppose I can look back and say at least I never had a serious injury. I am retiring with my knees intact and all my faculties still there - although some people might question that!"

In truth, when Le Tissier announced his retirement to his adoring Saints supporters, there was no major feeling of shock. The genius they had marvelled at for 17 years had wrestled for over two seasons with his body, so they were hardly surprised when the painful battle was brought to a conclusion.

IS IT THE END FOR LE TISS?

By Dave King
at St Mary's Stadium

More injury agony as Matt limps off

A DEJECTED Matthew Le Tissier limped off the St Mary's pitch las' night with a huge question mark hanging over whether the talismanic midfielder will ever wear ? Saints first-team shirt again.

Le Tissier's contract is up at the end of the season and the 33-year-old player was desperately hoping to use the reserve game against Charlton as a springboard to impress watching manager Gordon Strachan and earn a new deal.

But after half an hour, the calf injury which has blighted much of the Channel Islander's season, struck again. Loo 'ng absolutely di-traught, Le Tissier signalled 'eserve tea' 'ss Steve 'd club 's shinp 's head'

How Saints fans were given the news by the Daily Echo that a great career was in danger of coming to a sorry end. It emerged some time later that Le Tissier's mind was made up - and he had already informed boss Gordon Strachan that he could no longer battle on.

He had given too much to the club for them to beg him to try one more time and risk a disability in later life from wrecked knees or a ripped muscle. Instead, fans looked forward to playing their part in giving him the send-off he so richly deserved.

Hindsight was now proving a wonderful thing for Le Tissier as he looked through numerous career options. Surely this sad end to his football-playing days would have been avoided if he had listened to his body and bowed out with that stunning strike in the final game at The Dell. Then he could have been carried off into the sunset as a conquering hero - on the shoulders of his devoted followers.

But he claimed: "I really wanted to give it a shot at the new stadium. After so long waiting for St Mary's, I wanted to be part of it and that was the inspiration for giving it one more go. I haven't scored at St Mary's, so I can always say my last goal was 'that' goal at The Dell. It's not a bad one to end on."

Le Tissier was in reflective mood and admitted he could perhaps have done a bit more to stretch out his playing days - by ensuring his waistline did not stretch so much. Self-critically, he acknowledged that his diet during his final seasons at the club had not been sufficiently modified - despite one enlightening summer in Australia - to counter-act the limitations on training caused by his various injuries.

That meant he was slightly too heavy when he returned to full training and the strain to a body battling on too many fronts was increased. "Probably in the last few years, I have not kept myself in the condition I should have," he said. "It has always been a vicious circle. I was not training enough to keep the weight down and I was still trying to eat the same food that I ate before. I didn't modify my diet at times when I wasn't training, which was the worst thing, looking back."

While Le Tissier admits his eating habits were sometimes a problem, the damaged calf fibres were never going to allow him to return to the form of his younger years; not even if he had munched out on lettuce leaves rather than his favoured Big Macs.

> **'All the fans who turned up were incredible, but it wasn't just about last night, it's about the last 17 years'**
>
> Matthew Le Tissier after his testimonial at St Mary's last night

The supporters said their farewells at his testimonial - a star-packed, tearful affair, at which the likes of Gazza, Chris Waddle, Kevin Keegan, Alan Ball, Peter Beardsley, Ian Wright and Alan Shearer appeared in a high-scoring match between a Saints X1 and an England side. The turn-out of such famous faces showed just how high his standing was among his peers and he used the game to score a goal at a wonderful stadium that his injury hell had prevented him from gracing.

Ever since he netted in the last game at The Dell, Le Tissier had been keen to make his mark at St Mary's before being forced to call time. But, despite opening the shiny new ground in the company of another Saints legend, Ted Bates, he sadly failed to start a competitive senior game there.

Striving to regain full fitness, he made his first Premiership appearance of the season in the 3-1 home defeat by Aston Villa on September 24 - as a substitute for Marian Pahars. It was part of a run of four losses in the first five League games - a sequence which ultimately cost Stuart Gray his job as manager. Lacking full sufficient sharpness, Le Tissier was then given a spell in the reserves in an attempt to build up some stamina.

Second-string games against Spurs, Leicester and Wimbledon supplemented his workload in a period that brought another appearance from the bench for the first team as a replacement for James Beattie in the defeat at Derby in mid-November. He also featured against Derby's reserves and scored his sole 'competitive' goal at St Mary's in the 1-1 draw against Fulham's reserves a few days before Christmas.

That convinced new boss Strachan to give him a run-out as a substitute in a shocker of an FA Cup third-round tie against Rotherham at Millmoor. Going on for Austin Delgado with Saints 2-1 down and the game running away from them, Le Tissier tried to work his magic. But despite sending a late chip narrowly over the bar, he failed to inspire his side to a comeback and Strachan's men returned home well and truly bullied into submission by the Millers' physical style.

Le Tissier was now firmly back in the squad and went on in place of Pahars in the 1-1 draw at Anfield on January 19, when only the upright prevented Anders Svensson snatching a winner at the death. And he was asked to help keep Saints in front as they easily beat West Ham 2-0 on January 30. He replaced Kevin Davies, a then-record crowd of 31,879 watching him trot on to the pitch in his inimitable fashion without realising they were witnessing the master's farewell.

There was no hint at the time that the frustration of a calf injury was about to leave him with little option but to call it a day. But he failed to last the full 90 minutes of a reserve clash against Chelsea on March 4 and, just 15 days later, gave up the fight.

He had spent the season missing training sessions as his body struggled to cope with a succession of setbacks. And with his contract running out at the end of the season, he knew he needed to produce some significant performances to warrant a new deal. Even with his illustrious past, the board would have been hard pushed to splash out on a contract for a player who would not have started a game in nearly two years and hardly looked in good enough shape to change that painful fact.

His career ended without a fitting finale. He was on the bench for the season's last home game against Newcastle with the promise of a late sub appearance to allow him to say goodbye. But Tahar El Khalej's foolish lunge not only left Kieron Dyer fearing for his World Cup place, it also denied Le Tissier his chance to make a late entrance.

The defender was sent off after 55 minutes with his side 2-1 ahead. With £500,000 on offer for each place Saints finished higher up the Premiership table, there was no room for sentiment. Sending on an unfit Le Tissier could have cost Strachan the win and he had to disappoint him by leaving him on the bench as Paul Telfer added a third in the dying minutes.

Moroccan international El Khalej's recklessness had robbed a player who had served up some of the game's greatest moments the opportunity to sign off with one last touch of brilliance, one final trick, and perhaps one magical strike past the hopelessly flailing glove of a keeper. But, in a way, the refusal of his body to even allow him to be considered by Strachan was an apt ending.

His whole career had been spent fighting against forces he could not control in a bid to ensure his skills enjoyed the justice they deserved. From sitting on the bench under Chris Nicholl, to missing out on an England under-21 career and then watching the 'three wise men,' Graham Taylor, Terry Venables and Glenn Hoddle, deny him his birthright as one his country's greatest international players, Le Tissier had always been battling to express his true ability.

Luckily for Saints supporters, they had seen the real glory, the endlessly repeated 30-yarders, the last-gasp rescue acts, all those sure-fire penalties and the little tricks and nuances that were never picked up by the television cameras. And they had enjoyed the charm and wit of a loyal man, who made Southampton his home and who treated as equals those with far less talent than himself.

For them, Matt Le Tissier will always be a footballing God.

Goal Log

(Matches listed are in the League unless otherwise stated. Hat-tricks appear in bold).

1986-87

LE TISSIER'S SEASON:
Starts 13, Substitute Appearances 18, Goals 10.

1 . . . . .Nov 4 v Manchester United H Littlewoods Cup third round, won 4-1
2 . . . . .Nov 4 v Manchester United H Littlewoods Cup third round, won 4-1
3 . . . . .Nov 8 v Sheffield Wednesday A, lost 1-3
4 . . . . .Nov 25 v Hull H Full Members Cup second round, won 2-1
5 . . . . .Nov 25 v Hull H Full Members Cup second round, won 2-1
6 . . . . .Mar 7 v Leicester H, won 4-0
7 . . . . .Mar 7 v Leicester H, won 4-0
8 . . . . .Mar 7 v Leicester H, won 4-0
9 . . . . .Apr 22 v Sheffield Wednesday H, drew 1-1
10 . . . .May 5 v Watford A, drew 1-1

SAINTS' PROGRESS:
League - finished 12th
FA Cup - third-round defeat against Everton
Littlewoods Cup - semi-final defeat against Liverpool
Full Members Cup - third-round defeat against Norwich

1987-88

LE TISSIER'S SEASON:
Starts 13, Substitute Appearances 9, Goals 2.

11 . . . .Oct 6 v Bournemouth H Littlewoods Cup second round, drew 2-2
12 . . .Jan 9 v Reading A FA Cup third round, won 1-0

SAINTS' PROGRESS:
League - finished 12th
FA Cup - fourth-round defeat against Luton
Littlewoods Cup - second-round defeat against Bournemouth
Simod Cup - second-round defeat against Bradford

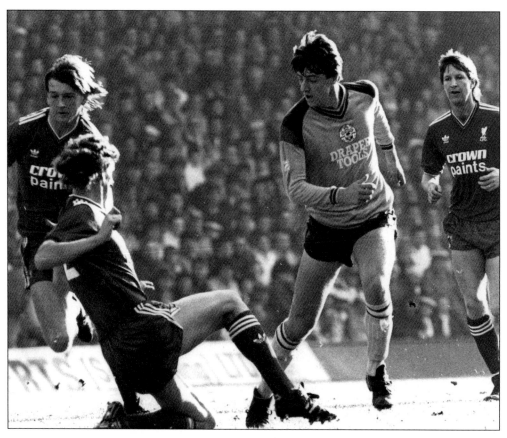

The young Le Tiss at Anfield in 1987 as the goals started to flow.

1988-89

LE TISSIER'S SEASON:
Starts 28, Substitute Appearances 8, Goals 11.

13 .... Aug 27 v West Ham H, won 4-0

14 .... Sept 3 v QPR A, won 1-0

15 .... Sept 17 v Arsenal A, drew 2-2

16 .... Nov 1 v Scarborough A Littlewoods Cup third round, drew 2-2

17 .... Nov 12 v Aston Villa H, won 3-1

18 .... Nov 12 v Aston Villa H, won 3-1

19 .... Nov 19 v Manchester United A, drew 2-2

20 .... Nov 22 v Scarborough H Littlewoods Cup third round, won 1-0

21 .... Dec 17 v Newcastle A, drew 3-3

22 .... Dec 17 v Newcastle A, drew 3-3

23 .... Dec 31 v QPR H, lost 1-4

SAINTS' PROGRESS:
League - finished 13th
FA Cup - third-round defeat against Derby
Littlewoods Cup - fifth-round defeat against Luton
Simod Cup - second-round defeat against Crystal Palace

1989-90

LE TISSIER'S SEASON:
Starts 43, Substitute Appearances 1, Goals 24.

24 .... Sept 30 v Wimbledon H, drew 2-2
25 .... Sept 30 v Wimbledon H, drew 2-2
26 .... Oct 14 v QPR A, won 4-1
27 .... Oct 21 v Liverpool H, won 4-1
28 .... Oct 28 v Manchester United A, lost 1-2
29 .... Nov 18 v Chelsea A, drew 2-2
30 .... Nov 18 v Chelsea A, drew 2-2
31 .... Nov 25 v Luton H, won 6-3
32 .... Dec 2 v Millwall A, drew 2-2
33 .... Dec 30 v Sheffield Wednesday A, drew 2-2
34 .... Dec 30 v Sheffield Wednesday A, drew 2-2
35 .... Jan 1 v Charlton A, won 4-2
36 .... Jan 6 v Tottenham A FA Cup third round, won 3-1
37 .... Jan 16 v Swindon H Littlewoods Cup fourth round, won 4-2
38 .... Jan 24 v Oldham H Littlewoods Cup fifth round, drew 2-2
39 .... Jan 24 v Oldham H Littlewoods Cup fifth round, drew 2-2
40 .... Feb 27 v Norwich H, won 4-1
41 .... Feb 27 v Norwich H, won 4-1
42 .... Feb 27 v Norwich H, won 4-1
43 .... Mar 10 v Derby H, won 2-1
44 .... Mar 17 v Wimbledon A, drew 3-3
45 .... Mar 17 v Wimbledon A, drew 3-3
46 .... Mar 17 v Wimbledon A, drew 3-3
47 .... Apr 28 v Coventry H, won 3-0

SAINTS' PROGRESS:
League - finished 7th
FA Cup - fifth-round defeat against Liverpool
Littlewoods Cup - fifth-round defeat against Oldham

1990-91

LE TISSIER'S SEASON:
Starts 42, Substitute Appearances 1, Goals 23.

48 .... Aug 25 v Aston Villa A, drew 1-1
49 .... Sep 15 v Sheffield United H, won 2-0
50 .... Oct 20 v Coventry A, won 2-1
51 .... Oct 30 v Ipswich A Rumbelows Cup third round, won 2-0
52 .... Nov 3 v Wimbledon A, drew 1-1
53 .... Nov 10 v QPR H, won 3-1
54 .... Nov 27 v Crystal Palace H Rumbelows Cup fourth round, won 2-0
55 .... Dec 8 v Norwich A, lost 1-3
56 .... Dec 15 v Aston Villa H, drew 1-1
57 .... Dec 26 v Manchester City H, won 2-1
58 .... Dec 29 v Tottenham H, won 3-0
59 .... Dec 29 v Tottenham H, won 3-0
60 .... Jan 5 v Ipswich H FA Cup third round, won 3-2
61 .... Jan 5 v Ipswich H FA Cup third round, won 3-2
62 .... Jan 12 v Luton A, won 4-3
63 .... Jan 12 v Luton A, won 4-3
64 .... Feb 23 v QPR A, lost 1-2
65 .... Mar 23 v Chelsea A, won 2-0
66 .... Mar 30 v Manchester City A, drew 3-3
67 .... Apr 1 v Liverpool H, won 1-0
68 .... Apr 9 v Arsenal H, drew 1-1
69 .... Apr 13 v Sunderland H, won 3-1
70 .... May 4 v Derby A, lost 2-6

SAINTS' PROGRESS:
League - finished 14th
FA Cup - fifth-round defeat against Nottingham Forest
Rumbelows Cup - fifth-round defeat against Manchester United
Zenith Data Systems Cup - third-round defeat against Norwich

1991-92

LE TISSIER'S SEASON:
Starts 50, Substitute Appearances 1, Goals 15.
71 .... Aug 24 v Sheffield United A, won 2-0
72 .... Sep 4 v Luton A, lost 1-2

73 . . . . Oct 9 v Scarborough H Rumbelows Cup second round, drew 2-2

74 . . . . Oct 22 v Bristol City A Zenith Data Systems Cup second round, won 2-1

75 . . . . Oct 26 v Nottingham Forest A, won 3-1

76 . . . . Oct 26 v Nottingham Forest A, won 3-1

77 . . . . Nov 26 v Plymouth A Zenith Data Systems Cup third round, won 1-0

78 . . . . Jan 4 v QPR H FA Cup third round, won 2-0

79 . . . . Jan 7 v West Ham Zenith Data Systems Cup area semi-final, won 2-1

80 . . . . Jan 11 v Sheffield United H, lost 2-4

81 . . . . Jan 29 v Chelsea A Zenith Data Systems Cup area final, won 3-1

82 . . . . Jan 29 v Chelsea A Zenith Data Systems Cup area final, won 3-1

83 . . . . Jan 29 v Chelsea A Zenith Data Systems Cup area final, won 3-1

84 . . . . Mar 11 v Crystal Palace H, won 1-0

85 . . . . Mar 29 v Nottingham Forest N Zenith Data Systems Cup final, lost 2-3

SAINTS' PROGRESS:

League - finished 16th

FA Cup - sixth-round defeat against Norwich

Rumbelows Cup - fourth-round defeat against Nottingham Forest

Zenith Data Systems Cup - final defeat against Nottingham Forest

1992-93

LE TISSIER'S SEASON:

Starts 44, Substitute Appearances 0, Goals 18.

86 . . . . Aug 19 v QPR A, lost 1-3

87 . . . . Aug 29 v Middlesbrough H, won 2-1

88 . . . . Sep 12 v QPR H, lost 1-2

89 . . . . Oct 7 v Gillingham H Coca-Cola Cup second round, won 3-0

90 . . . . Oct 7 v Gillingham H Coca-Cola Cup second round, won 3-0

91 . . . . Nov 22 v Blackburn H, drew 1-1

92 . . . . Nov 28 v Nottingham Forest A, won 2-1

93 . . . . Dec 19 v Everton A, lost 1-2

94 . . . . Jan 3 v Nottingham Forest A FA Cup third round, lost 1-2

95 . . . . Jan 26 v Middlesbrough A, lost 1-2

96 . . . . Mar 6 v Wimbledon A, won 2-1

97 . . . . Mar 13 v Ipswich H, won 4-3

98 . . . . Mar 13 v Ipswich H, won 4-3

99 . . . . Mar 20 v Arsenal A, lost 3-4

100 . . . Mar 24 v Nottingham Forest H, lost 1-2

101 . . . May 8 v Oldham A, lost 3-4
102 . . . May 8 v Oldham A, lost 3-4
103 . . . May 8 v Oldham A, lost 3-4

SAINTS' PROGRESS:
League - finished 18th
FA Cup - third-round defeat against Nottingham Forest
Coca-Cola Cup - third-round defeat against Crystal Palace

1993-94

LE TISSIER'S SEASON:
Starts 40, Substitute Appearances 0, Goals 25.

104 . . ..Aug 25 v Swindon H, won 5-1
105 . . . Aug 25 v Swindon H, won 5-1
106 . . . Oct 24 v Newcastle H, won 2-1
107 . . . Oct 24 v Newcastle H, won 2-1
108 . . . Oct 30 v Liverpool A, lost 2-4
109 . . . Oct 30 v Liverpool A, lost 2-4
110 . . . Nov 24 v Aston Villa A, won 2-0
111 . . . Nov 24 v Aston Villa A, won 2-0
112 . . . Dec 18 v Swindon A, lost 1-2
113 . . . Jan 15 v Coventry H, won 1-0
114 . . . Jan 22 v Newcastle A, won 2-1
115 . . . Feb 5 v Oldham A, lost 1-2
116 . . . Feb 14 v Liverpool H, won 4-2
117 . . . Feb 14 v Liverpool H, won 4-2
118 . . . Feb 14 v Liverpool H, won 4-2
119 . . . Feb 25 v Wimbledon H, won 1-0
120 . . . Mar 30 v Oldham H, lost 1-3
121 . . . Apr 9 v Norwich A, won 5-4
122 . . . Apr 9 v Norwich A, won 5-4
123 . . ..Apr 9 v Norwich A, won 5-4
124 . . ..Apr 16 v Blackburn H, won 3-1
125 . . . Apr 30 v Aston Villa H, won 4-1
126 . . . Apr 30 v Aston Villa H, won 4-1
127 . . . May 7 v West Ham A, drew 3-3
128 . . . May 7 v West Ham A, drew 3-3

SAINTS' PROGRESS:
League - finished 18th
FA Cup - third-round defeat against Port Vale
Coca-Cola Cup - second-round defeat against Shrewsbury

1994-95

LE TISSIER'S SEASON:
Starts 49, Substitute Appearances 0, Goals 30.

129 . . . Aug 24 v Aston Villa A, drew 1-1
130 . . Sep 12 v Tottenham A, won 2-1
131 . . . Sep 12 v Tottenham A, won 2-1
132 . . . Sep 17 v Nottingham Forest H, drew 1-1
133 . . . Sep 20 v Huddersfield A Coca-Cola Cup second round, won 1-0
134 . . . Oct 5 v Huddersfield H Coca-Cola Cup second round, won 4-0
135 . . . Oct 5 v Huddersfield H Coca-Cola Cup second round, won 4-0
136 . . . Oct 5 v Huddersfield H Coca-Cola Cup second round, won 4-0
137 . . . Oct 5 v Huddersfield H Coca-Cola Cup second round, won 4-0
138 . . . Oct 8 v Everton H, won 2-0
139 . . . Oct 15 v Leicester A, lost 3-4
140 . . . Nov 2 v Norwich H, drew 1-1
141 . . . Dec 10 v Blackburn A, lost 2-3
142 . . . Dec 10 v Blackburn A, lost 2-3
143 . . . Dec 19 v Aston Villa H, won 2-1
144 . . . Dec 26 v Wimbledon H, lost 2-3
145 . . . Jan 2 v Sheffield Wednesday A, drew 1-1
146 . .Jan 7 v Southend H FA Cup third round, won 2-0
147 . .Feb 4 v Manchester City H, drew 2-2
148 . . . Feb 8 v Luton H FA Cup fourth round, won 6-0
149 . . . Feb 8 v Luton H FA Cup fourth round, won 6-0
150 . . . Feb 18 v Tottenham A FA Cup fifth round, drew 1-1
151 . . . Mar 1 v Tottenham H FA Cup fifth round, lost 2-6
152 . . . Apr 2 v Tottenham H, won 4-3
153 . . . Apr 2 v Tottenham H, won 4-3
154 . . . Apr 12 v Chelsea A, won 2-0
155 . . .Apr 17 v Wimbledon A, won 2-0
156 . . . May 3 v Crystal Palace H, won 3-1
157 . . . May 3 v Crystal Palace H, won 3-1
158 . . . May 14 v Leicester H, drew 2-2

SAINTS' PROGRESS:

League - finished 10th

FA Cup - fifth-round defeat against Tottenham

Coca-Cola Cup - third-round defeat against Sheffield Wednesday

1995-96

LE TISSIER'S SEASON:

Starts 43, Substitute Appearances 0, Goals 10.

159 . . . Aug 19 v Nottingham Forest H, lost 3-4
160 . . . Aug 19 v Nottingham Forest H, lost 3-4
161 . . . Aug 19 v Nottingham Forest H, lost 3-4
162 . . . Sep 19 v Cardiff A Coca-Cola Cup second round, won 3-0
163 . . . Sep 19 v Cardiff A Coca-Cola Cup second round, won 3-0
164 . . . Nov 4 v QPR H, won 2-0
165 . . . Feb 7 v Crewe H FA Cup third round, drew 1-1
166 . . . Apr 6 v Blackburn H, won 1-0
167 . . ..Apr 13 v Manchester United H, won 3-1
168 . . . Apr 27 v Bolton A, won 1-0

SAINTS' PROGRESS:

League - finished 17th

FA Cup - sixth-round defeat against Manchester United

Coca-Cola Cup - fourth-round defeat against Reading

1996-97

LE TISSIER'S SEASON:

Starts 32, Substitute Appearances 6, Goals 16.

169 . . . Aug 21 v Leicester A, lost 1-2
170 . . . Sep 4 v Nottingham Forest H, drew 2-2
171 . . . Sep 18 v Peterborough H Coca-Cola Cup second round, won 2-0
172 . . . Sep 28 v Middlesbrough H, won 4-0
173 . . . Sep 28 v Middlesbrough H, won 4-0
174 . . . Oct 13 v Coventry A, drew 1-1
175 . . . Oct 19 v Sunderland H, won 3-0
176 . . . Oct 23 v Lincoln H Coca-Cola Cup third round, drew 2-2
177 . . . Oct 26 v Manchester United H, won 6-3
178 . . . Nov 2 v Sheffield Wednesday A, drew 1-1

179 . . . Dec 26 v Tottenham A, lost 1-3

180 . . . Jan 18 v Newcastle H, drew 2-2

181 . . . Jan 29 v Stockport H Coca-Cola Cup fifth round, lost 1-2

182 . . . Feb 22 v Sheffield Wednesday H, lost 2-3

183 . . . Mar 1 v Newcastle A, won 1-0

184 . . . May 3 v Blackburn H, won 2-0

SAINTS' PROGRESS:

League - finished 16th

FA Cup - third-round defeat against Reading

Coca-Cola Cup - fifth-round defeat against Stockport

1997-98

LE TISSIER'S SEASON:

Starts 29, Substitute Appearances 1, Goals 14.

185 . . . Sep 30 v Brentford A Coca-Cola Cup second round, won 2-0

186 . . . Sep 30 v Brentford A Coca-Cola Cup second round, won 2-0

187 . . . Oct 14 v Barnsley Coca-Cola Cup third round, won 2-1

188 . . . Nov 2 v Everton A, won 2-0

189 . . . Nov 8 v Barnsley H, won 4-1

190 . . . Dec 13 v Leicester H, won 2-1

191 . . . Feb 18 v Coventry H, lost 1-2

192 . . . Mar 7 v Everton H, won 2-1

193 . . . Mar 14 v Barnsley A, lost 3-4

194 . . . Mar 14 v Barnsley A, lost 3-4

195 . . . Mar 28 v Newcastle H, won 2-1

196 . . . Apr 18 v Aston Villa H, lost 1-2

197 . . . Apr 25 v West Ham A, won 4-2

198 . . . May 10 v Tottenham A, drew 1-1

SAINTS' PROGRESS:

League - finished 12th

FA Cup - third-round defeat against Derby

Coca-Cola Cup - fourth-round defeat against Chelsea

1998-99

LE TISSIER'S SEASON:

Starts 22, Substitute Appearances 11, Goals 6.

199 . . . Aug 29 v Nottingham Forest H, lost 1-2
200 . . . Sep 19 v Tottenham H, drew 1-1
201 . . . Oct 24 v Coventry H, won 2-1
202 . . . Nov 14 v Aston Villa H, lost 1-4
203 . . . Feb 27 v Manchester United A, lost 1-2
204 . . . Mar 20 v Sheffield Wednesday H, won 1-0

SAINTS' PROGRESS:
League - finished 17th
FA Cup - third-round defeat against Fulham
Worthington Cup - second-round defeat against Fulham

1999-2000

LE TISSIER'S SEASON:
Starts 10, Substitute Appearances 11, Goals 3.

205 . . . Sep 25 v Manchester United A, drew 3-3
206 . . . Sep 25 v Manchester United A, drew 3-3
207 . . . Apr 1 v Sunderland H, lost 1-2

SAINTS' PROGRESS:
League - finished 15th
FA Cup - fourth-round defeat against Aston Villa
Worthington Cup - fourth-round defeat against Aston Villa

2000-01

LE TISSIER'S SEASON:
Starts 4, Substitute Appearances 6, Goals 2.

208 . . . Sep 20 v Mansfield H Worthington Cup second round, won 2-0
209 . . . May 19 v Arsenal H, won 3-2

SAINTS' PROGRESS:
League - finished 10th
FA Cup - fifth-round defeat against Tranmere
Worthington Cup - third-round defeat against Coventry

(This was the summer in which Southampton moved from their old ground at The Dell to their new St Mary's Stadium).

2001-02

LE TISSIER'S SEASON:
Starts 0, Substitute Appearances 5, Goals 0.

SAINTS' PROGRESS:
League - finished 11th
FA Cup - third-round defeat against Rotherham
Worthington Cup - fourth-round defeat against Bolton

CAREER BREAKDOWN

GOALS:
League 161, FA Cup 12, League Cup 27, Other 9*. Total 209.

WHO SUFFERED THE MOST (Who his goals were scored against):
Aston Villa 12, Nottingham Forest 12, Tottenham 12, Wimbledon 10, Manchester United 9, QPR 9, Newcastle 8, Norwich 8, Sheffield Wednesday 8, Chelsea 7, Leicester 7, Liverpool 7, Oldham 7, Blackburn 6, Coventry 6, Luton 6, Huddersfield 5, Ipswich 5, West Ham 5, Arsenal 4, Barnsley 4, Crystal Palace 4, Everton 4, Middlesbrough 4, Swindon 4, Manchester City 3, Scarborough 3, Sheffield United 3, Sunderland 3, Brentford 2, Cardiff 2, Derby 2, Gillingham 2, Hull 2, Bolton 1, Bournemouth 1, Bristol City 1, Charlton 1, Crewe 1, Lincoln 1, Mansfield 1, Millwall 1, Peterborough 1, Plymouth 1, Reading 1, Southend 1, Stockport 1, Watford 1.

APPEARANCES:
League 443 (including 66 as sub), FA Cup 33 (3 as sub), League Cup 52 (8 as sub), Other 12 (1 as sub). Total 540 (including 78 as sub).

(*'Other' in the above paragraph and in the career goals breakdown higher up this page relates to the Full Members Cup, Simod Cup and Zenith Data Systems Cup).
NB: Saints were in the top flight throughout the Matt Le Tissier era.

Subscribers

Scroll of Honour

A

Dawn Adams
Matthew Aslett
Leon, Jo, Francesca &
Charlotte Aquilina

B

Adam Baker
David John Baker
Mike Baker
Darren Bartlett
Gordon P Bassett
David Oliver Batchelor
Miss J Bates
Andrew Beach
Gordon Bean
Christopher Beare
Richard Becheley
Matthew Bell
P C K Bickerstaff
Mervyn Birch
Ted Bishop
John Blackburn
Iain Blair
Billy Boulton
David Brindley
Vivienne Broadway
Glyn Brown
Rodney A Brown

Stephen Brunsdon
Julia Buchanan
Richard Buckingham-Smith
John Budd
John Budden
Russell Budden
Karl Bulman
Kenny Burgess
Carys Emily Bushnell

C

Cyril Cable
P J Canton
Ben Chamberlain
Stephen Cheffey
Mrs J Chesshire
Martin Churcher
Jim Clarke
Paul Clements
Paul Cobbold
Brian Coffin
David Cole
Philip Cooke
Simon Coombes
Mark Cooper
Richard Cooper
James Cornick
Geoff Cotton
Jamie Cotton

SCROLL OF HONOUR

Michael Cox
Wendy Crookes
Stephen Cross
Tim Cull
Andy Curtis
Christine Curtis
Jamie Curtis
Susie Curtis

D
Joe Davis
Paul Dear
Garry Denton
Clive Derwent
Richard Derwent
Lee Donnarumma
Chris Driver
David Driver
Jonathan Driver
Clive Dumper
Keith Durnford

E
Daniel Edmonds
Jane Erridge
Luke Evans

F
Darran Mackenzie Fawcett

Leslie Felgate
Michael Fenn
William Fenner
Simon Field
Ben Ford
Craig Foster
Kevin Foster
Lynn Foster
Jerry Fox
Matthew Franklin
Ross Freemantle
Lucy Fry

G
Shanette Gardner
Andy Gastrell
Robert Gibbens
Joseph Peter Gibbons
Richard John Gibbons R.A.
Robert Shaun Gibson
Nick Gilbert
Matthew Giles
Bobby Gill
Paul Gilliam
Philip Gilliam
Mark Griffiths
Brian Grist
Richard Grunsell
Yvonne Gunter

SCROLL OF HONOUR

H
Chris Hancock
Paul Harris
Steven Harris
Mark Harsant
Keith Hartnell
Michael Hartnell
Brian Hawkins
Graham Hawtree
Andy and Kevin Hayes
Linda Hayman
Clive Haythorne
David Herbert
Cliff Hibberd
Alan Higgins
Mike Higgins
Mike Hoar
Jon Holloway
Roy Honeybone
Ross Howard
Craig Paul Hulbert
Nick Humby

J
Daniel Jehan
Eric Jeram
Paul Johnson
Martyn Philip Jones
David Joy

Neil Kapur
Sam Keites
Tony Kellett
Matthew Kelman
Marcus David Justin Kinsella
John Kirk
David Knight

L
David Lance
Di Lavers
Mona Le Tissier
Melvyn Linter
Alan Linton
Roy Longman
Gavin Lovell
John Lovelock

M
John Magee
Terry Marshall
Geoff Martin
Mr & Mrs Martin
Nathan Martin
Carl Mason
Kirsty McDonald
Darren Milam
Lewis Milam
William Joseph Milligan

Scroll of Honour

Jean Mills
David Moore
Steven Moore
Michael Morant
Steven Morant
R C Mursell

N
Sheila Nadolski
Chris Nathans
Derek Neal
Paul Neal
James Neate
Trevor Newell
Matthew Charles Niblett
K R Nicholson
Geoff Nicoll
Sean Nutbeen

O
Nigel Offord
Sam Andrew Offord
The Old Family
David Onslow
Martin Andrew Orman
Barry Osgood
Nick Osman
Paul Over
The Owen Family

P
Alison Palmer
Craig Parker
Craig Parker
Gary Parker
Gordon Parrish
Chris Patching
Matt Paul
Michael Paul
Wendy and Laura Platt
Andy Poolman
Martyn Price
Rob Price
Louise Pugh
Lee Purkiss

Q
Keven Quick

R
David Rattey
Des Rebbeck
Jem Robbins
Barry Roberts
James Roberts
John Roberts
Kevin Roberts
Robin Rose
Chris Rowthorn

SCROLL OF HONOUR

Alan Ruthen
Ken Ruthen

S
Miss Emma Sainsbury
Carl Sandalls
Keith Sandalls
Brian Sandy
Matt Sansome
Lofty Saunders
Mr & Mrs S Shephard
The Simmonds Family
Malcolm Sims
Kay Small
Terry Smith
Phil Snarr
Paul Spacagna
Pete Spacagna
Jack Thomas Spencer
Mick Spencer
Natasha Spencer
Paul Spencer
Audrey Stacey
The Stevens Family
Clive Simon John Stickland
Peter Strange
Tim Strange
Mr & Mrs J Stranger
Joan Strugnell

T
E Tarbart
Claire Taylor
Derry Taylor
Robert Tilley
Steven Tilley
Shane Tirvengadum
Gary Tonner
John Trodd
Barry Tull
Joseph Twigg

U
Simon Upton

V
John Vallis
Peter Vear
Ben Vincent
Dominic Vitoria

W
Martin Walden
Mathew Walker
Stuart Wallace
David Warbrick
Zoe Warr
Michael Warren
Antony Warwick

Scroll of Honour

Graham Watford
Graham Wetherick
Connor White
Michael White
Ryan White
The Whiteside Family
Barry Whitlock
Ken Wilds
Glen Williams
Dave Willis
Craig Wilson
Dennis Wilson
John Wilson
Betty Wing
Malcolm Wing
Stephen Wood
Alan Woodward
David Woodward

Y
Ronald Yeates

Other titles by Thomas Publications are:

- The Bully Years (£8.99)
- Wolves: Exclusive! (£6.99)
- Sir Jack (£12.99)
- Forever Wolves (£16.99)
- When We Won the Cup (£15.99)
- Running With Wolves (£16.99)
- Wolves: The Glory Years (£16.99)
- Forever Villa (£17.99)

All these books are available by writing to Thomas Publications, PO Box 17, Newport, Shropshire, TF10 7WT, or by emailing info@thomaspublications.co.uk.

Further information about all titles can be obtained from our website, www.thomaspublications.co.uk.